7-31-2014 Stan,

My Birthday gift to you

Tony Virtue !!

:)

FOX VALLEY VET★RANS

A SALUTE TO HOMETOWN HEROISM

George Rawlinson

State Street Publishing
Elgin, Illinois

Cover Design: David Van Delinder
Photography: Gus Stuertze
Publicity: Sofia Hedberg

FOX VALLEY VETERANS
A Salute to Hometown Heroism

ISBN 0-9760216-0-9

Publisher: State Street Publishing
              506 S. State Street
              Elgin, Illinois 60123

SPONSORSHIP
FOX VALLEY VET≡RANS
A Salute to Hometown Heroism

State Street Publishing is pleased and proud to acknowledge the following donors. Without them, this book would not have been possible.

Their contributions honor all veterans, especially those who reside in the Fox Valley.

Part of the proceeds from the sale of this book will be donated to the local organizations that show support for area veterans.

In addition, complimentary copies of this book will be given to all age-appropriate area schools and libraries.

Platinum Patriot ($1,500 and above)
- EFS Bank
- Swanson Real Estate
- Durante Real Estate
- Bob and Dee Korby

Golden Patriot ($1,000-$1,499)
- Judy LoBianco Nelson

Silver Patriot ($500-$999)
- Barrett O'Connor
- Bearco Management Company
- Bruce Butler
- IMS (Industrial Motor Service)
- Juan Figueroa
- Eve Latino

Bronze Patriot ($150-$499)
- Richard A. Grieger
- Tim McCann
- Judy Steffen

Patriot ($50-$149)
- Melissa Barbosa-Guzman
- Ted Bonifas
- Ken Bruderle
- Tom Cross
- C. Neal Davis
- Dotty Dosé
- Scott Fitzsimmons
- Rick Floyd
- Dan and Karen Fox
- Bill and Karen Fuchs
- Phillip Graf
- John Juergensmeyer
- Michael Kerber
- Bob Martens
- Clare Ollayos
- Mark O'Malley
- Betty Rylko
- Jean Sauer Ferron
- Barbara Schori
- Anne Vodicka

ACKNOWLEDGMENTS

"It takes a village ... "

So said former first lady Hillary Clinton, now a United States senator from New York.

Her words were a call to arms—loving arms, a communal approach to raising happy, healthy children.

Books are something else entirely.

In writing *Fox Valley Veterans: A Salute to Hometown Heroism*, I've learned that authoring a quality book takes much more than a village.

It takes a valley.

For me, it took the entire Fox Valley—from Oswego to Lake in the Hills, with a number of stops in between. I interviewed veterans in Aurora, Batavia, Bristol, Burlington, Carpentersville, Elburn, Elgin, Geneva, Hampshire and St. Charles.

It takes a valley.

I didn't do this alone.

Ron Altman was with me every step of the way. He was the book's biggest fan and its toughest critic.

A veteran himself, Ron is also a military historian. He has read countless books on World War II, which is his area of expertise.

Through his company, the Military Connection, Ron has recorded many memories, which were formed from the youthful perceptions of an earlier generation. He has talked to a lot of World War II veterans, asking them to share their remembrances and recollections.

Months ago, he reminded me that there were still so many stories to be told. His words were the original impetus for this book, which grew to include veterans from other generations.

Ron went on twenty-eight of the thirty interviews featured in this book. He worked without ever expecting anything in return financially. On occasion, I was able to buy him lunch.

The book was his labor of love.

As an outside reader, Ron contributed thoughtful observations, adding his considerable breadth of military knowledge to the process.

He also shared his personal experiences as a veteran.

From the book's first word to its last, Ron was my mentor and motivator.

He remains my friend.

Not only did he help with the historical research, Ron provided me with valuable contacts. It was through his efforts that the book includes Guy Bodor, Jacob Schindlbeck, Amos Nicholson, George Von Hoff, George Gebes, Lee Laz, Marvin Miller, Dick Young, Jack Richardson and Tom Greaves.

Ron shared an unending supply of stories, facts, figures and ideas. So much help came from so many places.

Sofia Hedberg, the book's publicist, helped immensely. Her assistance was remarkable throughout the publication process.

Without her help, it would not have been possible to get these words into print.

Sofia worked late nights and odd hours. She sought out sponsorship, an essential element in getting a new publishing company off the ground.

But much more than that, she came to care about the thirty people profiled in this book as much as I did.

Her personal passion, professional efficiency, good cheer and honesty kept me balanced and mostly on schedule. She knew when to say yes and how to say no without hurting my feelings—a trick in itself. I've been called overly sensitive since kindergarten.

Sofia read the entire manuscript, making several suggestions along the way. We disagreed on many things, but her heart was always in the right place.

In the end, I learned a valuable lesson from her—learned, for example, that even when people don't see eye-to-eye, they can still see heart-to-heart.

Sofia made the telephone calls I didn't have time to make. She arranged meetings with potential sponsors. She tolerated my fits of frustration, anxiety and emotion.

In my eyes, she is a masterpiece of nature. A book is just as much about publishing as it is writing.

Others who helped make this book a reality include Gus Stuertze, a professional photographer whose inspiring images project power and perspective. His camera is a tool—like a pen, like a paintbrush.

From photograph to photograph, Gus captured the serendipitous, split-second confluence of subject, shadow, light and camera. He was always in the right place at the right time.

I am especially grateful to David Van Delinder, who did the book's cover design. His coolness under fire when our print schedule changed and changed again will live in my heart forever.

David's work is an art form. One of his strengths is in asserting values of goodness and wisdom. He has something to say. And what he says is all about making a human connection. He's funny. He's tough. In his world, humanity is worth more than a picture of humanity.

Look at David's cover. It reaches into your soul.

A special thanks goes to Dave Gathman, who edited this book. He caught countless mistakes and embarrassing errors. He provided interesting insights and added a great deal of the information included in this book.

Editing is the main work when writing good prose. It can be a painful process—eliminating words, sentences, even whole paragraphs.

Dave made it seem so easy.

I'm also indebted to Michael Camacho, who took the photograph that appears on the back of this book. Making me look somewhat sophisticated may have been the toughest assignment of all.

Others without whom this book could not have been accomplished include Jim Hedberg, Maxwell Swanson, Robert Mitchler, Molly Hubbard, Paul Linden, Bill Durante and Dean-o of Grandma Sally's restaurant.

My daughter, Karlin Rawlinson, remained my inspiration through the long days of writing this book.

She's still a teenager, but that will change in a few years. Certain things will never change, however. She will always be my greatest creation.

I'm extremely proud of her. She is a good student and a quality person.

People never know the love of a parent until they become parents themselves.

Finally, I want to thank the men and women who appear on these pages.

This book was written for them.

And for those who didn't return.

DEDICATION

To all Fox Valley veterans … and to those who will never read any of this because they died defending our country.

You kept America free.

You kept America great.

Your service is a marvelous monument to liberty. But it is not a block of marble or an elaborate edifice.

No. Neither one could ever equal what you gave America.

You are the heart and hope of a great land.

This book was written with appreciation and gratitude.

May our nation never forget your courage, commitment and sacrifice.

As always, the cause of freedom remains the cause of God.

PROFILES IN COURAGE
THE HEART AND HOPE OF A GREAT COMMUNITY

FOREWORD

June 2004

One of the great privileges of serving as Congressman for the 14th District is having the opportunity to meet with Fox Valley veterans. Sometimes those meetings involve serious policy discussions; other times we simply shoot the breeze. But one thing is constant: our veterans offer a unique perspective on life and country that is inspiring and well worth hearing.

That is why we need this type of written tribute, which intends to honor all the local men and women who served our great nation. We need to thank those who answered America's call, from the campaigns of World War II to the desert of Iraq—a span of more than two generations.

While the men and women in this book represent only a small percentage of our local veterans, their stories constitute an enduring legacy of courage and commitment. This book reminds us all in very personal terms of what it means to put country before self, and serves as another testament to the incredible service veterans have offered our union.

The men and women of the United States military represent the very best our nation has to offer. This book will introduce you to just a few of their stories, and demonstrate why veterans truly are our Hometown Heroes.

J. Dennis Hastert
Speaker of the House

INTRODUCTION

Up and down the Fox River, patriotism is a bright strand, twisted together in a rainbow of red, white and blue.

They're the colors stitched through the entire fabric of this book, which profiles thirty veterans from the Fox Valley.

Located about fifty miles west of Chicago, the area includes more than a dozen communities—Aurora, Elgin, South Elgin, St. Charles, Sleepy Hollow, Hampshire, Huntley and Carpentersville, among others. While the valley is a geographic fact, American courage knows neither latitude nor longitude. The veterans in this book embody cause and country.

They believe in America.

They served from World War II to Iraqi Freedom.

As a writer, I was blessed, having had an opportunity to talk to the people profiled in this book, which was six months in the making.

Any writer would be blessed.

"It was an honor," I'd say at the conclusion of each and every interview.

Indeed it was.

I wrote a book about otherwise ordinary people in the Fox Valley, all of whom did extraordinary things.

They are different colors and creeds. And of the thirty people profiled, four are women.

I tried to capture a wide range of experience, wanting this book to represent the very diversity that makes the Fox Valley what it is—a small slice of America, a region remarkable in content and character.

I sought out that diversity, asking for names and numbers at local veterans' posts, where I became a frequent visitor.

In the end, I found exactly what I was looking for.

The oldest veteran in this book is some sixty-five years older than the two youngest.

As a boy, George Gebes, born in 1915, helped herd cattle. The South Dakota native once worked as a drover, moving beef along a trail west of the Mississippi River.

He came to Batavia during the Great Depression, drawn to town by the promise of a job shoveling coal, which would feed and house him.

Shannon Sterk and Travis Cotner, both born in 1981, never knew a world without test-tube babies, nuclear power plants, microwave ovens and Trivial Pursuit.

They were born five years after *Viking I* landed on Mars.

Gebes was born before penicillin, the Band-Aid, the domestic refrigerator and the pop-up toaster. He was nearly twelve years old when Charles Lindbergh made the first solo, nonstop, transatlantic airplane flight.

Age aside, the three local veterans illuminate common themes—they keep the memory of service, sacrifice and duty alive in all of us.

Those themes are illuminated by every veteran in this book.

I am not a veteran myself. I've never even considered military service. But I do know how to listen to people. I've picked out a good group. They're representative of the Fox Valley. Not all were born in Illinois, but all live within the parameters of the book's target area—from Oswego to Lake in the Hills.

The Fox River rolls through the target area, providing it with a sense of sacred space. There is an allegiance and loyalty here that transcends the realities and boundaries of everyday life.

The veterans featured in this book have spoken for themselves, trying to tell their stories with uncompromising clarity, giving each profile a full measure of authenticity. They were there. I wasn't. They put their lives on the line. I didn't.

Editing this book has been painstaking.

Not only was a professional editor brought aboard early on, but each person previewed his or her own story, making corrections in the final copy. It was a cumbersome process—picking up and dropping off individual chapters—but certainly worthwhile in terms of accuracy.

The veterans opened up their hearts and souls to me. I just collected their words, writing down the best of what was said.

Their phrases, their word choices and their slang are indicative of the Fox Valley, where they themselves have some 1,500 years of combined history—about fifty years per person.

Their memories are unique. I chose the recollections that are highlighted.

Not all of the profiles are kill-or-be-killed battlefield stories.

It was important, instead, to dig deeper, to write with a greater sensitivity. L.C. West and Willie Lewis witnessed things that others in the book did not, for example.

Both men are African-American.

Mary Loechner was an Army nurse in World War II. She saw things that others didn't. During our interview, she shared so much.

The other veterans did, too.

They are hometown heroes—about half, in fact, are homegrown heroes. They carry themselves well. And in the line of duty, these thirty veterans did what was asked.

Their voices describe decades of American history. In each profile, I have incorporated what was happening at a particular time, trying to tell the bigger story.

Each person profiled is proud of his or her military

service. They remain motivated by it. The differences between them are not of feeling, but of age and experience. On a number of occasions, tears flowed freely.

As with people in general, some veterans were a little more hesitant to talk than others.

But that was okay. Their stories were worth waiting for.

It is, after all, only because of their sacrifices—sacrifices made by all veterans—that this book was possible in the first place.

I offer it as a small payment to them, knowing, of course, that the debt America owes its veterans can never be fully repaid.

This book is my gift to Fox Valley veterans. I am more grateful to them than they'll ever know. In finishing this patriotic project, I'm hopeful that I finally found a way to thank those who served.

George Rawlinson
Elgin, Illinois
June, 2004

CONTENTS

VIETNAM

DESERT STORM

IRAQI FREEDOM

Jacob Schindlbeck

---◆---

JACOB SCHINDLBECK

"It's our country. We can't contribute enough."

For Jake Schindlbeck, World War II was an essential theme throughout his life, although the experience was something he didn't discuss with his family for decades.

"What we saw, what we went through ... it was pretty horrific," said Schindlbeck, who was a working-class kid born in March 1921. "It took a long, long time before I could talk about the war. I still get emotional thinking about it."

Like other veterans from World War II, Schindlbeck shoved his military memories into the back of a desk drawer, where they lurked like dust balls for years and years.

The heroes and heroines of World War II were from a different era—without support groups or the benefit of public catharsis. In some sense, they never saw themselves as anything special. They were only doing what everyone else was doing.

Often called "the greatest generation," these men and women were linked by common morals—a shared sense of duty, courage and commitment, as well as love of family, friends and country.

Now in the twilight of his life, Schindlbeck says that

those same morals remain dear to him.

His parents came to the United States from Germany in the early 1900s.

Schindlbeck's Bavarian-born father found work at an Aurora brewery. He sold real estate, too.

"My father and I were very close," Schindlbeck said. "Financially, well ... we did the best we could. When the Depression came along, those were awfully tough times."

Tough times or not, the young Schindlbeck had an easy smile. It stretches like a rubber band across faded photographs from an earlier time.

Being an admittedly adventuresome sort, the longtime Batavia resident had a passion for flying, even early on. He first flew as a 7-year-old in 1928, climbing aboard an airplane piloted by an area barnstormer.

"There was a cornfield out near Randall Road and Route 38," Schindlbeck said. "My father, my sister and myself—we all took a ride. Cost us $5. I still remember that old airplane."

Other airplanes would come later.

Schindlbeck served in the U.S. Army Air Corps from January 1941 until October 1945.

"I enlisted almost a year before the war started," Schindlbeck said. "I was looking for something to do, something exciting. At that time, you could enlist for one year of duty, and then you would be discharged on an active reserve status."

Schindlbeck was first assigned to an ordnance division.

"We were the people who repaired and supplied guns and ammunition," Schindlbeck said. "Having had no college experience, I couldn't become a pilot. Anyway, I was sent to the Panama Canal, which wasn't what I wanted at all. We were out there doing nothing, living with the bugs. And me? I was looking for something thrilling to do."

Soon, he would get more thrills than he ever wanted.

After World War II started, Schindlbeck saw a posting on a bulletin board. It asked for pilot trainees.

Without even a high school diploma, he had to take a series of written equivalency tests. He passed them and entered a training program.

"I was always an avid reader; that helped," he said, referring to the required passing of those tests.

The Army Air Forces would become what was called the largest single educational organization in existence. It had a total strength of just over 20,000 when World War II began in Europe, representing about 10 percent of the Army. By 1944, it was up to 2.4 million personnel in its ranks, almost one third of the total Army strength.

Trainees had to be taught highly specialized skills. Be that as it may, time was of the essence.

By October 1942, U.S. training programs were graduating up to 100,000 pilots per year, and proportionally more aircrew.

For those tested, the most feared word was "washout," a process that began almost immediately. More than 50 percent of entrants failed one of the initial tests, which included a battery of physical and written examinations. Those who didn't pass were routinely packed off to the infantry,

"I wasn't quite 21 years old at the time," Schindlbeck said. "I had to get my father to sign a consent sheet for me. He said he didn't want to, but if it was what I wanted, he would do it. One of the reasons he left Germany was to get out of having to go into their army."

Schindlbeck became co-pilot on a B-29 Superfortress, an airplane that came into action in 1944. It was the largest combat aircraft of the war. It had an array of .50 caliber machine guns in remotely controlled turrets and a 20-mm. cannon in a manned tail turret. It could carry 10 tons of bombs, was pressurized and could fly faster than 360 miles per hour in excess of 30,000 feet. Its maximum range was 5,830 miles without bombs on board. It could bomb a target 1,600 miles from its base.

"We had an 11-member team," Schindlbeck said. "Today, I'm the only one left alive from that original crew."

A father of six, grandfather of 32 and great-grandfather of 12, Schindlbeck laughs when asked about the size of his family.

"I always tell people: We were like Hertz—we tried harder," he says.

Extra effort also propelled the B-29 crews.

U.S. officials promised Chiang Kai-shek a steady supply of the big bomber.

It was an assurance made at the Cairo conference in November 1943.

The Chinese government wanted the B-29 used in the China-Burma-India Theater of Operations. Baby Boomers who grew up during the Cold War might not know that the U.S. and China were allies against Japan, an arrangement made prior to postwar problems and the takeover of the mainland by Chinese communists.

Looking back to 1941, American opinion overestimated the contributions China could make to the war effort. Chinese potential was based not only on its population—then estimated at 500 million—but also on its geography.

The country provided an overland way to get to the Japanese, as well as an airbase from which American bombers could reach the enemy homeland. Schindlbeck was attached to the 444th Bomb Group, 58th Wing, which first operated in the China-Burma-India Theater.

"I flew 31 bombing missions," Schindlbeck said. "And about 40 trips carrying freight across "the Hump," the 20,000-foot-high Himalayan Mountains."

After arriving in India, the 444th participated in the first Allied air strike on the Japanese homelands since the famous mission led by Lieutenant Colonel James Doolittle in April 1942.

Doolittle's raiders piloted modified B-25 bombers, which flew from aircraft carriers.

Schindlbeck recalls first seeing the much-bigger B-29.

"I remember walking around it, looking at it, thinking that it would never get off the ground," Schindlbeck said. "It seemed much too big."

When the Pacific conflict began in 1941, the Japanese held a significant lead in numbers of airplanes. They also had many crewmen who were veterans of the China campaign.

The Japanese Army and Navy together had some 3,000 operational aircraft and twice that number of pilots with at least 500 hours flying experience.

The United States possessed fewer than 900 planes in the Pacific, of which a heavy proportion were destroyed during Japan's opening attacks against Hawaii and the Philippines.

The man in command of the Allied air offensive over China was General Claire Chennault, who had been an unofficial "adviser" to Chiang Kai-shek since 1937. In 1941, he put together a group of volunteer American pilots, known as the "Flying Tigers," who were paid $600 a month to fight for China, plus $500 for every "kill" of a Japanese airplane.

They flew the P-40 Warhawk. Their kills were many.

The B-29 did even more damage to the Japanese, becoming the ultimate air weapon of World War II.

The "Flying Tigers" were disbanded before Schindlbeck arrived in the China-Burma-India Theater. Chennault's command became the U.S. Fourteenth Air Force. His own status in China prior to 1942 was always a subject of speculation. Chennault claimed that he was a civilian advisor to the secretary of China's Commission for State Aeronautical Affairs—first Madame Chiang Kai-shek and later T.V. Soong.

By the time it was in production, the B-29 had become a 60-ton machine, capable of flying sixteen hours nonstop when loaded. The first Superfortress sent to India arrived in April 1944—two months before promised to Chiang Kai-shek.

Enormous airfields were built for the B-29 in both eastern India and western China.

"At one time, Japan controlled the entire coastline, from Burma all the way up to Manchuria," Schindlbeck said. "That was the reason almost everything had to be flown into China. The most expedient way in was across the Himalayas."

Fear figured into the dangerous missions.

"In the beginning, we had a lot of fighter opposition," Schindlbeck said. "Because of their range, our escorts could only go so far. Still, you did your job. Afterwards—when you began to feel safe— that's when you started shaking. And that's when you realized your pants were probably wet. In wartime, you sometimes have a two-month period of absolute boredom, followed by a couple of hours of sheer terror."

The first actual Superfortress raid took place on June 5, 1944, from India to the railroad marshalling yards of Bangkok, Thailand. Ten days later, another raid took off against Yawata, the Japanese steel center on Kyushu Island.

When Major General Curtis E. LeMay took over bomber command, the Superfortress was used for close-formation daylight raids—a tactic he had mastered while serving with the Eighth Air Force in England. It was at this time that the B-29s began to do their most insistent and devastating damage.

The planes were used against the factories and harbors of Japan's home islands, hammering the main cities one by one.

The unstated objective was to burn out important Japanese cities. In 1945, for example, tons of explosives made of jellied gasoline and magnesium—commonly called napalm—were dropped on Tokyo, Nagoya and Kobe, as well as other enemy cities with a population of more than 50,000.

In early March, 334 B-29s roared over Tokyo, raining napalm across the city. A quarter of all buildings were consumed by fire; 84,000 people were killed.

Five months later, on August 2, 855 Superfortresses wiped out six Japanese cities in a single day.

About a year earlier, Schindlbeck's B-29, called the Agitator, was shot down by a Japanese Zero fighter, which was patrolling an area between the Himalayas, flying below the mountaintops.

"It gets very personal when someone starts shooting at you," Schindlbeck said. "It was August 16, 1944. We were hauling gasoline. The airplane itself carried 7,400 gallons. And we had two bladders in each of the bomb bays, four bladders total, each one carrying 2,000 gallons of fuel. All together, we were carrying 8,000 reserve gallons. We were heading to our base in China."

Schindlbeck said that the Japanese Zero was hiding behind a mountaintop, waiting for an opportune time to strike.

"It was a nice clear day," Schindlbeck said. "He must have spotted us long before he attacked."

The B-29 was raked from wingtip to wingtip with 20-mm. shells.

"He hit us before we even saw him," Schindlbeck said. "Our outboard engine on the right side stopped immediately. Alongside that, the inboard engine was spitting and sputtering. The airplane had full power on one side, none on the other. We decided it would be best to leave the airplane."

Schindlbeck jumped out of an airplane for the first and only time in his life.

"We had been told to count to ten, then pull the cord," he said, laughingly. "I counted to ten—5 ... 10, then I pulled the D-ring."

The entire crew came out of the ordeal alive, after spending nearly two weeks on the ground. They found friendly Chinese villagers and awaited American rescue.

"Our B-29 crashed into the side of a mountain about five miles from the jump site," Schindlbeck said. "With all that gasoline, it was a horrendous explosion. You could see the fire from a long, long way off."

The B-29 crew walked down the mountainside, knowing that the watershed would lead them to a village. Nine days later it did.

"We had survival kits and lived off the land," Schindlbeck said. "When we got to that Chinese village, one of their people was sent to an American camp about 50 miles away. The villagers treated us very well, gave us lots of hot tea and rice. We managed all right, but to this day, I hate hot tea."

Villagers were paid $500 for every American returned alive.

"When we were finally picked up, that village made more money than they ever had before," Schindlbeck said.

American airmen carried "blood chits," which were printed notices in different dialects. In essence, these reward notices stated that "this foreign person has come to China to help in the war effort. Soldiers and civilians, one and all, should rescue, protect and provide him with medical care."

The reward for a dead American body was $100, significantly less than the $500 paid for a living airman.

And in terms of payment, the U.S. government kept its word. According to Internet information last updated in 2001, the greatest reward ever given went to the family that aided a B-29 crew shot down during the

Korean War. The crewmen, badly injured, were found by North Korean civilians. Yu Ho Chun found the blood chit in the pocket of one of the American fliers. He gave them medical aid and helped sail them to safety, navigating coastal waters for 100 miles. Two weeks after that, the North Korean Army found Chun, then tortured and killed him. But, 43 years later in 1993, the United States paid $100,000 to his son, Yu Song Dan.

After the Himalayan episode and a short stay in the hospital, Schindlbeck returned to the 444th Bomb Group and was assigned to another B-29, the Agitator II, flying more missions in Asia.

The 444th Bomb Group arrived on Tinian Island in May 1945.

"In the China-Burma-India operation, the B-29 flight and ground crews were still learning about the aircraft," Schindlbeck said. "By the time we were engaged in the air offensive against Japan, we had come into our own."

After the war, Schindlbeck returned to the wife he had married while home on a 30-day furlough in 1943—the only furlough he had during four years in the service.

"I had actually met Rose several years earlier," Schindlbeck said, smiling. "She lived in Chicago. We dated, but she said I was getting too serious. When I came home on leave in 1943, I borrowed my brother's car, put in five gallons of gasoline—which was all you could get because of the rationing—and decided to try to see her. I didn't even know if she still lived in that same house. But going there, it was the best thing I ever did. I had a real passion for her. We had two days together, then I didn't see her again for almost 2½ years."

Some say there is a single color in life, as on an artist's palette, which provides meaning and the true measure of oneself.

For Jake Schindlbeck, that color was Rose, the woman he fell in love with and married.

Rose Schindlbeck died in 1999. The couple spent more than 55 years together.

"I miss her terribly," Schindlbeck said, his voice cracking with emotion. "Not a day goes by ... it really was till death do us part."

Schindlbeck spent the years after World War II engaged in several businesses. He tried selling real estate, running the office his father had started.

"That was my first bankruptcy," Schindlbeck said. "I didn't know enough about sales."

For a short time afterward, he went into business as a construction contractor, finally finding work as a union painter, which he did for more than three decades.

"I even taught the apprentice class," Schindlbeck said. "Color mixing and matching. Other things, too. Staining, etching ... a variety of techniques."

Schindlbeck retired in 1983.

"I sat home for about a year," he said. "Then, like always, I started getting restless."

He returned to school.

"I got my real estate license back," Schindlbeck said. "I concentrated on VA and HUD homes. Sold a lot of them."

After helping raise their six children, Rose Schindlbeck went back to work outside the home.

"It was going to be for one summer, but Rose stayed there 20 years," Schindlbeck said, adding that his wife worked at an area manufacturing plant.

One of Schindlbeck's adult children died in an automobile accident in the 1970s, something he has difficulty talking about.

"All in all, I've led a good life," Schindlbeck said. "Even through the hardships, you learn to keep moving, to keep getting up every day, trying to do something productive."

Outside Schindlbeck's Batavia home flies an American flag, which he sees as an almost sacred symbol of patriotism.

The onetime B-29 co-pilot spends several days each month as a volunteer at the Aurora Airport, headquarters of an air classics museum.

"I'm a tour guide there, at the Air Classics Museum," said Schindlbeck, who handed in his pilot's license after being diagnosed as a diabetic. "I've always had a real fondness for flying. I enjoy the time I spend at the museum. We get a lot of school kids there. They get an appreciation for aviation and for the American military."

Regardless of his advanced age, Schindlbeck remains one of the military's most impassioned veterans.

"My time in World War II, sometimes it's still tough to talk about," he said. "So many men never made it home. I was one of the lucky ones."

As a young man, at a time when Schindlbeck should have been learning lessons about the workaday world and raising a family, he was among an assemblage of men and women asked to save the world.

But Schindlbeck downplays the importance of his

individual role in World War II.

"I went where I was told to go," he said. "I did what I was told to do. I did it to the best of my ability. I wanted to get home. I had a bride and a job waiting for me. The way I see it, you could say that World War II was payback time. It was what we did for the privilege of living here in this country."

The war effort was all around the young men and women who came of age in the 1940s.

Even after a late start and against all odds, they answered their country's call, defeating the two ruthless military machines of Germany and Japan.

"We weren't looking for glory, just an opportunity to do our part," Schindlbeck said. "To me, the only heroes of World War II were the guys who didn't come home alive."

He remembers a sign over an Allied cemetery in Burma, the country called Myanmar today. "I was on burial detail, which was very, very difficult to take emotionally," he said. "There were Americans, Canadians, Senegalese and British being buried. And there was a sign over the cemetery entrance. I'm paraphrasing now, but it said something like this:

When you go home, tell them of us, and say—
For your tomorrow,
We gave our today.

Marvin Miller

MARVIN MILLER

"It was kill or be killed."

He is a quiet man, now slump-shouldered and slow-moving, yet there is something elegant about Marvin Miller.

His unlined face looks like a portrait in oil.

During World War II, he was an inexperienced American infantryman, plunged into a strange and different war, fighting in the jungle against seasoned Japanese troops.

"I was part of the Mars Task Force," said Miller, an Iowa native born in May 1926.

Miller moved to Chicago as a boy, graduating from Lane Technical High School in time to be drafted into the U.S. Army.

He has spent the last 30 years in Aurora.

"The one thing I really remember about Iowa as a youngster is learning to shoot a rifle—a .22," said the Fox Valley widower, who was married three times. "But I never shot at the good animals, only at rats and possums. I couldn't imagine killing a squirrel or rabbit."

He could kill Japanese soldiers, however.

He had to.

Miller was an expert sharpshooter, sent to the Burma jungle in southeast Asia.

"If I saw an enemy soldier in my sights, I could hit him, even at 1,000 yards. It was windage and elevation," said Miller, whose hands and voice tremble today.

Tremors aside, his mind has stayed sharp.

"I have Parkinson's disease and severe advanced arthritis," he says softly. "When the weather's decent, I can get out of the house. Other than that, I'm here."

He remembers being "over there," too.

"I spent five months walking and shooting, walking and shooting," Miller remembered. "If our sergeant said, 'Take the shot,' I took it."

Miller was handed a Bronze Star "for meritorious service in ground combat against the armed enemy during World War II."

He understood what was required of him.

"I wasn't a hero, just another soldier," Miller said. "So many men made the 'ultimate sacrifice' in World War II. They're the heroes."

One of them was a friend of Miller's, a soldier killed by a sniper's shot to the head, fired as the two Americans sat sharing a K-ration.

"He just slumped over, his head hitting my shoulder," Miller said, recalling the incident. "You never forget something like that."

So many memories—things that come back like lightning, each flash piercing another recollection.

"Jungle warfare was bad, real bad," Miller said. "War isn't about parades and flag waving. It's about a heavy cost, much heavier than they tell you at the draft board."

Miller was drafted in June 1944.

He was 18 years old.

The Mars Task Force helped replace Merrill's Marauders, which came into existence in 1943.

A type of Ranger outfit, the Marauders were originally formed to operate behind enemy lines in Burma.

By 1944, the Japanese had been forced onto the defensive. Nevertheless, they were fighting a stubborn delaying action against the Allies.

The goal of Merrill's Marauders was the destruction of Japanese communications and supply lines, which would play havoc with enemy forces while an attempt was made to reopen the Burma Road.

"They had a lot of casualties," Miller said, referring to Merrill's Marauders, a volunteer outfit made up of about 3,000 Allied soldiers, most of whom were American. "But what they did was very important to our success in Asia."

The Marauders—with no tanks or heavy artillery to support them—walked hundreds of miles through the dense jungles of Burma, often having to cut and chop a path of their own. In five major and thirty minor engagements, they defeated the veteran forces of the Japanese 18th Division, which had conquered Malaya and Singapore.

The behind-the-lines operation of Merrill's Marauders peaked with the capture of the Myitkyina Airfield, the only all-weather airfield in Burma.

"They saw significant action," Miller said.

He did, too.

Miller helped chase the Japanese through thick jungle canopy, crossing some of the most forbidding terrain on Earth.

"The jungle could get extremely dark," he said. "Sometimes, even in the afternoon, you'd swear it was midnight. It made things dangerous."

Other dangers were even more severe.

Poisonous snakes and leeches the size of a man's hand awaited Miller in the jungle.

"You picked out a buddy, both guys stripped down and you took turns checking one another for the smaller leeches, like the ones that got on your back and buttocks," Miller said. "If one of them got in your ear or rectum, that could cause a serious problem."

Then there were the cases of malaria, dysentery and typhus, which weakened and killed advancing Allied troops.

"Quite often, you moved through knee-deep mud," Miller said. "Even at its best, the ground was spongy and swampy. Your boots were almost always wet. We slept on the ground—no tents or sleeping bags, but you tried to cover up with something."

Mosquitoes materialized by the thousands.

Sleeping wasn't easy. Along with inclement conditions, the Japanese repeatedly engaged in a war of nerves, laughing and chattering things.

"We're coming to get you. Time to die, Joe," Japanese soldiers would call out.

They also used firecrackers to keep the Americans on edge, hoping to draw their fire. It was an attempt to trick young soldiers into revealing their position.

For GIs in World War II, learning to adjust to life in

the jungle was difficult. Each day was often sheer agony, especially during the rainy season.

But those difficulties paled in comparison to the other horrors Miller met in the jungle.

"Some say the Japanese were brutal," he said, closing his eyes momentarily. "Me? I think they were just desperate, an army on the run."

In trying to slow down the American chase, Japanese soldiers would wipe out passing villages.

"To this day, what's most vivid is the sight of a Japanese bayonet sticking out of the stomach of a pregnant woman," Miller said. "It was gruesome."

By all accounts, the enemy was cold, clever and calculating.

"We were Christians, the Japanese knew we'd stop to bury the dead, tend to the wounded," Miller said. "I saw more mutilated people than any young man should ever have to."

War was not a dashing adventure.

Not when you had to grab a shovel and scrape up the remains of your buddies. Or pull their lifeless bodies out of some swollen river, flooded by an Asian monsoon.

"Death was part of our day-to-day life," Miller said. "It sought us out."

Being a skilled sharpshooter, Miller also was a seeker, a soldier trained to kill.

"It was war," he said. "You're not particularly proud of taking someone's life, but you did it. You believed in America, I guess."

Even so, all these years later, Miller still struggles to talk about his combat experiences. More than five decades passed before he said a word publicly.

"When you kill someone, you not only take away everything they've got, you take away everything they'll ever have," he said. "You fought for friends in your unit. You fought for your country."

F. Scott Fitzgerald, the great American writer, once called World War I "the last love battle." The author of *The Great Gatsby* died just a year before Pearl Harbor. Had he lived, he would have seen his fellow countrymen engaged in a greater love than ever existed before.

But love was only part of World War II. People also had to be tough. Before fighting against Germany and Japan, Americans had been tempered and strengthened by the Great Depression of the 1930s, which was a day-to-day struggle. Survival itself was at stake, just as it was overseas against the enemy.

In 1940, two out of every five American draftees were rejected—most of them victims of malnutrition. The World War II generation saw themselves as in it together. No strings were being pulled for anyone, not even President Franklin Roosevelt's sons—all four of whom were in uniform.

While the America of the 1940s was woven with many strands, it was pulled together tightly.

That said, combat makes men anxious. No war is glorious. It is ugly; often dreary, deeply disturbing and miserable. And no matter how just the cause, war brutalizes those who fight it.

Because when your life is at stake, it's almost impossible not to subscribe to the law of the jungle—that's right, kill or be killed.

Miller made it out of the real jungle alive, but barely. On his trip out of hell, he volunteered to drive a truck, which would take him to the Burma Road. It ran for 717 miles and had twenty-one treacherous curves in one stretch.

The Burma Road was a single lane built by hand by 150,000 men, women and children. With the Japanese in occupation of Asian seacoasts, it was one of China's only links to the world.

Miller's truck hit a land mine on the Burma Road. He was seriously injured, and had to spend a month in a Chinese hospital, followed by additional rehabilitation in the U.S.

He reenlisted in an elite Army outfit—the 82nd Airborne paratroopers.

"The food was good," Miller said, laughing at the recollection. "I thought it was quite an honor making it into the 82nd Airborne. I'm proud of that."

He served with the paratroopers in Germany after World War II.

Before reenlisting and going to Europe with them, Miller married a "church girl" he'd met while stateside.

"We had six children and were married nine years," Miller said. "We were back living in Iowa. She started running around, got herself a boyfriend."

His words are matter-of-fact, without any trace of anger. Even so, such emotion can boil over.

While Miller doesn't seem the type to let that happen, he did cut ties to his family in Iowa and returned to Chicago.

"After she left with the children, I just sort of went my own way," he said. "I didn't care anymore."

Miller married a second time. That marriage lasted five years.

"But the third time was a charm," he said.

Miller married Marilyn Does. The couple had three children, then moved from Chicago to Aurora, where she was supervisor of nursing at Mercy Center. She died from breast cancer in 1987 at age 49.

Photographs of happy times together line the living room wall of Miller's home on Root Street in Aurora.

"She was a good woman," Miller said of his third wife. "People were real proud of her."

Proud of Miller, too.

His granddaughter framed the Bronze Star that also hangs on the living room wall in Miller's home.

Like many men of his generation—like many men in this book—Miller firmly refused to talk about the war for decades. Only recently, after prompting by family members, has he started to open up.

Miller is characteristic of his age. Men spent their time concentrating on daily life rather than on the past.

"We never went public with our feelings," he said. "Making it through the war was enough."

After coming home, Miller made his living as a mechanic. He operated an auto repair and sales shop in Aurora.

His youngest daughter, Karen Shafer, said she urged her father to start talking about World War II.

In addition, over the past few years, he has made contact with some old Army buddies. He also was reunited with children from his first marriage. And failing health reminds him he won't be around forever.

"I talked to someone from Merrill's Marauders on the telephone," Miller said. "He was going through ... I don't know, maybe mental problems. He started screaming. Nothing in particular—just wasn't doing very well, you might say."

But the man wouldn't want to be pitied, Miller said.

Good soldiers never do, he adds, his voice stronger than it had been before.

Miller has seen grown men cry—men who were scared to death during World War II. They had nothing to be ashamed of, he says.

Approaching 80 years old, he seems adverse to any overstatement or posturing.

"I respect the men who served in World War II," he said. "That's why I really wanted to talk."

Although it took years for him to tell it, Miller's account of World War II is something precious. It is of the common fighting man, who often turned out to be a person of uncommon valor. Think of almost any American soldier, how he lived through the hardships and horrors of battle.

That those rough and ready men survived is a blessing. And as time goes on, the preservation of their stories becomes more and more important

George Von Hoff

GEORGE VON HOFF

"I made a pact with God."

Who wouldn't?

On May 8, 1942, Batavia resident George Von Hoff was just a scared, skinny 21-year-old on board the USS Lexington.

"I joined the Navy in July 1940, more than a year before Pearl Harbor," Von Hoff said. "We would have been right there in the thick of it, but our ship was out on maneuvers."

Japanese attack airplanes certainly would have gone after the Lexington, a 41,000-ton aircraft carrier, one of three operating out of Hawaii.

So beloved its crew called her "Lady Lex," the ship sank almost five months to the day after Japan's surprise air attack against America—December 7, 1941.

The following spring, Japanese planes played another strategic role, striking the Lexington during the Battle of the Coral Sea, the first famous air-sea confrontation, which would become a phenomenon peculiar to the Pacific between 1942 and 1945. Neither side's surface fleet sighted the other—the engagement employing carrier-based aircraft.

On that fateful day in early May 1942, two

torpedoes and three bombs hit the Lexington. Fires burned below deck. The "gallant lady" had to be abandoned.

"It was hell ... it was pure hell," remembers Von Hoff, who jumped 90 feet into the ocean. "It's hard to explain how terrified you are. At age 21, you sure don't want to die."

He watched as U.S. Marines burned to death on the Lexington's deck.

"It was a bloodbath," Von Hoff said. "My battle station was as a firefighter, and I had plenty to fight. All of us did. A lot of Marines died while trying to shoot down the Japanese Zeros. They were strafing our deck. And many men died as aviation fuel exploded. Guys were burning up. They looked like hot dogs. It was just terrible."

Because of uncontrollable internal explosions, the Lexington was doomed.

Fearing for the safety of men working below, Captain Frederick C. Sherman ordered all hands to the flight deck and gave the order to abandon ship.

Sherman and his executive officer, Commander M.T. Seligman, were the last to leave the Lexington.

It was while looking down at the ocean from ninety feet up that Von Hoff made his pact with God, promising to lead a completely Christian life in the future.

"Promise or not, I was worried about the sharks," Von Hoff said. "Three days earlier, we threw some rotten beef overboard. We watched as sharks came in for the meat. You should have seen them gobbling it up. That's what was going through my mind before I jumped from the Lexington. I was scared stiff."

Some 2,700 seamen on the aircraft carrier were rescued by accompanying ships. Only 216 men were lost.

After the Lexington was abandoned, an American destroyer torpedoed the ship to avoid its capture by the enemy.

Von Hoff has a framed photograph of the burning Lexington. He has had the picture enlarged.

"It was taken by our ship's photographer from an American cruiser—the USS Chester—which rescued him," Von Hoff said.

The Batavia resident swam to the USS Hammann, a nearby destroyer, which rescued about 500 men at the Battle of the Coral Sea.

"It's ironic," Von Hoff said. "The Hammann is the same ship that saved many of the Yorktown's crew just before it was sunk at the Battle of Midway."

Within one month, the Hammann had rescued crews from two different aircraft carriers in two different battles. Shortly after that second rescue, the Hammann was itself sunk. It went down while tied alongside the Yorktown, assisting in its salvage.

"Old Yorky," which was hit and crippled on June 4, 1942, immediately developed a 26-degree list to the left side. Water rushed in, but hopes were to tow the ship home and save it. The Hammann was assigned to help in that towing operation, which included the use of a minesweeper.

On June 6, the Hammann suffered a massive explosion and sank after a Japanese submarine scored a torpedo hit.

Literally cut in half, the ship went down in less than four minutes. Eighty Americans were lost at sea, more than one-third of the Hammann's crew.

Given its rescue history, the Hammann was appropriately named. Charles Hazeltine Hammann (1892-1919) was a naval ensign and Medal of Honor recipient.

In 1918, while piloting a seaplane in southeastern Europe, he landed on the Adriatic Sea to rescue Ensign George H. Ludlow, whose aircraft had been shot down by Austro-Hungarian forces during World War I.

Although Hammann's plane was not designed for two people and despite the threat of enemy attack, he successfully completed the rescue and returned to base at Porto Corsini, Italy.

Hammann lost his life while on active duty. He had recently turned 27 years old.

Von Hoff has lived into his eighties. The Chicago native was born in June 1921.

"We moved to Batavia early on," Von Hoff said. "I had a paper route in grammar school. As a teenager, I worked at a movie theater, then at a bowling alley."

In trouble at age 16, he ran away from home, hopping a train, then hitchhiking to Florida.

It all started so foolishly.

"I went to a sports store in Aurora with three friends of mine," Von Hoff said. "We all had to steal something small. They took fishing lures. If my memory is correct, I took a pair of galoshes."

What was typical teenage mischief turned into something serious.

"Some parent found out what we did," Von Hoff said. "So, on December 22, we decided to run away. It would have been better to just own up to the trouble we caused."

Von Hoff and his friends spent Christmas on the run. The boys ate by stealing meat and cheese.

More than a week went by, but they were eventually apprehended.

"At night, we'd sleep in used car lots," Von Hoff said. "Well, what happens? One night, when we were sound asleep, the police caught us."

Returning home wasn't easy. But just as gems aren't polished without friction, boys aren't perfected without tribulation.

"My dad was really mad," Von Hoff remembered. "I didn't think about it at the time, but years later I realized how scared my mother must have been."

Back home in Batavia, Von Hoff played on his high school football team.

"I played on the varsity as a sophomore," he said. "I was a good athlete. They used to call me 'The Flying Dutchman,' which was a compliment."

After graduating from high school in 1940, Von Hoff got a job working construction.

"I was just a common laborer," he said. "After working about a week, I found out that the plumbers were making twice as much as I was. And here I'm doing the really hard work."

Von Hoff decided to learn a trade.

"I enlisted in the Navy in July 1940," he said. "I knew they'd teach me something that would help me make a decent living when I got out. Back then, you had to join for six years. They didn't want to take me at first because I had bad teeth. I had to have 'em fixed, which I did before going in."

Just before Von Hoff graduated from boot camp,

the chief in charge asked for volunteers to go on board the Lexington.

"It's a funny story," Von Hoff said. "The chief wanted eighteen sailors. I almost missed out because I was number nineteen. I guess he just miscounted. A simple mistake changed my life."

Von Hoff first went to Bremerton, Washington, which he didn't like much.

"It rained almost every day," he said.

He was uplifted, however, after an assignment to the V-2 Division—aviation structural mechanics.

"We worked on everything in an airplane except for the engine," Von Hoff said. "I was happy, learning how to weld and rivet."

After Pearl Harbor was attacked, the Lexington looked for the Japanese fleet out in the Pacific, spending about a week in the hunt.

"It sounds silly now, but I wasn't too worried about Japan," Von Hoff said. "It's such a small country. I didn't think that the Japanese were a very powerful people. After the Coral Sea, my opinion changed completely."

The Battle of the Coral Sea was one of the half-dozen most significant battles of the Pacific war.

Having conquered nearly all of Southeast Asia, Japan was at the apex of its power. Still trying to recover from a series of devastating defeats, the Allies were just beginning to develop the skills needed to survive militarily, then to strike back.

Allied strategy at this time focused on a defensive force in terms of U.S. Army and Marine strength on New Caledonia—well to the south of the Solomon

Islands—and Australian air and ground strength at Port Moresby, in southern New Guinea.

In April 1942, Japanese forces left their stronghold of Rabaul, north of New Guinea, and launched a two-pronged amphibious invasion of Tulagi in the southern Solomon Islands and Port Moresby—the last Allied base between Japan and Australia. In so doing, they brought the U.S. carrier fleet to battle for the first time in World War II, although American ships had previously launched air attacks, including the Doolittle raid.

Historians remain divided about Japan's long-term intentions. In practice, the Japanese military planning structure was extremely complex, with ill-defined areas of responsibility and acrimonious debates between Army and Navy.

Nonetheless, if successful at Tulagi and Port Moresby, it seems reasonable to assume that the Japanese would have invaded northern Australia.

Three Japanese fleets set sail in the South Pacific. They were pointed toward Tulagi and Port Moresby.

The force included two big aircraft carriers, Shokaku and Zuikaku, both Pearl Harbor veterans, as well as heavy cruisers and another aircraft carrier, the smaller Shoho.

Alerted by radio intercepts, the Allies countered with three main task forces: USS Yorktown—already at the Coral Sea—USS Lexington and a joint surface group.

The carriers USS Hornet and USS Enterprise were heading south after the Doolittle raid on Tokyo, but arrived too late to take part in the battle.

The Japanese occupied Tulagi without incident on May 3. The Yorktown closed on the island, launching three successful strikes against Japanese shipping and aircraft there.

Carrier and land-based airplanes of both the U.S. and Japan searched for each other's fleet in the Coral Sea.

The Lexington's aircraft attacked and sank Shoho. The next morning, the large Lady Lex could not avoid the torpedoes that sank her.

The Battle of the Coral Sea was historic not because it was a decisive victory for either side, but because opposing fleets fought without their ships seeing one another.

In tactical terms, the Japanese had had a narrow victory: one small carrier lost and a large carrier damaged, against the loss of the Lexington and damage to the Yorktown.

"But from our point of view, after five months of continuous Allied defeat, a battle that came out about even was close enough to a victory to claim it as one," Von Hoff said.

In addition, the seaborne invasion of Port Moresby was averted, which was key to Allied strategy. The loss of Moresby may well have meant the loss of Australia, certainly a substantial blow to the Allied cause. As a result of the Coral Sea battle, the Japanese were forced to attempt taking Moresby overland. The subsequent delay was long enough to allow veteran Allied soldiers to gather along the narrow Kokoda Trail, which crossed the Owen Stanleys, a mountain range extending southeast and northwest on New Guinea.

As the Japanese came within thirty-two miles of Port Moresby, the Australians counterattacked, along with American reinforcements, driving the Japanese back over the mountains. The enemy retreat turned into a rout. Japanese by the thousands died of starvation and disease. A Japanese general died in a river crossing. By November 1942, however, the Allies also became bogged down. They too were hollow-eyed with jungle fever and hunger.

With the Allied forces stalled at Buna, General Douglas MacArthur airlifted in some 15,000 fresh troops to help stimulate the campaign.

In December, he sent in a new general, Robert L. Eichelberger, telling him to take Buna or not to come back alive. By the end of January 1943, Buna was in Allied hands.

While the Buna campaign was a U.S. Army initiative and did not get as much notice as Guadalcanal, for example, the fighting was every bit as savage, and the cost in dead and wounded was even higher. The long push up the northern coast of New Guinea began next. New Guinea is the world's second biggest island: the campaign would take two more years.

Von Hoff's combat experience ended at the Battle of the Coral Sea.

"The promise I made to God before I jumped into the ocean ... all these years later, I can honestly tell you I've honored that commitment every day of my life," he said.

Von Hoff spent twenty years in the U.S. Navy, becoming a chief petty officer. He was stationed in California.

While home on leave in December 1942, he married a local girl—a St. Charles resident. He had met her just two months earlier.

"She came out to California, of course," Von Hoff

said. "Anne and I, we were always a happy couple."

They returned to Batavia in 1960, raising a family there. Von Hoff began teaching Sunday school at Bethany Lutheran Church.

"I was a changed man," he says, adding that faith is like radar, seeing through the fog—picturing the reality of things at a distance, things the human eye cannot detect.

Anne Von Hoff died several years ago.

"She was a wonderful wife," Von Hoff said. "I tell you, in fifty-four years she went to the doctor with the kids, but only once for herself. She had very good health, then she was gone."

The father of four adult sons—one of whom pitched professional baseball for the Houston Astros, another who became a colonel in the U.S. Army—Von Hoff said his wartime memories sometimes still haunt him, especially during Fourth of July fireworks shows.

He remains proud of his military service.

"I have had a good life, mostly handed to me through God," Von Hoff said. "My sons are all strong Christians. That's a real positive. Losing my wife was one of the down times, but you accept it, knowing it's all part of a bigger plan."

Thinking back across more than six decades, Von Hoff said that Edward "Butch" O'Hare was one of the most unforgettable people he has met.

"He was a real friendly sort of guy," Von Hoff said. "He almost single-handedly saved all of us."

O'Hare was a Medal of Honor recipient and the man for whom Chicago's O'Hare International Airport is named.

The famous naval aviator was a pilot on board the USS Lexington. In February 1942, less than three months before the Battle of the Coral Sea, the Lady Lex had been assigned the dangerous task of penetrating enemy-held waters to make a strike at Japanese shipping.

But before the planned attack, the Lexington was discovered by a four-engine Japanese flying boat, which relayed the ship's location.

Japanese bombers attacked.

"I had come up on the flight deck," Von Hoff said. "I had firefighting duties. Along with that, down below is not where you want to be when you're being bombed."

Von Hoff became an eyewitness to history.

"We launched all of our available Wildcat fighter planes," he said. "Our scouts located the first nine Japanese planes. They were about thirty miles away. Six of the Japanese airplanes were intercepted and shot down. The Lex brought down two more with antiaircraft fire."

The Japanese kept coming, however.

"The second group of nine planes was spotted shortly thereafter," Von Hoff said. "The Lex sent six more planes up. O'Hare and his wingman were the first ones in the air. They found the Japanese planes, but the wingman developed problems with his guns and returned to our ship. O'Hare was up there all alone, the only thing between us and the bombers. One by one he attacked them until five were downed. He was firing and flying full-throttle into their formation."

By this time, other U.S. pilots were able to catch up

with O'Hare and finish off the other three incoming Japanese planes and one straggler.

Having help from the additional American airmen was a good thing for the Lexington. O'Hare was out of ammunition.

"With all that action going on, all the ship's crewmen were on deck cheering," Von Hoff said. "You'd have thought O'Hare just scored the winning touchdown in some big football game. He did us proud."

O'Hare was promoted to lieutenant commander. He became the U.S. Navy's first aviation ace, but he never saw the end of World War II.

In November 1943, O'Hare went down during the first aircraft carrier-based night fighter operations of the U.S. Navy—a tactic that he helped develop.

"We were all sorry to hear that O'Hare was lost," Von Hoff said. "He was a good man and a great aviator."

Von Hoff also is a good man—just ask anyone in the Batavia area. Among many other things, he has been that town's Sports Fan of the Year.

"Through the years, I've been real involved in youth sports," he said. "Tennis, swimming, baseball—lots of recreational activities. And each and every day, I read a chapter in the Bible. You know, back at the Coral Sea, I knew we weren't supposed to try and make a deal with God, but I prayed and prayed anyway. God came through and I've kept up my end of the bargain."

Von Hoff has a Batavia gymnasium named in his honor.

It's not anywhere near as big or busy as O'Hare International Airport, named for Von Hoff's World War

II acquaintance, but the longtime church and community contributor said he's happy nonetheless.

"I was never a hero, just one of the lucky ones who came home," he said.

And Batavia residents have been lucky, too.

Men and women such as Von Hoff are any village's greatest asset. They don't try to see through people, but to see people through.

And after all is said and done, what the human heart gives away is never gone. It is kept in the hearts of others. In and out of the military, Von Hoff has given a great deal.

Art Richoz

ART RICHOZ

"Every war is the war to end all wars."

He comes across as a friendly man, nice and neighborly—totally unassuming.

"Good to meet you," Art Richoz says, the words as freshly perked as morning coffee. "I'm honored ... having a chance to talk about America."

Conversation comes easily. Richoz is said to be a man of deep conviction. Those who know him best say that his heart is like an apple tree, its boughs bent with the thickest fruit.

Through the earlier stages of his life, Richoz was part of a generation that faced historic challenges. Their achievements were of a magnitude the world had never before witnessed. By and large, these were people who knew the difference between right and wrong.

"We believed in hard work ... we valued honesty," said the lifelong Fox Valley resident, who was born in Carpentersville and spent his entire adult life in Elgin. "People took charge. There was a strength and stability to family life, no matter what we were going through at the time."

Richoz, who was born in October 1922, was tempered and toughened by the Depression.

And like other World War II veterans, he believed in cause and country, believed that America was fighting for decency and democracy.

Overwhelmingly, these veterans were high school or college students when America went to war. They were drafted or enlisted in 1942, '43 and '44. At a time when they should have been tossing baseballs, they were throwing grenades. Some survived, others didn't. In both Europe and the Pacific, they came as liberators, not conquerors.

"I entered the service in July of 1944," Richoz said. "On Christmas Eve, I boarded the ship to go overseas."

Saying goodbye to his newlywed wife wasn't easy, remembered Richoz, who would later receive a Bronze Star and Purple Heart, among nearly a dozen ribbons and medals.

He had married a lifelong Elgin girl—Elinor Radde—on December 19, 1942.

"When my orders came, I was told to catch the train at Union Station in Chicago," Richoz said. "I asked Elinor not to come, telling her how hard it was going to be—you know, saying goodbye. I sure didn't want to leave her. She said she wouldn't cry at the station. Anyway, she came to see me off. Don't forget, she'd only been my wife for two years. And she's standing there holding our two-month-old son. Tears came to both our eyes. I hugged her, then promised I'd come home alive."

Richoz recites that promise word for word.

"Don't worry, honey," Richoz recalls telling Elinor nearly sixty years ago. "I'll be back. There's no German who'll keep me there."

Although Richoz was drafted into the service, he

had tried to enlist several times before.

"I was a tool and die maker," Richoz said. "Because our company—the Illinois Watch Case factory—had been turned into a defense plant, I received an automatic deferment from military service."

The watch case company—the same one where Richoz's father worked and where his father's father preceded them both—began manufacturing mortar shells, which were important to the war effort.

"I tried enlisting on a number of occasions," Richoz said. "Each time it was the same story: 'We need you here,' they'd tell me."

Richoz became an extremely skilled worker. He had left high school at age 16 to get a job, something that was at a premium in 1938.

Starting out, he ran errands, eventually becoming an apprentice tool and die maker. By the time World War II erupted, he was certified in that occupation.

Some saw the automatic deferment as a blessing. Richoz didn't.

"My brother was serving in the Italian and African campaigns," he said. "We lost an uncle at Luzon. Having helped with the mortar shells, I felt I had done my part here. Now, let me go there, let me try to help overseas."

Even with all the military medals and commendations, Richoz remains proud of an award the factory won for manufacturing mortar shells.

His automatic deferments came every six months.

"This one day, I went down to St. Charles, trying to enlist again," Richoz said, adding that he ran into the Carpentersville postmaster, who was on the draft board.

The man, who had been in World War I, knew Richoz.

"Art," he said, "I don't understand you. There are three months left on your current deferment. Your company has already applied for another one. If you do what I ask, you'll go back to work and forget you ever came here. It takes a long, long time to train a tool and die maker. It takes no time at all to teach someone to pull a trigger. You'll be doing more for your country by going back to work."

Unable to fight his way into the military, Richoz went back to the company and helped manufacture mortar shells. But deferment or not, the American military needed men. Richoz was drafted.

He would thus see World War II from a dual perspective: first, as part of the home front manufacturing effort, later as a combat infantryman.

In at least some sense, Richoz embodies the "we" generation of World War II. There was a commitment to the notion that America's needs came before individual desires.

Take the U.S. Army, for example. At 175,000 men, it hardly existed in 1939. Five years later, at more than 8 million strong, it was far and away the best-equipped military force in the world, especially in tanks, artillery and other heavy weapons, as well as jeeps and trucks. In 1945, U.S. industry built half of all the weapons produced worldwide.

By that time, Richoz was in France and Germany.

It was at the port city of Le Havre—west, northwest of Paris—that he first saw what war looked like up close. Ships had been sunk in the harbor. Buildings were blown apart.

Men were, too.

One evening, within those early days and nights, Richoz was awakened by the sound of a truck engine.

"I heard some sort of noise," he said. "These two trucks were slipping on the ice, trying to get up a hill. There was a freezing rain. We were in an old barn."

The trucks were loaded with dead soldiers, piled up "like logs," said Richoz, who had gone outside the barn to track down the noise.

He went back inside the barn and immediately wrote a letter to his father-in-law.

"Dad," the letter started, "When I left the train station, I told Elinor not to worry—that I would come home, that I would be back alive. The things I saw tonight made me question that promise. I'm sure that these soldiers promised their wives and their mothers and fathers that they'd come back, too. They're not going to make it. I realize now, that could very well happen to me. I don't want you to tell Elinor this now, but should I not come back, I want her to know that I did not go into battle blindly. I knew what I was doing. Staying alive may be beyond my control at this point. Tell her, though, that I did everything in my power to get back home."

Was Richoz frightened?

"I was very, very, very concerned," he said. "I prayed harder than I had ever prayed in my life."

At the beginning of Richoz's time in Europe, the Allies had driven the Germans back to or near their western border. General Dwight D. Eisenhower hoped to do even better. But gasoline shortages and the Siegfried Line had stopped his troops and a counteroffensive in the Ardennes had thrown them back, at least temporarily. Much had been gained,

43

however. The Allies had liberated France and Belgium—killing, wounding or capturing hundreds of thousands of Germans, some of them woefully inadequate as soldiers, some of them still superb.

Richoz engaged in hand-to-hand combat during his time in France. Later, he was involved in what was the worst battle he had experienced.

He was there at the Siegfried Line, a formidable obstacle along Germany's western border.

German soldiers had reached home. Men who saw no point in fighting to retain Adolf Hitler's conquests in France were ready to defend their homeland. The fighting was particularly fierce. German officers began taking the terrified survivors from their rout in France and organizing them into squads, platoons, companies, battalions and divisions. What was once little more than a mob force became an army again.

While Hitler hated being on the defensive, German troops were prepared for vicious and savage fighting at their border.

The last hundred days of the "thousand-year" Third Reich had now begun.

The Siegfried Line ran along the Rhine River.

Richoz was part of L Company—179th Infantry Regiment, 45th Division, U.S. 7th Army. He was a member of the famed "Thunderbirds," which was one of four National Guard divisions activated in 1940 by President Roosevelt, foreseeing war on the horizon.

Many members of the original Thunderbirds were of Native American ancestry, hailing from Arizona, Colorado, Oklahoma and New Mexico. After activation, replacements for the 45th came from all across the United States.

The Thunderbird symbol was a red square containing a golden bird with outstretched wings.

The division slogan was "Semper Anticus," meaning "Always Forward."

It was a slogan Richoz believed in.

"People who offer their lives for their country understand a thing or two about patriotism," said Richoz, adding that such an allegiance is not the fear of something, but the love of something.

"Being an American, to me, it's a blessing," he said.

Richoz nearly paid the ultimate price for that blessing. Just as there are no points of a compass on the chart of true patriotism, memories of service and sacrifice can be rekindled with a question.

Richoz doesn't hesitate when asked about being shot. "My luck ran out on March 29, 1945," says the Elgin grandfather of four, who retired in 1987. "I was wounded about 150 miles inside of Germany."

Richoz's company was advancing up a hill during the battle he'll never forget.

He was hit by a German machine-gun, the bullets damaging his jaw and shoulder, destroying his right eye, which was replaced with a plastic one.

Today, Richoz is legally blind.

Upon being hit, the young American experienced the sheer ghastliness of war.

"All I could think of was getting home," Richoz said. "I thought of my wife and son. I thought of my folks."

Richoz's ears were ringing. He saw stars, then felt as if he were burning up. He hit the ground. Bullets whizzed past him.

A medic came over to help him, cutting off the sleeve of his jacket, putting sulfa drugs on the wound.

"I kept saying, 'My eye, my eye,' but he couldn't do anything with it," Richoz said. "He told me my wound was serious. He said, 'Richoz, I'd like to take you back, but I just can't do it. There are too many here who need me. I'm going to aim you down the hill. You just keep crawling. And stay close to the ground, they're firing at you and me both.'"

The last thing Richoz remembered was someone picking him up and putting him on the hood of a jeep. When he awoke, he was in a tent. Later, he was transported to a field hospital.

As far as Richoz recalls, he was in four field hospitals.

One of his best buddies overseas was Californian Richard Rios, who was wounded the same day as Richoz, although the Elgin infantryman didn't know it at the time.

Richoz was in an ambulance, being transferred to another area for additional medical attention a day or two after being wounded.

He didn't realize until years later that one of the other soldiers in the ambulance was his friend Rios, who also survived, making it home to California after the war.

"He was hit in the stomach, a terrible, terrible wound," Richoz said. "He kept trying to touch it, fidgeting with it. He was trying to get at that wound. He went under the bandages, which wasn't a good idea. I couldn't take seeing that. I finally grabbed his hands, hugged him and held his arms as tight as I could, right up against his body. 'Hold on, soldier,' I said. 'We're on our way home. God is with us. We're on our way home.' "

It was dark in the ambulance and Richoz was heavily medicated, explaining why he didn't recognize Rios.

Decades later, when Elinor began putting her husband's World War II memories and mementos together, she found an old letter from Rios, written some 58 years earlier. It told of how Richoz's friend had been shot in the chest and stomach. It specified a date and time. It mentioned the ambulance ride.

"Turns out, the soldier I was trying to console was my friend Rios," said Richoz, who has since tried to contact the California native. "I never caught that when I first got the letter years ago."

As of early 2004, the two have not communicated.

"If he's still alive, I hope to find him—somehow, someway," Richoz said.

Buddy relationships are common during war. Soldiers have always understood the importance of individual bonds. Group bonds, too.

As in any closely knit family, the death of any member is a loss felt by all.

Richoz remembers the sting of watching young soldiers die—young soldiers who had become friends. More than once, he had to lower his head to hide the tears.

At the same time, soldiers learn to accept the death of comrades as an inevitable consequence of war. They are saddened by the loss, but cannot dwell on it.

The living have to keep right on living.

Despite being seriously wounded, it's what Richoz

did.

He and Rios shared foxholes, swapped stories and went scrounging together. The terrible downside of any friendship is the death of a good buddy—or, as in Richoz's case, losing contact with someone who was once a close comrade in arms.

A month before Richoz was wounded in 1945, the military situation required that the principal Allied leaders meet for the purpose of making basic decisions on the shape of the postwar world.

The Nazi position was hopeless. Germany was going to be overrun, occupied and forced to accept an unconditional surrender.

The site chosen for this most fateful Allied summit meeting of World War II was Yalta, on the Black Sea shore, in the Soviet Union's liberated Crimea.

In February 1945, President Roosevelt met with British Prime Minister Winston Churchill and Soviet Premier Joseph Stalin. The three men gathered with their staffs in palaces that were once used by vacationing czars, but by then were in a sorry state, due to the German occupation. While the palaces were still standing, the rest of Yalta had been destroyed.

A major aim of Roosevelt's was to get the Soviet Union involved in the war against Japan. In return, he was prepared to make concessions to Stalin in Manchuria. Roosevelt's critics claimed later that he sold out Chiang Kai-shek and the Nationalist Chinese. Others, however, said that there was nothing Roosevelt could have done to hold back the Red tide in northern Asia.

Among other issues at Yalta, the Big Three also ratified previous agreements made among the foreign ministers about the shape of postwar Germany. These agreements divided Germany into four zones of occupation—the Big Three plus France—with Berlin inside the Soviet zone but divided into four sectors. Although they could not agree on a fixed amount of reparations to be extracted from Germany by the Soviets, it was accepted that Germany would provide labor as well as funds for reconstruction.

With the Yalta meetings going on, Richoz was advancing with the 45th Division, squeezing Germany even tighter.

The German collapse was accelerating on all fronts when Richoz was wounded.

Although wars are fought with weapons, they are won with men. Like Richoz and countless others, those on the American side did their best at a time when their best was needed.

He left Germany on April 3, 1945—one month before the actual surrender ceremony, which took place in a modest schoolhouse at Rheims, in northeastern France, on the Vesle River, about 83 miles from Paris.

In New York, Washington, Los Angeles, Chicago and across the land, Americans celebrated V-E Day. President Harry Truman made a radio broadcast to remind people of the tasks ahead: "We must work to bind the wounds of a suffering world—to build an abiding peace, a peace rooted in justice and in law. We can build such a peace only by hard, toilsome, painstaking work—by understanding and working with our allies in peace as we have in war."

Roosevelt had died on April 12, 1945. He was tired and prematurely old.

Nonetheless, the shock was profound. In those pre-television days, the public actually saw little of the president, and few Americans realized how FDR had sacrificed his health for the nation. For most of the 12 million soldiers and sailors in the U.S. Armed Forces, Roosevelt was the only president they could remember. In terms of history, if he could be properly criticized for not doing enough to prepare America for the war, he must be praised for being a great wartime leader. It was Roosevelt who shook the lethargy out of the American people.

Richoz came home to his wife and young son. A daughter would be born after the war.

Both children became schoolteachers.

"I'm so very, very proud of them," Richoz said.

He has been married to Elinor for more than sixty years.

She is the unquestioned love of his life. Through good times and bad, they've found out that the best thing to hold onto is one another.

In marriage, being the right person is just as important as finding the right person, Richoz says, smiling.

Listening to him, it's easy to hear the idealist inside. Even after having been kicked around by the Depression and losing an eye in World War II, he had an undying affection for his country.

That feeling continues today. In the world according to Richoz, patriotism never goes out of fashion.

After World War II, Richoz went to work at International Harvester, and was involved in the making of one of the largest crawler tractors ever built.

He stayed at International Harvester only a short

time, however.

"It was a long commute," Richoz said, referring to the hourlong drive to and from the plant in Melrose Park.

He took a tool and die job with McDonough Manufacturing in Elgin. He had to make a number of adjustments because of the loss of his right eye, but Richoz thrived at the local company.

Over the years, the strain of those adjustments caused him to lose his remaining vision.

Nonetheless, he calls McDonough the best place he ever worked.

"It was like an extended family," he says of his time there.

It was at McDonough that Richoz worked on a component for the Mercury space program.

"I did the tooling that helped put the first American into space," he said.

Astronaut Alan Shepard was a World War II veteran and a U.S. Navy pilot. He became the first American in space on May 5, 1961, riding the capsule "Freedom 7" to an altitude of 117 miles.

McDonough also assisted in putting John Glenn into orbit. Richoz helped on that one, too.

"My contribution can't compare to what the scientists did, but I'm proud to have helped," he said.

Ask Richoz about being a World War II hero and he shakes his head.

"No," he says, "But I served in the company of heroes."

He thinks back to other young Americans, the ones who didn't make it home.

The biggest price people pay for war is what might have been.

"We were cold and frightened and exhausted a lot of the time," Richoz remembers of his combat experience in World War II. "But we were young and strong then ... You wouldn't want to go through it again, but you're proud of having served your country with honor."

Any regrets?

"Sure," Richoz says. "You feel for all the good guys who never got to come home."

In 2002, Richoz received all the military honors he so richly deserved. His original Purple Heart, which was lost decades earlier overseas, was replaced. And he found out he had also qualified for the Bronze Star, as well as six other medals. If he had been given the awards during World War II, the additional service points would have resulted in an earlier discharge date. In all branches of the military, these things often slip through the cracks.

But Richoz's not complaining.

U.S. Speaker of the House J. Dennis Hastert handed him the medals in a small ceremony attended by family members.

Duty, honor, country and courage—those hallowed words defined what was a rallying call for the young Richoz. Years and years later, they still define him.

His disability is a daily reminder of the war. So is the integrity with which he carries himself.

Neither money nor medals can repay him for what he has done.

"Looking back, I was just one tooth on a gear," he says, referring to his time in the service. "Every tooth is important. Remove one tooth from that gear, and the gear will stop turning."

Without Richoz, the Fox Valley would have been diminished.

Young and old alike, its citizens should be profoundly grateful that he has made his home here.

George and Mary Loechner

GEORGE AND MARY LOECHNER

"Women wear uniforms, too."

Forget the old adage about a woman's place being in the home. World War II changed all that.

To begin with, women entered the workforce in record numbers. Just say "Rosie the Riveter" to someone who lived through that era. The knowing response will be an acknowledgment that the war was an about-face for both sexes.

With so many men in the military, young women spent more and more time together. A support system developed, something that their mothers didn't have.

In addition, the wartime housing shortage forced young women to share space. They lived together out of necessity—often five or more to one home, with one bathroom and one kitchen.

Gasoline was rationed, not so much to save fuel, but to save rubber, which was almost impossible to get after the Japanese overran Southeast Asia. Across America, the speed limit was set at thirty-five miles per hour—again, to save rubber more than fuel. Accordingly, carpooling became a national phenomenon.

A world away, Mary Loechner was stationed on Tinian Island, site of American airfields, from which U.S.

planes were sent to drop atomic bombs on the Japanese cities of Hiroshima and Nagasaki in August 1945.

The lifelong Elgin resident was an Army nurse, having enlisted in November 1944.

"I was very adventurous," said Loechner, who was born in January 1923. "During my professional training at St. Joseph's [Hospital], Japan attacked our country. Everything changed. When I was in high school, I wanted to become an airline stewardess, but was considered too tall. Years later, as the planes got bigger, they wanted taller girls. It was water under the bridge by then. I had turned to nursing. Anyhow, being young and daring, I didn't have any fear—none of us did, really. Maybe we were just dumb kids, I don't know. But more important than that, we wanted to do our part. There was no question that women should serve somewhere, somehow. We were all involved."

From the St. Joseph School of Nursing in Elgin, Loechner, who is 5 feet 7 inches tall, became a cadet nurse at Edward Hines Hospital, located outside Chicago.

And as a cadet nurse, Loechner was part of the first group of such women in Illinois.

She went through nursing and cadet school with her best friend, Marian Weise. The two met in the third grade, and stayed close through the years, even though Weise moved from the Fox Valley before high school started.

Years later, they would go to Tinian at the same time, having asked that they serve together, which was not an uncommon request during World War II.

For one family, the same sort of request proved tragic.

The story of the U.S. Navy and the Sullivan

brothers is well remembered by people who are of a particular age—old enough to have made it through World War II.

The Sullivans were living in Iowa when Pearl Harbor was attacked. The oldest brothers were George, 28; Francis, 27; Joseph, 24; Madison, 23; and Albert, 20.

When a family friend, Bill Ball, was killed at Pearl Harbor on the USS Arizona, the five oldest brothers decided to enlist in the Navy to avenge his death. They insisted on serving together, despite an official policy separating brothers, and persisted until their request was finally approved. The oldest, George, summarized the brothers' philosophy: "If the worst comes to worst, why, we'll all have gone down together."

Eleven months later, on November 13, 1942, they were crew members on the USS Juneau. A Japanese submarine hit the cruiser with a torpedo. The ship sank instantly.

The U.S. Navy portrayed the Sullivans as heroes who went down with their ship. It sent the parents of the five young men on a nationwide speaking tour. They stopped at factories, encouraging workers to reach higher levels of productivity. In April 1943, Mrs. Sullivan christened a destroyer named for the now-famous brothers—USS The Sullivans.

Genevieve, the only Sullivan sister, joined the Navy as a member of the WAVES—Women Accepted for Volunteer Emergency Service. A sixth son, Jimmy, enlisted in the Navy on the day he turned seventeen.

But there was a problem, completely kept from the public. At least one of the five oldest Sullivan brothers did not go down with the Juneau. With some 140 other members of the crew, George Sullivan managed to get into one of the ship's rubber rafts. The men were adrift at sea for many days. Only ten of the crew survived. The others died of thirst, exposure and shark attack. The U.S. Navy in the Pacific War had an often grossly inadequate rescue service. Critics claim that they didn't put enough planes and ships to work when conducting search and recover missions, adding that the Navy never wanted to admit this.

In addition, while some say that the Navy exploited the Sullivan situation, it failed to learn from the experience. Two and a half years later, on July 30, 1945, the cruiser Indianapolis was sunk by a Japanese submarine. Before the ship went down, distress signals were sent. Messages were either ignored or unnoticed. Whatever the cause, there was no search. Hundreds of crew members were killed by exposure and shark attack. If Navy officials had handled things differently, more Americans would have survived the ordeal.

The Indianapolis had just completed a top-secret mission, delivering a key component of the first atomic bomb to Tinian, located in the South Pacific, about 1,500 miles south of Japan.

"Even though we were there, we didn't know anything about what was going on," remembers Loechner, whose husband, George, received the Bronze Star, the Purple Heart and four bronze battle stars, having seen significant action in North Africa and Anzio, an Italian fishing port.

The Loechners live in the same attractive Elgin home that they had built when they were married after World War II. Construction cost $6,000.

They have three children, as well as grandchildren and great-grandchildren.

George Loechner is confined to a wheelchair, having had a heart attack and stroke.

His wife, who is in good health, outranked him in World War II.

"My wife was a lieutenant; I was just a dogface soldier," said George Loechner, who worked as a draftsman at the Elgin National Watch Company after World War II.

Rank aside, Mary Loechner says her husband is the one who walked into and out of the valley of death, surviving through toughness, tenacity and extraordinary heroism against the enemy. Luck was part of it, too.

"He was the one involved in heavy combat," she says. "I did my part and I'm proud of it, but I never went through what he did."

They have been married for more than 55 years. There is a give-and-take to their conversation. Talking to them, it becomes clear that chains do not hold a good marriage together. It is the threads—thousands and thousands of tiny threads—that sew people together through the years.

Mary Loechner's military threads take her back to Tinian.

The Army Nurse Corps, established in 1901 and thus the oldest female branch of all the military services in the United States, grew to unprecedented numbers after Japan's attack on Pearl Harbor. To meet the demands of total war, the corps expanded to more than 57,000. Members served in almost every corner of the globe, meeting a difficult and dangerous series of challenges. As with most of the World War II generation, their contributions were wrapped in patriotism, service and sacrifice.

"After you heard the news about the attack on Pearl Harbor, you wanted to do your share," Mary Loechner said. "It wasn't just your brother's war or your future husband's war. It was my country as much as theirs. It was just as much my war as it was theirs."

Most Americans got news of the surprise attack from the radio. The vastness of the country meant that its inhabitants got up and carried out their Sunday morning rituals in successive stages, east to west, as the sun rose. People in Richmond and Philadelphia were finishing breakfast as residents of Cincinnati brushed their teeth. Those in St. Louis opened their eyes to the morning light while citizens of Seattle and San Francisco slept on, blanketed by what was left of the night.

And for those at Pearl Harbor, morning always came later than that. When the Japanese attacked at about 8 a.m., it was already afternoon in New York.

Early or late, many Americans attended Sunday services that morning—half the population of 130 million were church members.

Radio is what also linked American to American. Radio, in fact, was the Paul Revere of its day, spreading the news of a cold and calculated Japanese attack. Many who heard the first bulletins telephoned friends and family members. They joined a swelling audience who were tuned to radios of various shapes and sizes.

Years later, it was from the radio that Mary Loechner heard about the atomic bomb blast over the still-intact city of Hiroshima, southwest of Tokyo.

The news came crackling from a radio owned by one of the nurses.

Earlier that evening, Loechner and the other nurses assigned to Tinian were ordered to stay in their Quonset huts through the night. Under no circumstances were they to leave the barracks.

"We were told about a 'big mission,' nothing more," Loechner said. "We didn't know how big, however. For being right in the middle of what was happening, we were the last to know anything."

She was doing laundry when the atomic bomb was dropped after 8 a.m. on August 6, 1945.

No one even knew what an atomic bomb was at the time, Loechner said.

A B-29 bomber from the 509th Composite Group, with a specially trained crew commanded by Colonel Paul Tibbets, was chosen for the Hiroshima mission. Their plane was called the Enola Gay.

Loechner and the other nurses were not briefed beforehand about the 509th Composite Group. Almost everyone on the island was kept in the dark, including the 200,000 troops stationed there. The mission was one of the best-kept secrets in history. Enola Gay crewmen lived by themselves in a compound on another part of the island.

On that historic day in August, Tibbets released over Hiroshima a uranium bomb called "Little Boy." He reported later: "As far as I was concerned it was a perfect operation."

On August 9, three days afterward, a plutonium bomb known as "Fat Boy" was dropped over Nagasaki.

As with the earlier operation over Hiroshima, an atomic weapon was loaded into the bomb bay of a B-29, but not the Enola Gay. The second airplane, called Bock's Car and piloted by Major Charles Sweeney, also flew from Tinian.

In the course of those three days, two cities were

leveled.

The destruction of each exceeded the most careful conclusions made by scientists assigned to the atomic bomb project. Reality was worse than they had predicted. At both Hiroshima and Nagasaki, it was hours before the mushroom clouds, flames and smoke cleared, opening enough air space to permit adequate photo reconnaissance.

Those are not pretty pictures.

While life came cheap at the end of World War II, the losses at Hiroshima and Nagasaki were not as great as previous Japanese losses in Tokyo. It was the inherent shock of the atomic event—one airplane, one bomb, one city—that overwhelmed people.

Allied scientists had harnessed the very same force that powers the stars. Some 80,000 lives were snuffed out at Hiroshima; another 35,000 at Nagasaki.

"We felt bad for the Japanese people, but knew that the bomb ultimately saved American lives," Loechner said. "We celebrated when we heard the news about Hiroshima, figuring that the war was over."

Before the first bomb was dropped, more than 2 million Japanese troops and countless civilians were prepared to defend their homeland and Emperor Hirohito.

They would use their bare hands if necessary.

What's more, additional Kamikaze missions were on the horizon. The Japanese decision to fight to the death endangered the nation. It was an official decision.

Estimates of the dead and wounded that would ensue from a U.S. ground invasion ran very high, up to one half million American casualties. Japan figured to lose at least that many men and women.

In July 1945, there was some discussion among American leaders on what preliminary warning should be addressed to Tokyo prior to the employment of the two bombs being assembled on Tinian. At the end of the month President Truman issued the Potsdam Declaration, defining terms for Japan's surrender.

Two days after it was issued, Japanese Premier Suzuki announced that his government would ignore the demand that Japan surrender unconditionally or face complete destruction.

The declaration was not an explicit warning that the United States possessed weapons of mass destruction and would use them. Truman was unwilling to be exact, thinking that Congress had tolerated an unknown project costing nearly $2 billion and might object to an explanation offered an enemy government without informing the legislative body that paid the bill.

The "Little Boy" bomb that was dropped over Hiroshima was 28 inches in diameter and 120 inches long. Weighing 9,000 pounds, its explosive power was the same as that of 20,000 tons of TNT.

After the first bombing, Loechner and a group of other nurses were invited to meet the crew of the Enola Gay.

"Everyone went to a victory mass on the island," Loechner said. "After that, we had a breakfast for the whole crew."

Some of the nurses went inside the airplane. The Elgin woman was able to take Tibbets' seat, sitting there for a minute or two, looking out the window.

"Thinking back, it gives you a real sense of history," Loechner said, adding that she introduced herself to Tibbets, a man whom she described as "nothing out of the ordinary." However, she adds, that observation was based only on a quick hello and an accompanying handshake.

"Because you didn't know them all personally, the pilots seemed to be of the same mold," she said.

Other than the atomic bomb event, Loechner's time on Tinian was fairly routine, she said. "I was a general nurse. We took care of everyday things ... various sicknesses. Hepatitis was one of them. The seriously wounded went to Hawaii, then were sent stateside."

Before being sent to Tinian, Loechner served as a nurse at a hospital for returning veterans. That hospital was in Battle Creek, Michigan. She saw countless amputees—young men who had lost an arm or leg during combat, for example. Many were double-amputees.

While not nearly as dramatic, daily life at Tinian was full for the nurses.

"We were almost always busy," Loechner said. "You'd get up early in the morning, then put on your fatigues and go to work. We never wore white because of the threat of snipers. We were well guarded. Oh, and another thing. There were all these little lizards on the island. They never bothered you, though. They were actually kind of cute. "

Loechner grew up a tomboy in Elgin. She lived near Bluff City Cemetery. It was on cemetery property that she learned to ride a bicycle.

"I'll bet that there's still a lot of skin from my knees and elbows out there somewhere," Loechner said, remembering the winding roadways of the cemetery. "Bluff City was our playground, even in the winter."

She greatly admired Amelia Earhart, the first

woman to fly across the Atlantic Ocean. The famed American aviator disappeared in July 1937, shortly after leaving New Guinea on a planned trip around the world.

Although aviation excited her, Loechner wanted to be a nurse from an early age. She tended to small animals around her house.

"I used as much Mercurochrome as I could," she said, smiling. "I thought it could cure just about anything."

That same spirit of hope and healing carried her through World War II.

Because of its proximity to Japan, Tinian was going to be an American hospital base.

"With an expected invasion of Japan, the American military was figuring on a lot of casualties," Loechner said.

In July 1944, U.S. Marines had taken Saipan in a series of bloody battles. It was from Saipan that they assaulted nearby Tinian, which was secured about a month later.

Although the island was somewhat secure, it was common knowledge that some Japanese were still living in coral caves on Tinian.

From time to time, nurses were able to go down to the beach at Tinian. Recreation gave them a chance to break from their regular routine. In a 1995 book about women who served in the military during World War II, a decades-old photograph of Loechner is among many featured. Written by a nationally known author, Olga Gruhzit-Hoyt, the book is called *They Also Served*.

The book is available at several local libraries.

On page 51, Loechner, then a dark-haired 22-year-old, is pictured with two other young nurses, one of them her close friend Weise, with whom she enlisted. The other woman, Elise Beger, also was a friend.

While Weise and Beger are deceased, back in 1945, they looked like pinup girls. So did Loechner. In the snapshot, the three nurses are wearing bathing suits and sitting side-by-side in the sand.

Beger's bathing suit was made of fabric from a parachute. She had not brought a suit of her own to Tinian.

Shoreline coral had been bombed out, allowing American military personnel an occasional opportunity to go swimming. The Tinian beach became a popular place.

"It was very tropical there," Loechner said of the island. "I was on Tinian for about five months."

She's proud of her time in the service.

"I would do it again in a minute," Loechner said, adding that military service is a reward in itself. The longtime nurse, who retired nearly twenty years ago, apparently initiated a family trend.

"My granddaughter served at the Persian Gulf during Desert Storm," Loechner said. "She was an MP, just out of high school. Third generation girl to enlist."

One of Loechner's daughters also was in the military. She served as a helicopter mechanic.

After Tinian, Loechner was sent to Japan. The war was over and nurses were assigned to help set up and staff a makeshift hospital in a Japanese post office near Nagasaki.

"We took care of American servicemen, maybe

someone who was hurt in a jeep accident," she said. "We weren't there to treat the Japanese, but you felt sorry for them. So many were badly burned."

Loechner visited the city of Nagasaki shortly after it had been destroyed by the atom bomb.

"Everything was flat," she said. "You know those pictures of Mars we're seeing now? Well, those photographs remind me of Nagasaki ... total devastation, wiped out completely."

Loechner said she knew nothing of radiation, knew nothing of its dangers.

"Even so, we wouldn't worry much, if at all," Loechner said. "You truly thought you were invincible. And along with friends of mine at the time, I thought I could do anything a boy could do."

Loechner grew up with an older brother, Joseph Goldner. He also served during World War II. He came home alive, too.

"All in all, I feel I've been blessed by a guardian angel," Loechner said. "I think of war as a necessary evil, like what we're going through today in Iraq. When you think about Hitler and all the terrible things he did, it would've been better to have had him out of power much, much earlier."

After the war, along with being a wife and mother, Loechner stayed in nursing.

Among other places, she worked in a maternity ward at St. Joseph Hospital.

"With all the death that the war brought, I wanted to help bring new life into the world," Loechner said.

Whether in the military—like Loechner was—or working stateside during World War II, women were able to acquire expertise in very complex, very challenging jobs. Their return to traditional roles never negated the pride they'd felt as a result. Many women resolved that prospects for their daughters were going to be a great deal better than their own had been before the war.

In many respects, then, World War II became an early combat zone for female equality in the workplace, even as they shared the burden of defeating Axis tyranny with men.

Likewise, World War II was the major turning point in the relationship of women to the armed forces. For the first time in American history, the military services set out to recruit large numbers of women to fill not only essential nursing positions, but to meet military requirements across a vast array of officer and enlisted skills. Before it was over, some 400,000 American women had answered the call of the Army, Navy, Marines and Coast Guard. By all accounts, this great endeavor exceeded all but the most optimistic expectations, and paved the way for women's permanent integration into the U.S. Armed Forces.

In 1985, Loechner went back to Japan, her visit coinciding with the 40th anniversary of the bombings. She stopped at a peace museum in Hiroshima.

"I'm happy, of course, that American lives were saved by our using the atomic bomb, but you feel so sad for the Japanese civilians," Loechner said. "You wonder what else could have been done to end the war. The bombings caused such destruction, disfiguring people for generations."

Regardless of her admittedly limited participation in one of history's most momentous events, Loechner learned something about the future. Having witnessed the aftermath of an atomic bomb blast, she, better than most, understands the costs of war, how they greatly exceed any potential gain, especially if mankind is ever to progress.

And judging by the past, there will be no veterans of a World War III. No survivors, either.

Ed Burnitz

ED BURNITZ

"We were shaped by tough times."

As the United States learned on September 11, 2001, two vast oceans, east and west, do not insulate a country from the danger of terrorism.

Decades earlier, the same sort of lesson was driven home. Back then, the terrorist was economic chaos.

"I never went to high school," says Carpentersville resident Ed Burnitz, his tone strong and steady, with words coming out like bullets. "It was the Depression. Things were tight at home. I wanted to help out."

Burnitz's mother was against his quitting school. She eventually relented.

"I told her, 'Mama, we need the money,' " said Burnitz, who dropped out of school after only the eighth grade. "My first job was delivering telegrams. It wasn't much, but every penny counted."

Burnitz counted, too, serving in the U.S. Army during World War II. He was part of the American military machine that rolled through Europe, stalling and stopping, however, at a number of German checkpoints.

About a decade earlier, it was the U.S. economy that had stopped.

The American stock market collapse of 1929 signaled the beginning of a radical change in fortune for the United States. That change coincided with the rise of sinister forces in the heart of Europe and Asia. Hitler was plotting to take over Germany with his rabble-rousing Nazis—the National Socialist German Workers Party. Japan was starting to flex its political and military muscle. The tiny island nation was grabbing larger and larger slices of Chinese territory.

To Burnitz, who was born in April 1923 and grew up on Chicago's North Side, those distant developments were of little consequence when measured against the frightening family problems that the Depression dumped on the dinner table every night. More often than not, those problems replaced a balanced meal.

"We were barely surviving," he said. "We lived in a rundown apartment near Wrigley Field. I'm one of five boys. My parents struggled to feed us. Dad was out of work for a long, long time. He was never the same after the Depression."

From delivering telegrams, Burnitz became a car hiker.

"Believe it or not, some people did have money in those days," he said. "To my thinking, if you owned an automobile and had a nice home, you were really rich. I got to know some of them folks, like this big business executive. I was paid to bring him his car. The only problem was, I didn't have a driver's license. I was too young."

Later, but before being drafted, Burnitz did get a driver's license.

"It's lucky the police never caught up with me," he said.

Burnitz entered the service in 1943. He was an Army rifleman.

"Growing up in the Depression wasn't much of an honor, but it did make you see things through ... you had to face your problems," Burnitz said. "Later, when I lost friends in battle, I was able to handle those losses without falling apart. And when all hell broke lose, you never chickened out."

The Depression was a great leveler. Most Americans were in the same boat—a boat that was sinking into chaos.

The numbers were staggering. In three years stocks lost 80 percent of their value. The Ford Motor Company employed 128,000 workers in 1929; by 1931 that number had dropped to 37,000. American farmers who had sold a bushel of corn for 77 cents in 1929 were getting only 32 cents a bushel by 1932.

When Roosevelt became president that same year, the American economy was in a free fall. One of the sad side effects was a plague of unemployment, bankruptcy and foreclosure. Perhaps the saddest side effect was trying to ride out the storm through what was a sea of broken dreams.

From Wall Street to Main Street, hardship meant more than statistics. It became a state of mind, a matter of horizons.

Seasons changed and so did the years. Taken together, they rushed away like leaves in a storm.

And the storm of all storms was coming.

At the start of the 1940s, the U.S. Army was not only small in number, but also limited in tanks and airplanes. With war igniting in Europe and the Pacific, flames would soon engulf the world. America needed firefighters. In the months before World War II, the military was handing out only garden hoses.

"When my time came, getting into the Army ... well, it was okay with me," Burnitz said. "We had enemies. They wanted to rule the world. As bad as things were at home, you still didn't want anybody breathing down your neck. You didn't want Hitler or the Japanese bossing us around."

After basic training, Burnitz was shipped overseas.

He would receive the Bronze Star and three Purple Hearts, the first of which was awarded for action at Anzio, where Americans were pinned down along a beachhead for four months.

"That was a hellhole," Burnitz said, referring to Anzio, located 35 miles southeast of Rome and birthplace of the emperors Nero and Caligula. "We were trying to hold a position. The Germans just kept shelling us."

Anzio came close to being an Allied disaster. The initial amphibious landing in January 1944 went well, but the operation's commanders did not capitalize on it. Surprised Germans then had ample time to assemble troops and artillery on the high ground surrounding the beachhead's perimeter. Their continuing counterattacks nearly succeeded in wiping out the beachhead.

The original purpose of the Anzio landing—to take pressure off the main drive toward Rome—failed. The Allies were trapped on the beachhead, every inch of it under German artillery attack. And the weather wouldn't cooperate. After foxholes filled with rainwater, the only protection came from surface shelters built out of sandbags. At the same time, soldiers sought safety in the few buildings that had not been pulverized into rubble.

Some say the fierce fighting at Anzio was equal to the battles fought at Gettysburg and Stalingrad. It was an important engagement. American troops would defeat the Germans and move on to Rome, but the cost was substantial.

All told, the Americans suffered 59,000 casualties at Anzio, many of them victims of shell shock.

Burnitz was wounded when shrapnel tore through his ankle.

"At times you were scared because the shells seemed to keep coming and coming," Burnitz said. "I lost a real close friend at Anzio. A Spanish boy from Waco, Texas. Real quiet kid. He had a heart of gold, but a good, good soldier. That was a hard one to take."

Burnitz was a member of the Thunderbirds. He and Art Richoz—profiled earlier in this book—were part of the same 45th Division, although the two didn't know one another at the time.

The two men met years and years later, strangers sitting side-by-side at an area doctor's office in 1999.

They struck up a casual conversation, then became friends.

Richoz was shot in the face during World War II. On the same day—March 29, 1945—Burnitz was shot in the back of the head. The bullet tore through his helmet, causing a serious wound, which was nearly lethal.

"We were in the trenches near a German training camp," Burnitz said. "There was a small building out front. You could see the door open and a machine gun sticking out. I told the guys, 'We gotta get out of here or we're gonna get it—we're gonna get hit.' We jumped up and rushed the building, broke three windows and threw grenades in."

As Burnitz backed away from the smoke-filled building, he was wounded.

"There was blood, of course, and a hole in the back of my helmet, but I was lucky," Burnitz said. "The doctors told me that the shot would have killed me if I'd have turned around."

Burnitz had been lucky before.

To his thinking, divine providence saved him months earlier.

It was in August 1944 that he heard "the voice."

His company was in France at the time.

"A lot of people think that I'm crazy, but the voice saved my life," Burnitz said. "I honestly believe it was my brother warning me about an incoming shell."

But Burnitz's brother, Robert, had died weeks earlier in the Pacific Theater.

"My being here today, you can call it 'special dispensation,' which I have had through the years," Burnitz said. "Long story short, I was in Southern France, sitting on a hill, taking time to relax. It was a beautiful day. Next thing I heard was, 'Eddie get into that foxhole right away!' Less than a second later, a shell hit the exact spot I had just jumped away from."

Burnitz says he asked around.

"I talked to everybody, but no one knew anything about a warning," Burnitz said, adding that the voice he heard was urgent and official-sounding, something like that of a radio announcer.

"Without hearing it, I would have been blown to smithereens," Burnitz said. "Maybe it's just believing in God, but I'll swear it was my brother's voice I heard.

My mother had already lost one son. Losing another would have been too much for her."

Of the five Burnitz brothers, four of them served in World War II. The youngest wasn't of age.

One of Burnitz's brothers, Walter, is the grandfather of major league baseball player Jeromy Burnitz, who has hit more than 230 career home runs through the 2003 season. He has played for the New York Mets and the Milwaukee Brewers, among others.

"Jeromy calls me 'Uncle Eddie,' " Burnitz said. "I go out to see him when he's playing in Chicago. He's a real Cub killer."

Burnitz saw the effects of what real killers can do.

His division helped liberate Dachau, the German concentration camp.

"By the time I was there, all the people had been released, but you could see signs of what they went through," Burnitz said, shaking his head when asked to explain those sights. "It's all in the history books. Besides, it's not an easy thing to talk about."

Along with the Kafkaesque images, Burnitz said the smell of Dachau is something he'll never forget.

"That type of death, it has a very powerful odor," he said.

The Dachau camp, named for a nearby town in Bavaria, was Germany's first concentration camp, started in 1933. Thousands of people died there, many in brutal medical experiments.

Dachau is particularly distinctive because it was there that Nazi SS personnel—Adolf Eichmann and Rudolf Hess—trained for work in newer camps such as Auschwitz.

That very name casts a dark, dark shadow. It hisses, too, like air whistling out of a punctured tire.

Auschwitz worked like this: Trainloads of Jewish people in sealed boxcars were packed so tightly and for so long without food or water that the dead had nowhere to fall. The trains arrived regularly. Guards threw open the doors and began shouting at the Jews to get out and line up. They were marched to an SS doctor who made a visual scan and pointed either to the gas chamber or to the labor camps. Infants, young children, pregnant women, the sick, the elderly and the disabled were sent to their immediate death. Between 20 and 40 percent were sent to the labor camps, remaining there until they were physically used up. Once weakened and exhausted, they were sent to the gas chambers, too.

At Auschwitz in 1944, 10,000 Jews were exterminated each day. Between 2 million and 4 million Jews and another 2 million non-Jews had been gassed by the time the camp was liberated. Total figures are guesswork because by then the SS had evacuated the camp and destroyed the gas chambers and crematoria, burning all applicable records at the same time.

What isn't guesswork is an event that happened during the liberation of Dachau, which Burnitz revisited some decades later.

As Americans approached one of the outlying camps of the Dachau system, the SS officer in charge ordered that the remaining 4,000 slave laborers be put to death. The guards had nailed the doors and windows shut, then hosed down the wooden barracks with gasoline and set the buildings on fire. The prisoners were cremated alive.

Dachau was huge. It would take an hour just to

walk around all the grounds. The original barracks had to be torn down in 1965 when the camp was turned into a memorial.

While the barracks buildings were badly decayed, the camp headquarters is now a museum.

"I visited there long after the war," Burnitz said. "Everything was changed. It was cleaned up. If you saw it when I did almost sixty years ago, you'd know how horrible the whole thing was."

Take the case of Dr. Siegmund Rascher, who did medical experiments at Dachau. One involved freezing people in cold water or air, then trying to warm them up with hot water, which was allegedly meant to help the German air force, presumably in adjusting to the temperature changes associated with flying. He also subjected people to high altitude simulations until they died.

After Germany surrendered, Burnitz was part of the American occupying force.

When he returned home to Chicago, he found work as a motorman, becoming a city bus driver as public transportation evolved.

He met his wife, Lucille, after the war.

"I tried getting a date with her younger sister first," Burnitz said. "I met Rosie [Lucille's sister] in a coffee shop at Belmont and Clark. It was called The Skillet. Anyway, we arranged a New Year's Eve date. When I got to her place, who opens the door—my future wife. I liked her right away. And here's the kicker: Rosie had set up a second date in advance. She was a real pistol, that one."

Ed and Lucille Burnitz were married in 1950.

Ed retired in 1985. Lucille died of cancer in 2000.

They had two children, as well as grandchildren.

"It was difficult, of course, losing Lucille, but we had a good life together," Burnitz said. "I just wish she had given up those cigarettes."

Burnitz moved to Carpentersville in 1960. He still lives in the same home he and Lucille bought for $16,200.

"A lot of city guys were moving out this way," Burnitz said. "If you had a family, coming west was a pretty smart thing to do. It was better for the kids. And you got a better house for your money."

In the 1960s, with middle age approaching, some of those same guys started playing golf. They tried talking Burnitz into taking up the game

"I said to them, 'You guys gotta be nuts,' " Burnitz remembers, laughing loud enough to drown out a military marching band. "I spent World War II chasing Germans across Italy, France, North Africa ... you name it. Now you want me to chase a little white ball? Forget about it."

If patriotic promises mean anything, what won't be forgotten are the things that Burnitz did for his country.

He's much, much older now. His hearing isn't what it used to be. He moves with a certain stiffness, yet he still stands at attention during special events—Memorial Day and the Fourth of July, for example.

His war is becoming a fading memory. Be that as it may, waves of emotion wash over an old soldier. He is alone but not entirely lonely.

He has been through things that succeeding generations know only from books and movies.

While Ed Burnitz is just one person, he represents

many more, including an almost endless number of young men who never made it back, never came home to their families.

"They were good guys," Burnitz said, recalling the men in his division. "You wonder why some made it and others didn't."

Embers again glow in the ashes of his memory.

"We fought for our country ... we fought for freedom," Burnitz said. "I'd do it again, no questions asked."

Amos Nicholson

AMOS NICHOLSON

"I could see something coming."

'

Sleeping battleships and cruisers had little warning when the Japanese attacked. Torpedoes slammed into their hulls. Gaping holes were blasted open. Water rushed in, turning the Pacific Ocean into an adversary.

Pearl Harbor—December 7, 1941?

No, this earlier attack occurred just before midnight, February 8, 1904—the opening blow of a war between Russia and Japan.

The war had its roots in the simultaneous determination of both Russia and Japan to develop "spheres of influence" in the Far East, mainly at the expense of China.

Japan had already fought a very successful war against the crumbling Chinese empire in 1894-95, imposing a severe treaty.

"Even before Pearl Harbor, you had an idea that Japan was interested in its own expansion," said Amos Nicholson, who was born in November 1916.

He has lived in Aurora for more than 80 years.

In the decades before World War II, Japan was indeed interested in expansion.

When forcibly opened to the West by an American naval squadron in the 1850s, Japan was a cloistered society, feudalistic in its structure and dominated by barons, known as the samurai.

In interacting with the West, Japan obtained schooling in contemporary technology, economics and military practices.

About a generation later, facing the hard times of a global depression, Japan turned to totalitarianism. Military men offered the tempting elixir of conquest abroad.

In 1931, the Japanese Army used a minor incident as a pretext to seizing Manchuria, a huge province bounded by Russia and Korea.

Not only was Manchuria large, it was rich and industrialized.

Through the 1920s, Manchurian military power was controlled by Chang Tso-lin and Chang HsUeh-liang, two Chinese warlords.

Back home in Japan, its own military had taken complete control of the government by 1933. Internal terrorism and political pressure were the military's methods of choice.

The Japanese policy was now to expand into China. Japan invaded China proper, capturing its principal cities.

Western democracies sat still—paralyzed, some said. The Japanese Army was known to be brutal. There were atrocities in Nanking, including rape and the massacre of almost 200,000 civilians. The American people were horrified by the pictures and stories coming out of China, but the majority remained resolutely isolationist.

Nicholson, however, enlisted in the Army Air Corps. "I joined in November 1941, a month before war was declared," he said. "I always loved mechanics and airplanes. The training I was promised could combine both."

It was a promise the Army Air Corps kept.

Nicholson went through basic training and aircraft mechanics school at Keesler Field in Biloxi, Mississippi.

During World War II, 142,000 aviation mechanics and 336,000 recruits were trained at Keesler Field. The majority of B-24 Liberator bomber mechanics were Keesler graduates.

Following the war, the aircraft mechanics school was moved to Sheppard Air Force Base in Wichita Falls, Texas.

Nicholson was shipped overseas in July 1942. Transportation came by way of a French luxury liner, the S.S. Louis Pasteur.

"We were zigzagging across the ocean for thirty-three days," Nicholson said. "You traveled that way to avoid enemy submarines."

In the spring of 1943, Army Air Corps Sgt. Amos Nicholson found himself in the Libyan Desert.

Although he was a trained mechanic, Nicholson also was a gifted amateur artist.

While attending school in Aurora years earlier, he won a scholarship to the Art Institute of Chicago.

"I was only there a short time," Nicholson said. "My parents couldn't afford the train fare."

During the Depression's darkest days, the Nicholson children went to school hungry on many mornings.

"My father worked hard, but there wasn't much money coming in," Nicholson said. "He mixed paints at a factory. He also delivered milk."

The fourth of five children, Nicholson was good with his hands. He could sketch at an early age. And he was quite comfortable with mechanics.

"I used to tinker with things all the time," he said. "Let me tell you about my first car, which cost me $6."

Six dollars?

"That's right," Nicholson said. "It was an old Model T Ford. It had running boards. I fixed it up and got plenty of use out of that car."

The Army Air Corps got plenty of use out of him.

While in Libya, he was told to paint pictures on the noses of the B-24s that were flying from the American base there.

It wasn't exactly the career move he had anticipated.

"I was a crew chief, not a professional artist," Nicholson said. "But they told me to paint, so I painted. It was either that or start peeling potatoes."

Airplane art is a tradition. It is associated with a desire to celebrate the instruments of war. These instruments could include a warrior or the warrior's weapons. History is filled with examples of this tradition: Egyptian chariots and Viking ships being two instances.

Native Americans and Zulu warriors used face and body paint, which was applied for a variety of reasons: protection from evil, personal identification or to receive supernatural powers from a given god.

Throughout the 20th century, the instruments of war became more and more sophisticated. During World War II, for example, airplane production increased tenfold.

Nose art became a popular form of expression. The reasons for decorating an airplane were numerous, including sexual deprivation, teasing the enemy and hoping that the particular painting brought good luck.

Nose art also made an airplane easier to identify. Simple serial numbers lacked personality.

Aircraft nose art did not begin as an American phenomenon, although it did reach its apex during U.S. involvement in World War II and Korea. The Italians and Germans are credited with initiating the tradition. The first recorded example appeared as early as 1913. It was a sea monster painted on the nose of an Italian flying boat. The Germans, late in World War I, added a painted mouth to the area under the propeller spinner of an airplane's nose.

During World War II and Korea, Army Air Force officials tolerated nose art in an effort to boost the morale of individual crews.

"Nose art took on many forms," Nicholson said. "Female pinups, animals, and graffiti were popular."

Nicholson specialized in cartoon characters— specifically, Snow White and the Seven Dwarfs.

As part of the 98th Bomb Group, 343rd Squadron, Nicholson spent time in North Africa and Italy. He had his picture taken strolling down a Tel Aviv street with four friends. He also posed in front of the pyramids in Egypt.

"Our planes helped the Eighth Army at the Battle of El Alamein," Nicholson said. "That was an important engagement, an important Allied victory."

German forces at El Alamein were led by Field Marshal Erwin Rommel, the Desert Fox. Known as a man of mercurial temperament and tremendous energy, he often displayed brilliance in the tactical handling of his forces. He led from the front and was on the move constantly. By all accounts, the men of his Afrika Korps loved and respected him and would follow him anywhere.

Despite spectacular victories in the desert, after Rommel lost El Alamein in the late fall of 1942 he became what Hitler called a "defeatist." Others called him a realist. He urged Hitler to end the war, but to no avail.

Rommel fell from Hitler's favor. When an assassination attempt against Hitler failed, Rommel was implicated. Although he was against the assassination itself, he was in favor of having Hitler arrested. What's more, he knew the conspirators.

In October 1944, SS troops surrounded his house and a German officer confronted him with a choice of suicide or trial. Rommel took the poison handed him. He told his wife and 14-year-old son—who grew up to be the mayor of Stuttgart—that Hitler was charging him with treason and that he would be dead within fifteen minutes. Publicly, his death was attributed to wounds suffered earlier in the year, the result of a car crash after attack by British fighter aircraft.

Hitler gave him a state funeral, not neglecting to send his condolences to Frau Rommel.

The Fuhrer remained a master manipulator. Had Rommel not taken the poison and instead demanded a public trial, Hitler had promised retribution against the field marshal's wife and son.

With Hitler, reality was a thing to be tossed around. Like loose change, it was of little consequence.

While obviously not on the same historical level, Nicholson had his own reality, although he tried treating it with appropriate respect.

"It was my job to help keep our planes in the air," he said. "It wasn't easy. We did the best we could. We did it with what we had ... I remember patching bullet holes with empty cans."

Jack Piper, a line chief, asked Nicholson to transform their assigned airplanes into the "Snow White Squadron," apparently an idea that came from an affection for the Disney film and having seen the title character on another aircraft.

In terms of the Snow White characters, Nicholson started by painting "Dopey" on the left front of an airplane called the "Arkansas Traveller," named after a colorful cartoon of the day, which was the Aurora resident's first actual attempt at nose art.

The Arkansas Traveller was a raunchy razorback cartoon, done at the request of a pilot from that same state—Arkansas, that is, although raunchy can also be a state of mind. Just ask any fan of the Janet Jackson/ Justin Timberlake Super Bowl show in January 2004.

By Nicholson's account, the southern swine had quite an impact.

"The guys seemed to really like it," he said, referring to the painted hog.

So much so, in fact, that he would paint more than a dozen airplanes.

Thinking back to the Arkansas Traveller, Nicholson smiles—quickly and quietly, like the flicker of an old home movie.

His cartoon creation of the Traveller included a small sign: "To Berlin." In addition, the snorting pig pulled a little cart, which was loaded with a bomb.

"It wasn't a real good painting," Nicholson says. "I didn't clean the metal. If there was a clump of something on the airplane, I knocked it off with the side of my brush. I painted over dirt and everything else, thinking that my artwork wasn't going to last long. The lacquer I used dried quick, so if I made a mistake I had to do it over with some fast finger painting."

Nicholson used camelhair brushes bought in Libya. All of his artwork faced frontward, toward the nose of the airplane.

After the Arkansas Traveller and the first Dopey, Nicholson painted "Happy," another of the seven dwarfs.

"If a plane was down for maintenance, I would have a chance to paint it," he said.

No matter how well maintained, some of the American airplanes didn't come back. That's what war is all about.

The original Snow White crashed on May 10, 1943. Nicholson painted that same cartoon character on another airplane.

No surprise. Several other cartoon characters were used more than once. If one Dopey was shot down, that same dwarf was used on a second airplane, although some of the pilots were superstitious about that.

90

"I had heard that some of the guys grumbled a little bit," Nicholson said.

And why not?

Being a crewmember or pilot aboard a World War II airplane was like sitting atop a volcano. Things erupted all the time.

Not even "Prince Charming" was safe. That airplane crashed on return from a low-level raid on the Ploesti oil fields, which was an Allied disaster. The Liberator bomber was being escorted by the "Witch," another aircraft identified by its nose art, with the character coming from the same story.

In the Ploesti raid, Nicholson lost almost an entire crew of friends. Only one man survived.

"On practice missions, I was flying as an engineer with that crew," Nicholson said. "The regular engineer had gotten sick. The pilot—his name was Gooden—asked me if I'd be his engineer on the next flight. The target was still secret. It didn't matter much, I was willing to go anywhere with those guys. Well, a day or two later, the pilot came back and said operations wouldn't approve the switch. Being a mechanic and crew chief, they said I was 'indispensable.' "

Either way, the regular engineer felt healthy enough to fly on the day of the Ploesti attack. He climbed aboard the American bomber, but never made it back from the raid, dying with others on the B-24.

"They crashed in Yugoslavia ... or some other place, I don't really remember right now," Nicholson said. "You just shook your head and got back to work. What else could you do?"

If not for the refusal from flight operations, Nicholson might have been on that airplane. If so, he almost certainly would have died with the others.

Ploesti, an oil-producing center in Romania, was what powered a sizable segment of Hitler's army. Without fuel, German forces would have grinded to a halt.

The oil fields were an obvious target. The Germans knew it, and Ploesti was heavily defended.

Nevertheless, an Allied attack was launched on August 1, 1943. The raid engaged 178 American bombers taking off from Libya. The B-24s made a 1,500-mile flight across the Mediterranean and German-occupied territory, encountering successive fighter attacks long before reaching their target.

The American crews fought their way through. In due course, refineries and oil tanks at Ploesti were engulfed by brilliant orange flames. Leaping like dancers in the air, ribbons of fire shot skyward. Billowing black smoke spread across the target area. The damage was substantial, but losses were worse. Nearly 450 of the 1,733 men on the mission were killed. Only 33 of the original 178 planes were fit for flying again.

The refineries were repaired. The Americans had lost at Ploesti.

Win or lose, however, the war continued. Living quarters in the desert were crude. Amusements were scarce. From time to time, movies would be projected on a screen set up on the back of a truck.

Another type of amusement involved such things as painting Hitler's face on a urinal at the base.

"Now that's entertainment," Nicholson says, smiling.

He married his high school sweetheart in May 1945.

Rita Nicholson died in early 2004.

The couple had two children, both boys. One is an air traffic controller and lives in the area; the other is a camera operator who works on the West Coast, among other places. Both sons are married. Nicholson has one grandchild.

Moments may be temporary, but memories last and last.

Above all else, memory is a complicated thing—a relative to truth, but not its twin.

Nicholson kept a locket of Rita's hair in his wallet through the years—before, during and after World War II. She had clipped that lock of hair in 1936.

He has also saved one of his World War II V-Mail letters, which was sent to Rita from overseas.

On the envelope is Nicholson's drawing of a B-24. It is dropping hearts all over a sentimental poem.

"Even today, I still know the words—I can recite them by heart," Nicholson says, looking away from the poem. The tone of his voice serves as a romantic reminder—love, it seems, isn't always like electricity, flaring for a second, then dropping in voltage along a flatline.

When the stars are aligned just right, it can last forever.

After World War II, and after marrying Rita, Nicholson reenlisted. He served as a crew chief, engineer and safety inspector during the Korean War.

"I never cleared an airplane unless I was absolutely sure of its flying ability," he said. "You never wanted to put someone in harm's way because of a mechanical malfunction—or anything related to the aircraft's operation, for that matter."

Nicholson was based in Japan. He and Rita lived there during the Korean War. She worked as a secretary, a civilian employee attached to the military.

"Our oldest boy was born in Tokyo," Nicholson said.

When the family returned to the United States in the 1950s, Nicholson became a painting contractor. He specialized in decorative stenciling, staining and graining, among other things.

His Aurora home is tastefully adorned, a reflection of the love he and his wife had for art.

While he didn't see action during World War II, Nicholson played an important role in the Allied effort.

"Common ground was an American ideal," Nicholson said, adding that the war was a great melting pot.

Common goals were important, too.

There was a huge appetite for wanting to help out. Whether on the frontline, on the home front or at a secure military base, Americans were keenly aware of the need to see things through together.

National unity remains one of America's most priceless assets.

Think of America as a tune, with the patriotic passages sung together. Like a roof-raising spiritual, it can carry an audience through unsettling times.

Some songs deserve an encore. Put America at the top of that list. Just ask a veteran.

L.C. West

L.C. WEST

"I've tried to forget the ugly incidents."

What was it like, being black as an international nightmare was unfolding?

What was it like, being black during World War II?

Just for a moment, silence lays like a sleeping cat—coiled and content, yet likely to scratch if rubbed the wrong way.

"You're asking about discrimination?"

Sitting across a kitchen table and bent forward at the waist, L.C. West repeats each word slowly, stopping at the last one.

In retrospect, the opening questions of this interview sound somewhat abrupt, perhaps even insincere.

"Well ... we lived through it," West says, adding that bigotry becomes like the pupil of an eye—the more light poured upon it, the more it will contract.

A longtime Elgin resident and World War II veteran, West comes across as a soft-spoken man, poised and polite. He has coffee-colored skin, an easy smile and an active mind. Thoughts tumble over and over, like a week's worth of wash.

West was a steward and cook in the U.S. Navy.

He was assigned to duty on several islands in the Pacific Ocean, including Midway.

"I cooked for the officers," he said. "It was good duty. We got to eat the same food that they did."

Breakfast might include ham and eggs. Dinners were even better—steaks cooked to order, for example.

"Most of the regular guys got beans, but the officers ate like kings," West said.

Being African-American, West wasn't treated as a member of the royal family, however.

"Most of the officers were nice, but you heard certain things," said West, who was born in February 1922.

The Arkansas native, who grew up in Illinois, has been in Elgin since the end of World War II.

"As a boy, we lived downstate, not far from Cairo, Illinois," West said. "After the war started, I tried to enlist, but because I had walking pneumonia, they told me to come back later. My mother didn't want me to go. She was worried. You know how those things are."

In the meantime, his draft notice arrived. West was inducted into the Navy, not knowing where he might end up.

"I just wanted to get in the service," he said. "Things were far from perfect stateside, but you had hope. And you stuck it out—you and your country, in sickness and in health, through thick and thin."

For West, hope had as many lives as a clever cat. He rolled with the punches, so to speak. He tried to walk away from Jim Crow, both at home and in the U.S. Navy.

Along with the treatment of Japanese-Americans, the unbecoming conduct toward black people is a permanent stain on the American record during World War II.

In the South, for example, blacks could be drafted, but they were overwhelmingly turned away when it came time to vote.

Without question, the war brought great changes—not because of the liberty-loving will of the American people, but because of industrial demands. With labor scarce and high wages available in the factories, Southern blacks began the greatest mass migration in U.S. history, moving from Montgomery to Milwaukee or Chattanooga to Chicago.

But even with jobs available, blacks were the last hired and the first fired. On average, they received lower pay than white men.

In the U.S. Army, they got equal pay but nothing else. The great majority of African-American soldiers were put in supply services, where they drove trucks or unloaded things. The common perception was that blacks couldn't fight. It was almost impossible for a black soldier to get a commission. There was little reward for doing well, yet ample punishment for making mistakes.

After being drafted, West was sent to a U.S. naval base in Norfolk, Virginia.

"We were out one day," West says, referring to a group of African-Americans he was with in Norfolk. "We wanted to catch the streetcar. Well, when we got on, the driver said we'd have to sit in the back. If not, he wasn't moving. It's just what was happening at the time."

Other things were happening, too.

Writing in *Yank* magazine, Corporal Rapiered Trimmingham recounted an incident from April 1944. He was traveling through the South, moving from one base to another. He and five other black soldiers stopped to get a cup of coffee. They were refused service, but a lunchroom manager at a Texas train depot said that they could go around back for a sandwich and something to drink. As they did, about two dozen German prisoners of war, with two American guards, arrived at the same station. They entered the lunchroom through the front door, sat at the table, talked, smoked, ate their meal and apparently had a grand old time.

Shakespeare said that a man may smile and smile, yet be a villain. Hypocrisy is the child of ignorance.

West isn't the confrontational type, but "how many times could you turn the other cheek?" he asks, clearly not needing an answer.

At least in some sense, for many African-Americans, World War II wasn't about defending democracy, but getting a share of the democracy they never had.

When West came home, his older brother told him about a job opening in Elgin.

"I had been staying in Chicago, but Johnny [his older brother] told me about a company out this way," West said. "They needed workers; I needed a job."

He has worked in a factory and as a meatpacker, becoming a supervisor at a local plant, which closed years ago.

"It's funny," he says. "When I was a boy living downstate, my dad was a farmer. I didn't like him having to slaughter any animals, but we had to eat. And then I end up as a boss in that meatpacking plant."

It was at an Elgin party that he met Mary Wheeler, whom West would marry in 1948. Call it a sign of the times—the Elgin party was segregated.

The Wheeler family has been in Kane County since 1870.

L.C. and Mary West have children and grandchildren.

Mary West worked at the Elgin State Hospital, starting there in 1952. The facility was subsequently renamed the Elgin Mental Health Center.

"It was a good job. I enjoyed working there," she said.

But in Elgin, being black was an entirely different matter. Never mind that the family lineage was deeply rooted in the past.

"Elgin was a racist city," Mary West said. "When I went to Elgin High School, blacks couldn't sing in the choir. And outside of school, we were refused service in several restaurants."

Things didn't improve dramatically after World War II, even though her husband was a veteran.

"In the early 1950s, we tried buying a little land at 408 Ann Street in Elgin ... We wanted to build our first home," Mary West remembered. "We were turned down. They said it was a 'whites only' property."

Mary West and her husband asked the members of a white church to buy the property. In turn, the church members sold it to them.

"When we built the home and moved in, things got scary," Mary West said.

Their windows were shot out. Crosses were painted on their sidewalks.

"We weren't leaving," Mary West said. "In the long run, those things went away."

A few years later, in 1956, Elgin was named an All-American City, one of eleven cities selected from a field of 164 entering the competition. Applicants were judged on effort and initiative shown by residents in working together for civic betterment. Judges must not have interviewed the West family, or those who wanted to run them out of town—or at least out of the neighborhood.

L.C. West is a longtime member of the Veterans of Foreign War. He was a commander of Elgin VFW Post 1307. His oldest son, Alan, died of a heart attack at age 33.

He was in the military and serving overseas at the time of his death.

L.C. West says there's nothing abstract about any death, particularly when a loved one dies at an early age.

Losing someone special always hurts. Even so, West remains upbeat.

"I believe in America ... I want everyone to have a piece of it," he said. "I know that there have been racial problems through the years, but you're always thinking about a better tomorrow."

That tomorrow wasn't realized at the end of World War II. With the defeat of Germany, Italy and Japan, peace came, but ugly prejudices remained a fact of day-to-day life.

At war's end, African-American servicemen sometimes saw themselves as forgotten laundry left on a back yard fence, said West, who isn't prone to such statements. He doesn't much care for verbal wrangling, but believes that justice delayed is decency denied.

While his future was brightened by the war, he came home to an America clouded by racial intolerance.

"I liked cooking in the Navy," he said. "But it was almost impossible to find a good job doing that after the war. Being black, there weren't a lot of restaurants where you could even apply for work."

West was part of the war effort, although not in a combat situation.

"I would do anything asked by my country," he says. "I would have fought if they told me to, but the way it ended up, they made me a cook."

West, like other African-Americans in World War II, serviced the service. For the most part, they handled food, clothing and equipment.

But when given an opportunity, blacks often went above and beyond the call of duty. During the Battle of the Bulge, General Eisenhower was forced to give African-American troops the chance to serve in frontline units on a non-segregated basis. Thousands volunteered, including sergeants who gave up their stripes to fight for their country. Historians say they did remarkably well overall, and thus started the U.S. Army on the task of reevaluating its use of black soldiers.

The Tuskegee Airmen also distinguished themselves during World War II.

Earlier, in July 1933, Dr. Albert Forsythe and Charles Anderson made history by becoming the first black pilots to fly across America. Eight years later, Anderson would make history again, helping to form the legendary Tuskegee Airmen, the first black military aviator group.

Anderson, a Pennsylvania native, taught himself to fly by watching other pilots. In 1941, first lady Eleanor Roosevelt visited the Army Air Corps base at Tuskegee Institute, Alabama. Anderson was asked to fly her around. Many aviation historians credit the short flight as the inspiration for training the first African-American military pilots, many of whom would go on to serve their country as members of the 332nd Fighter Group, later known throughout the world as the Tuskegee Airmen.

Anderson became the group's chief flight instructor.

More than 950 black servicemen were trained as pilots at Tuskegee. The squadron proved to be a dangerous opponent to the enemy. The Airmen completed 1,578 missions throughout North Africa and Europe, shooting down enemy planes, bombing enemy trains and escorting bomber pilots to their missions.

American bomber pilots called the Airmen the "redtail angels." Not only had they painted the tails of their airplanes red, the Airmen never lost a pilot they were assigned to escort.

When World War II ended, the Tuskegee Airmen had received 150 Distinguished Flying Crosses and eight Purple Hearts.

Other African-Americans didn't do as well with receiving their medals, however.

Fifty years after the war ended, African-American soldiers received long overdue recognition for their service in World War II. On January 13, 1997, seven veterans were awarded the Medal of Honor that was originally denied to them because they were black.

For his time in the U.S. Navy, West received an Asiatic Pacific Ribbon and a Victory Ribbon. He was discharged in November 1945.

World War II was an "act of faith," he says, decades removed from the event. "Black or white, there wasn't any hiding place from the problems that faced America ... I'm grateful for having participated in the war effort."

From the beginning of World War II until its conclusion, freedom was expensive. It cost money. It cost blood. It called for courage, commitment and endurance, not only in servicemen, but also in every man and woman who was free.

That they were determined to remain free is something America can never forget.

George Gebes

GEORGE GEBES

"Each day is a bonus."

Appreciation is a memory of the heart.

World War II veterans share a closeness unknown to all outsiders, including writers.

Even at an advanced age, they remain connected—well-worn strands that look like the rainbow braid twisting through a telephone cable. Almost instinctively, these veterans know someone is at the other end.

The relationships are different than the ones they have with newer friends, even family members. Their trust in one another is unquestioned. They know each other's life stories. They're saddened when time takes a group member away.

George Gebes made a promise on the island of Iwo Jima. He was with the U.S. Navy then, serving aboard a Landing Ship Tank—commonly called the LST.

Gebes was in charge of the auxiliary engine room, located in the deepest part of the ship.

Space was cramped and the temperature could get as hot as the inside of an oven. Diesel engines were noisy. Conversation came in shouts and surges.

Up top, things were worse—at least they were on the volcanic scab called Iwo Jima, a flyspeck of an island that today is part of Japan's sovereign state.

But in the early weeks of 1945, Iwo Jima was captured and controlled by U.S. forces.

In terms of human blood and guts, victory carried an enormous price tag. There were no frontlines on Iwo Jima, just one rocky plateau after another, almost all of them heavily fortified by the Japanese.

"After seeing all those dead American Marines on the island, I made my pledge," Gebes said. "If God got me home, I would do something in their honor."

What Gebes did was really something, although he would never say so. Modesty is a further reflection of his character. He is a reluctant witness to the accomplishment that he helped initiate.

When he came back from World War II, Gebes got the ball rolling on a project that required raising $3,600—money that was used to buy land along the Fox River in Batavia.

"The land wasn't for me, but to put up a permanent memorial for the boys at Iwo Jima, for all veterans," Gebes said. "We wanted a place for them to meet, a place for them to remember the ones who couldn't come home."

The property was almost solid brush back then. Gebes had his eye on a nearly seven-acre stretch of riverfront land.

To get it, he formed the Batavia Overseas Club, originally made up of World War II veterans, friends and family members. About a dozen World War I veterans also joined.

"We were determined to raise enough money to buy that land and build what we wanted, which would be something special for those who served their country," Gebes said.

After borrowing enough to purchase the Fox River property, Gebes drew up plans for a building, which still stands today. A second building, larger than the first, was added decades later.

Born in South Dakota in July 1915, Gebes came to Batavia in the 1930s.

He had come to shovel coal.

"My uncle owned a greenhouse here in Batavia," said Gebes, whose father was a homesteader, beginning back in 1906. Long deceased, his South Dakota ranch has expanded to 7,000 acres. It's still in the family.

Gebes was supposed to work three months in Batavia, then go home.

Money was tight; jobs were scarce.

Gebes stayed decades longer than those first 90 days, but they weren't spent at his uncle's greenhouse.

"While here in Batavia, I was lucky enough to find another job," he said. "It came just as the first finished up. And I would be doing the same thing—shoveling coal. So instead of going home, I worked at a foundry, which made castings for sewer systems. My pay was $15 a week, plus room and board. Boy, I thought that was great."

Gebes had to work for the money.

"Every day, there I'd be, shoveling out a railroad car filled with coal," Gebes said. "By quitting time, you were dog tired."

Be that as it may, work has been Gebes' constant companion through the years.

Before entering the Navy, he had become a carpenter, which was his longtime profession after World War II. Shoveling coal came to an end.

"Along with owning the ranch, my dad was a carpenter, too," Gebes said. "You could say I was always mechanically inclined. It came naturally to me. I enjoyed being in the trades."

He met and married Francis Lies before World War II.

They have three children, eight grandchildren and seven great-grandchildren.

"We got married in 1938," Gebes said. "I met Francis through a church group."

Talking to Gebes is a reminder of how important integrity is to the people of his generation.

God looks at the clean hands, not the full ones, Gebes said.

His were dirtied only through hard work, which, being a carpenter, was always on the level. Ask anyone who knows him.

In building the original VFW Hall at 645 River Street in Batavia, Gebes organized a group of volunteers who worked nights and weekends.

"We'd get together after our regular jobs," Gebes said. "I'm proud that I honored my commitment, the one I made back at Iwo Jima."

VFW Post 1197 is one of the most active in the Fox Valley, perhaps in the entire Midwest. As of February 2004, hundreds of packages—which contain toiletries and other related items—have been shipped from

Batavia to the troops serving America in Iraq, which was liberated about a year earlier.

At Iwo Jima, liberation came an inch at a time. The island is only eight square miles, about a third the size of Manhattan.

Only about 775 miles from Honshu, the largest island of Japan, Iwo Jima was of strategic importance to the Allies, especially to the B-29 offensive. Nonetheless, it was a small island to have had such a big battle.

From the shoreline to the top of Mount Suribachi, 100,000 men spent more than a month trying to kill one another there, making it one of the most intense and closely fought battles of World War II.

Eighty thousand American men fought above ground, twenty thousand Japanese fought from below. They were hidden in a sophisticated system of tunnels that crisscrossed the island, rendering them all but invisible to the U.S. Marines.

A number of surviving Marines, in fact, said they never saw a live Japanese soldier on Iwo Jima. They were fighting an enemy they couldn't see.

Being on a large LST, Gebes was not part of the first invasion wave at Iwo Jima.

"By the time we hit the island with equipment and supplies, the beach was pretty secure," Gebes said. "It was a terrible, terrible mess, though. We helped bury the dead and tried to take care of any wounded we came across. Those things—young men crying out for help, young men blown apart—you never forget them."

Gebes and two shipmates decided to crawl up Mount Suribachi, where on February 23, 1945, after three days of intense combat, American military men hoisted the Stars and Stripes and photographer Joe

Rosenthal of the Associated Press took one of the war's most famous photographs.

"We'd heard about the flag," Gebes said. "You couldn't see it from our LST, but we knew it was up there."

Gebes' captain told him that there was still some danger of sniper attack. The Batavia man, who then had a wife and two young children back home, decided to climb to the top regardless.

Standing near where the flag was raised at the edge of an extinct volcano, Gebes could view the entire two-mile beach area, where an American armada had discharged boatloads of attacking Marines, many of them dead by the time he stepped ashore.

Wind whipped across the mountaintop.

And from a crouched position, Gebes stood straight up.

"All I wanted to do was salute that flag," he said. "And after we crawled to the top of Suribachi, I gave it my very best salute, then went over and touched it."

Gebes calls that moment one of the most important in his long life.

"With what we'd seen along the shore, touching the flag was a spiritual experience," he said, choking back emotion. "I've been to the parades and heard the speeches, but that flag stands alone in my memory. It's a monument to those lives of sacrifice and service."

Gebes freely admits that he cried and cried at the touch of that flag. The other men did, too.

"We stayed up there for about half an hour," Gebes said. "Even then, before history told the Iwo Jima story, you knew you were standing atop sacred ground."

It is fitting, then, that the Batavia VFW is an extension of that sacred ground.

Of the six men who raised the first flag on Iwo Jima, only two of them walked off the island. One was carried off with shrapnel stapled up and down his side. Three were buried there, heroic ghosts of the bloody battle.

The six men who raised the flag are representative of the furious fighting on Iwo Jima. If Rosenthal's famous photograph showed any six men atop Mount Suribachi, the picture would be the same: two-thirds casualties. According to a published report, two out of every three men who fought on the island of agony were killed or wounded.

The LST that Gebes served on was new to World War II, as were other specialized landing craft. They were limited almost exclusively to the British and Americans. Hitler had none; it was one of the reasons he couldn't cross the English Channel in the summer of 1940.

Early on, the U.S. Navy wasn't much interested in landing craft; aircraft carriers and battleships were more to their liking. But in 1939, the U.S. Marines, anticipating island battles in the Pacific, forced the U.S. Navy to sponsor a design competition. What the Marine Corps was looking for was a boat that could take a rifle platoon off troop transports straight onto the beach. Andrew Higgins, a small boat-builder in New Orleans, had an answer: he came up with a flat-bottomed boat 36 feet long and 10½ feet wide, propelled by a diesel engine. It could carry a platoon or a squad and a jeep. The ramp was metal but the sides and square stern were plywood. Even in a moderate sea, it would bounce and shake. All the while, swells broke over the ramp and sides. It was called Landing Craft Vehicle and Personnel (LCVP).

Higgins was as adept at mass production as he was at design. His factory began with 80 employees in 1940. Four years later, that number swelled to 30,000.

His company produced 20,000 LCVPs, which carried fighting men ashore in the Pacific, North Africa, Sicily, Italy and Normandy. Eisenhower called Higgins "the man who won the war for us."

Higgins also built Patrol Boats (PTs), Landing Craft Tanks (LCTs) and the LSTs.

Gebes served aboard just one LST in World War II.

"I was with that same ship from start to finish," he said.

Not only did the ship see action at Iwo Jima, but also at Okinawa, among other places.

"We came under attack a number of times," Gebes said. "The younger guys got nervous, but I'd tell them not to worry about the bullets and bombs they heard. You worried about the one you didn't hear. That's the one with your name on it."

Gebes was 28 years old when he entered the U.S. Navy.

"A lot of the other guys were still in their teens," Gebes said. "They called me 'Dad,' which was kind of funny, I guess. I was just a young man myself, but to them I seemed old and experienced."

He was hurt after an enemy attack on the LST. Decades later, in 2004, he was scheduled to receive a Purple Heart.

"I spent five weeks in the hospital," Gebes said,

thinking back to the 1940s. "Being on an LST, you were always watching for a kamikaze strike."

No wonder, really.

The LST was a big ship, as big as a light cruiser, 327 feet long, displacing 4,000 tons. It was also sluggish; the crews said LST stood for "Long, Slow Target." But it was capable of crossing the ocean, then grounding at a beach and discharging tanks or trucks. When it did beach, two bow doors opened to the sides and a ramp was lowered to allow the vehicles to drive ashore. It could carry dozens of tanks and trucks in its cavernous hold, with LCVPs on its deck.

The LSTs, their great jaws yawning open, came onto the beaches to supply fighting divisions with whatever they needed. The LST was as critical to the battle in northwest Europe as to the Pacific battles. It was far more valuable than Hitler's secret weapon, revealed a week after D-Day Normandy, the V-1. Without the LST and its smaller cousin, the LCVP, the Allies could not have gotten ashore on any Pacific island or European beach.

After World War II, Gebes came home and returned to work.

At the same time, the U.S. Navy veteran was absolutely determined to honor the commitment he'd made on Iwo Jima.

"I was a carpenter with a young family," Gebes said. "I didn't have any money to speak of. We were living paycheck to paycheck, but I had a million dollars worth of resolve. I was going to get whatever we needed to buy that land for our memorial."

He went to a local bank, asking about a loan.

"The banker laughed," Gebes remembered. "He

said, 'You don't have any collateral. I can't give you a penny.' That just made me more intent. The Navy teaches you that you can do more than you think you can. It's what comes from being part of a team."

The postwar team—the Batavia Overseas Club—started selling bonds.

Apparently, Gebes knew something the Batavia banker didn't—that the heart of a man cannot be determined by the size of his wallet.

"We were paying 3 percent interest on a three-year bond," Gebes said. "The money mostly came in $25 and $50 at a time. I asked everyone I knew to help out. You went door-to-door when necessary. It only took a month. We raised the $3,600 needed for that land. And when the bonds came due, we paid back every dime, interest included."

The property purchase was finalized in 1947. By 1948, the land was cleared and the first foundation poured.

"Before the World War II guys got involved, the Batavia VFW only had about 15 members—World War I veterans, I suppose," Gebes said. "We really got going, bringing in fresh faces and ideas."

The first meeting at the new building was held around a potbellied stove.

Today, more than 55 years later, Gebes still stops at the VFW Hall nearly each and every day.

"Being here, it's my life," he says, sitting in the original building, now used as a clubhouse. "I help open things up, cut the grass ... whatever's needed."

Gebes said that accomplishment is more about attitude than aptitude.

"The Navy expected you to attain something, to achieve excellence in all you do," Gebes said. "You accepted your responsibility and worked without complaining. When something had to get done, you reached beyond your rank and rate of pay to do it. Your hard work was for the guy next to you, for the Navy and for the nation."

Along with membership in the VFW, Gebes has been involved in community activities and events throughout the Batavia area.

Not only is he a past post commander of the VFW Hall he helped build, Gebes is a recent recipient of another honor—he was Batavia Citizen of the Year.

Both before and after World War II, Gebes served his country and community well. He put more into life than he expected to get out of it. He drove himself while leading others. And more than anything else, he counted his blessings—at home and at Iwo Jima, where consideration for fallen brothers and faith in God came together.

A goal should be lofty and laudable. With the construction of the VFW Hall in Batavia, Gebes achieved something special—something worthwhile and rewarding.

"I had help from a lot of good people," he says, referring to the building of the hall.

While talking to Gebes at the end of a two-hour interview, conversation turns to another goal—an ultimate one, incidentally.

Well, what's left? Where will a long life of dedication bring him?

Heaven—if quality time on Earth means much, that is.

After all, the ones who give should get back in kind.

And Gebes gave plenty.

Richard Besancon

RICHARD BESANCON

"As a Christian, I believed in what we were doing."

He remembers firefights tearing through a European afternoon—the screaming, shouting and swearing of soldiers lying along the side of a road. They clung to life like shipwrecked sailors on a rock. Nonetheless, some of the GIs died. It didn't matter how young or how tough they had been.

Dog tags would be collected later.

Still, somehow or another, scared young American men kept doing what they were supposed to do. It was part of their training. They advanced under a sheet of deadly fire, crisscrossing from one side of the road to the other.

Some vomited whenever they took time to think, or catch their breath, which amounted to the same thing. Yet valor overcame the terror that waited up ahead.

Richard Besancon was just 18 years old. He had been raised on the family farm in Ohio. Chores were important, especially early in the morning. Baseball and basketball were played for fun, although at a championship level in high school.

"It was a happy childhood," Besancon says. "Simple, yet very fulfilling."

He came to the Fox Valley decades ago, wanting to do something important. For him, that meant teaching and preaching.

Besancon became a philosophy professor at Judson College, a small school nestled near the Fox River in Elgin. He taught there nearly forty years, retiring in the late 1990s.

Several years later, Besancon still lives only a stone's throw from the campus.

Judson is a Christian college, highly regarded in both approach and application.

And if you were looking for the prototypical philosophy professor, Besancon would be a likely candidate. He is soft-spoken and scholarly, someone who thinks that the best books have no ending. Talking to him is an education in itself.

Most of the time, Besancon's eyeglasses are at the end of his nose, making him look like a wise old uncle.

But back in 1944, he was a front point scout, attached to the Rainbow Division, which was the nickname given to the 42nd Division of the U.S. Army.

The Rainbow nickname was used because its men came from all over the United States.

"I was a Rainbow replacement," said Besancon, who was one of six children, a family that included his twin brother, Robert, who was also in the military. And so were two other brothers, one of whom went to West Point.

All four Besancon boys came home alive.

Theirs was a Baptist background, going to church on Sunday; trying to live like Christians through the week.

Real religion is a way of life, Besancon says. It isn't a white cloak cleaned for use on the Sabbath, then tossed into a closet of disinterest, staying there the rest of the week.

Although a devout Christian, he never considered applying for a 4-E: conscientious objector status.

"For me personally, I just wanted to do the right thing," Besancon said. "It's what I learned at home, at school and at church. World War II was a moral undertaking. I thought that serving in the military was a responsible choice. For other Christians, things certainly could have been different. You live according to principles. Sometimes, those principles have to be defended."

A Bronze Star recipient, Besancon saw no contradiction between faith and fighting, not when he was fighting for freedom.

Fascism was antithetical to everything democracy stood for. Before World War II—in Italy, Germany and Japan—the ground was fertile for tyranny and totalitarianism. It was the same sort of soil that covered Russia, where Stalin consolidated power by purging Soviet army officers and intellectual elite, among others.

Stalin's small frame, withered left arm and pocked face concealed a monster. His ideology was dark, distorted and dictatorial.

With the temperament of a Spanish inquisitor, he was devoid of humanity or guilt, and was sustained by an icy faith. He could do horrible things by day, then sleep like a baby at night.

As evidence that international affairs make strange bedfellows, Stalin was not only a brutal tyrant, he was also an American ally.

Hitler wasn't.

Besancon, born in May 1926, studied the things that helped sustain the power and popularity of the Nazi Party. During his time teaching at Judson, he used an authentic Nazi flag to create classroom discussion.

This isn't just any Nazi flag. It's as impressive as it is intimidating—large and loathsome, a reminder of death, despair and hatred. It hung inside a Nuremberg office.

Made of red silk, the flag is emblazoned with a black swastika, the ancient hooked-cross religious symbol that once represented health, happiness and prosperity. It was assigned a whole new meaning under Hitler.

Besancon keeps the flag in a plastic bag at his home.

Attached to the Rainbow Division, Besancon went through Nuremberg, part of an Allied sweep through Germany.

"Nuremberg was where the Nazis staged their annual party rallies," Besancon said. "Hitler wanted to be seen as a man of destiny, someone ranked alongside Alexander, Caesar and Napoleon."

Hitler, a former corporal in the German Army, had a fanatical belief in his own mission, however murderous and misguided it was.

The annual party rallies at Nuremberg began in 1933, after Hitler became Germany's chancellor. They continued until the beginning of World War II.

In essence, they were little more than goose-stepping orgies. The rallies were held in early September and lasted a week. Torchlight parades and other nighttime pageants were frequent, for Hitler believed that "in the evening people's willpower more easily succumbs to the dominating force of a stronger will."

The climatic event of each annual rally was a speech by Hitler himself. He would send listeners into an emotional frenzy, meeting them there at the same time. The theme was ancient German heroes. They were invoked to promote a sense of national unity. The Nazis—with filmmaker Leni Reifenstahl, who died at age 101 in September 2003—produced a monumental motion picture of the 1934 rally entitled *Triumph of the Will*. The documentary dramatized Hitler's hypnotic appeal, the way he voiced the fears and resentments of the German people. Those who saw him in action never forgot his eyes, which would become round and shiny, like the glass-bead buttons of a stuffed animal.

Some said they were tunnels to the devil.

At Nuremberg, Besancon took the flag as a souvenir.

"After we made sure the building was clear of Germans, it was taken down," he said.

Later, Besancon packed it away and has had it all these years.

To an extent, the Nuremberg rallies were the culmination of Hitler's rise to power, which was rooted in the fighting and flawed peacemaking of World War I.

Nuremberg also was the site of the war crimes trials, which established a new foundation for the law of nations—above all that every person is responsible for his or her own acts.

Those acts were part of an extended engagement. Historians wrote of a world war that began in 1914, had a long armistice from 1918 to 1939, and was resumed and continued until 1945.

What American President Woodrow Wilson hoped

would be the "war to end all wars" turned out to be the starting point for even greater devastation.

Colossal mistakes were written into the Versailles Treaty, which essentially ended World War I and created the League of Nations—the first major international association of countries. A total of 63 states were members, although not all simultaneously.

The treaty made Germany pay an enormous sum for the war. This, in turn, forced the Weimar Republic— named for the eastern German city where it was founded—to take such drastic economic measures that it had almost no support at home.

The economic consequences of the treaty were disastrous. At the end of World War I, the German mark was worth about twenty-five cents; by November 1923, its value had shrunk a billion times. Workers in Essen took their pay home in barrels, and some three hundred paper factories and one hundred fifty printing establishments were unable to turn out notes fast enough to keep the economy off the barter basis.

The man who profited most from this situation was Hitler, an Austrian born rabble-rouser. The Nazi party remained relatively small until the economic slump of 1929. They had received fewer than a million votes in the elections of 1928, but in 1930 they got more than six million, and by 1932, almost fourteen million.

Hitler was adept at intrigue. He made political alliances with wealthy industrialists, with nationalist politicians and with army generals. He got himself named chancellor by then-President Hindenburg in January 1933.

The next month, when a fire destroyed the Reichstag—Germany's national capitol building in

Berlin—the Nazis used it as excuse to jail, beat and torture their opponents. Political parties were gagged; churches made subservient. A bloodbath within the Nazi Party eliminated all internal opposition to Hitler.

He was in complete control.

When Besancon entered France in February 1945, that control was greatly diminished.

The young soldier saw significant action, however, including fighting in the Vosges Mountains, located in eastern France.

Was that a major engagement?

The question seems to bother Besancon, but not to the point of having him raise his voice.

"When an enemy soldier shoots at you, it's always a major engagement, at least it is in your mind," Besancon said. "You're fearful, but you acted like a soldier. There was good reason for our involvement in the war."

The talk turns back to Christianity, specifically being able to reconcile faith and fighting.

"I saw a place for a Christian in the military ... I still do," Besancon said. "I think it does dictate some things: for instance, you don't shoot someone if you can take that person prisoner. We had our share of knuckleheads on the American side. One guy told me that he never took a German SS soldier prisoner, 'I just shoot them,' he said, as if he were bragging. Well, that type of GI didn't do us any good. All they did was give the enemy the feeling that they couldn't surrender."

When it was originally formed, the SS, short for Schutzstaffel, was assigned to guard Hitler.

In December 1940, Heinrich Himmler established the Waffen, or fighting, SS. This new army grew rapidly and within six months expanded to more than 150,000 men.

The cold-blooded killing of an SS soldier was just another radical extension of the "them or us" syndrome. It became a question of what was needed to survive.

Besancon certainly saw things that spoke to the darker side of men at war. The heat of battle brings on atrocities. A soldier who has just lost his closest friend, for example, decides to gun down an enemy who runs up a white flag only after running out of ammunition.

Right or wrong, those things happened.

"I remember when Lieutenant Skidmore was killed, I told this fellow that we would work our way behind the German line," Besancon said, adding, however, that he didn't want others involved in the plan.

They might have been thinking strictly of revenge, Besancon said.

Regarded as decent, disciplined and courageous, Skidmore had been shot and killed in Furth, a German city northwest of Nuremberg.

Besancon picked up Skidmore's carbine. Along with the second soldier, they did indeed get behind enemy lines, opening fire on the Germans.

Earlier, as they snuck through a cellar on their way to outflanking the Germans, the two Americans took a civilian prisoner. While not thought to be much of a threat himself, the older man might have alerted the enemy.

"Some of our own soldiers might have shot that old man," Besancon said. "We didn't. I figured that he was so scared he wouldn't want to alert anyone."

The old man kept quiet. Besancon's instinct was correct.

So was his instinct to survive. Once engaged in the business of war, he didn't lust for the role of hero. Few, if any, did, Besancon said.

"I don't think that there was a feeling on anybody's part that they wanted to be the first to Berlin," Besancon said. "You wanted to do your job and come on home."

There were "war lovers," however. Many frontline groups had at least one soldier who seemed to enjoy killing. Others admitted that they liked blowing things up.

Fear triggers an adrenaline rush, not the same as pleasure, though exhilarating nonetheless.

While their thoughts might have been lofty, Americans fighting World War II didn't spent their time talking about democracy, freedom or the Constitution. A foxhole isn't intended as an arena for a great philosophical discussion. Men engaged in combat spent their time thinking in terms of how to stay alive. Whispered conversations centered on hot food, clean clothes, warm places to sleep and those they'd lost. Abstractions have nothing to do with wartime situations, Besancon said.

War is often about utter and absolute luck, or faith, depending on a person's beliefs.

Besancon says God interceded in what would have been his death—an almost accidental death that would have been the result of friendly fire.

"It was at night in the forest, and we were out of our foxholes pitching grenades," Besancon said. "At the same time, we were being shelled by the Germans. There was a lot of noise and confusion. Coming back, we were trying to find our secondary line of defense, going up through the woods. I was walking up diagonally. I heard a click. And it's here that I think the Lord gave me instantaneous recognition. When I heard that click, I recognized it as the safety on an M1. Immediately, I said, 'Don't shoot, it's us.' Later, I talked to the soldier who came close to shooting me. He said that there was a moonlight patch. I stepped into it and he saw me. He had a bead on my head. If I hadn't said something he was ready to squeeze the trigger. I'd have been dead in an instant."

Besancon said the Lord saved him. The Lord also kept him Christian when he might have strayed.

It was when Lieutenant Skidmore was killed.

"Back at Furth, we were engaged in a heavy street fight, darting from doorway to doorway," Besancon said. "Someone shouted, 'Skidmore's shot.' I ran to him from across the street. He was badly wounded—he knew it and so did I. 'Lieutenant,' I told him, 'I will pray for you.' He said, 'Thanks, Dick.' He was shot in the midsection. Some of the guys were getting very, very angry. They were cursing and cursing. I moved off into a little room to pray. I asked the Lord to give them patience, also to calm my own adrenaline. I prayed and said, 'Lord, help us do what should be done in this situation.' I knew Scripture said 'Love your enemies,' but we had to shoot at them, too."

Skidmore lived only a little longer, then died. He had been married ten days before shipping overseas.

Besancon made it through World War II.

He came home and went to college on the GI Bill.

In was while at a Baptist college that he met his future wife.

Richard and Vannye Besancon have three children and one grandchild. They were married in August 1950.

Along with being a retired philosophy professor, Besancon is an ordained minister.

And along with the Nazi flag from Nuremberg, he brought back other souvenirs.

"We were young guys," he says, smiling. "We wanted to brings things home. In addition, our orders were to confiscate anything with a swastika."

Besancon confiscated more than a dozen Nazi belt buckles and medals, including the heralded Iron Cross and a set of German air force wings.

"They came from an abandoned warehouse," Besancon said. "They were never handed out."

During the interview, Besancon points to an inscription engraved on one of the Nazi belt buckles, which he keeps in a box.

"Gott Mit Uns," he says, tracing each letter with his right index finger. "It means, God With Us."

But God wasn't with Hitler, who helped engineer man's most convulsive effort to destroy himself. His twisted ambition was aided and abetted by the indecision of others, many of them American. The docile indifference of free men enabled them to convince themselves that the bell tolled only for those on the other side of the ocean.

It also tolled for thee.

Some said it was appalling. All told, on both sides, military and civilian, from 1939 to the end of World War II, there were as many as 50,000,000 dead. Two continents were in ruins.

In the summer of 1945, General Eisenhower flew from Berlin to Moscow at 800 feet on a clear day. He did not see a building still standing, not a single one.

Human wreckage was worse.

The majority of the dead were in their teens and twenties.

In North Africa and Europe, including Italy, the U.S. Armed Forces incurred 765,694 casualties, including 177,062 dead. In the Mediterranean and the Atlantic, the U.S. Navy incurred 10,204 casualties, including 5,462 dead. The total for the war against Germany and Italy was 775,898 casualties; 182,524 dead.

World War II, for all its cost, did not settle major ideological issues. It took fifty years of Cold War to do that.

The various captive peoples in the Soviet Empire were consigned to a life as horrid as their lives under Nazi occupation from 1941 to 1945.

Given today's global realignment, the communists came to accept something that the Nazis learned more than a generation ago. They could conquer, but not convince.

Years after World War II, Besancon wrote a poem, telling of an 18-year-old American soldier staring at the lifeless body of an equally young German soldier.

ODE IN BEHALF OF A FALLEN FOE

He will not sit in halls of learning
    Yet he was the object of some parents' yearnings
Made for better things than to be a tyrant's pawn,
    He was cut down like an unwary fawn.

His face now pressed against the earth,
    Blonde tresses disheveled
And blood-smeared girth
    Bore stark witness of war's cruel curse.

To those now, like those then,
    Who see the carnage of youthful lives
Dashed into unseeming waste
    Join resolve now to honor Him
Who is the Truth
    Above every battle's din

For life is a trust
    That causes one to see
The tragedy of commitments
    That do not honor Thee.

Gene Bonk

GENE BONK

"Death is inevitable, immortality is not."

He remembers the unsung soldiers, All-American boys who would die at Omaha Beach. Many of them were killed while wading ashore, cut down by German guns.

The code name for the bloody beach was Easy Red, an appropriate color given all that happened there on June 6, 1944.

In the reddening water along the seashore, Gene Bonk could not distinguish the living from the dead. He pushed through the surf.

"I still hear their voices, all these years later," said Bonk, then a 22-year-old master sergeant. " 'Help me, help me,' they called out."

It was a gray day, with clouds crowding the sky. Dawn would break to the sound and fury of history. Heroism meant meeting great challenges. Ordinary men were asked to do extraordinary things. They were soldiers of democracy. And America owes them for preserving and protecting its most cherished possession: freedom.

On D-Day, the Allies had some 175,000 fighting men scheduled to go ashore at Normandy. Hundreds of thousands in Britain and America were set to follow.

Reinforcements began coming on June 7. Bonk was there the day before, part of the earliest invasion group.

"I hit the beach at 7 a.m.," says Bonk, who grew up on the North Side of Chicago, moving to the Fox Valley decades ago.

Today, Gene and Jane Bonk live in Bristol, just outside of Aurora. They have four children, six grandchildren and two great-grandchildren.

Gene Bonk went 50 years without talking about his role in World War II. In 1994, at a local D-Day anniversary commemoration, the combat veteran talked about his experience for the first time publicly.

"It wasn't easy," he said. "But I realized that the young people needed to hear from someone who was there, someone who went through the worst of the worst."

For many World War II veterans, the memories of combat have receded. But for Bonk and others like him, memories don't die. They are the howling demons that have ruled their nights for years and years.

Bonk saw young men under his command cut down. Some of them were right beside him, as close as twilight is to darkness. He would regret those losses the rest of his life, but in those moments, he kept going, moving inland toward the Germans.

That was his training; that was his mission.

General Eisenhower was the supreme commander of Operation Overlord, the Allied code for the invasion itself.

Along with the 175,000 fighting men, D-Day involved 1,000 transport planes, as well as 5,000 ships. About 6,000 fighters and bombers were overhead.

Even today, some sixty years later, the scope of Overlord defies imagination. Think of trying to move the Wisconsin cities of Green Bay, Racine and Kenosha across Lake Michigan in one night, relocating every man, woman and child, with every vehicle, in the trip.

Eisenhower's intention was to enter France, then undertake operations aimed at the heart of Germany, destroying that country's armed forces along the way, which would end the war in Europe.

Eisenhower personally picked the time and place of the Allied assault, although weather certainly proved to be a factor.

The Allied armada came out of eleven ports in southern England. In the months before the invasion, that area of the country became one huge military encampment. Ports filled with transport ships; airfields became packed with fighters and bombers. The pleasant countryside was cluttered with parked tanks, trucks and jeeps. By early June, nearly 3 million Allied soldiers, sailors and airmen were ready to finally meet the Germans in a fight to the death.

So many stories of the invasion were lost because the sea and sand closed over the young men who might have told them, sealing their lips forever.

Bonk becomes quiet when asked about the horrors of D-Day. Tears flow freely.

"I'm sorry," he says, "I get emotional thinking about things—the war and the terrible losses that were necessary to win it. These were good guys, young and brave, called to duty. They shared a common core, and a lot of them died together. But we were united in something bigger than all of us put together. Those guys on the beach, they were my family. It's as simple as that."

There was nothing simple about getting inland on Omaha Beach, however.

Surprise was critical to the invasion of France because the Germans had fifty-five divisions, eleven of them armored, while Eisenhower could put only eight divisions ashore on D-Day. If the Germans knew where the attack was coming, they could surely hurl it back into the sea.

After analyzing intelligence reports, Eisenhower chose Normandy. Defenses there were nowhere near as formidable as at the Pas de Calais, where the Germans assumed the Allies would attack on the direct line from England to Berlin.

The Allied intelligence reports were based largely on thousands of reconnaissance flights over the French coast. It was a game of cat and mouse. Germany had its own intelligence reports. The Allies mounted an elaborate deception scheme, one that drew on the talents of Hollywood and the British film industry, to produce cardboard equipment, hoping to convince the enemy that the invasion force was gathering at Dover for an attack on the Pas de Calais. By all accounts, the Germans were deceived.

Nonetheless, their Atlantic Wall of concrete fortifications extended quite a distance. For six months, half a million men labored, constructing giant pillboxes and hazards of every variety.

In addition, advance barriers were set up along French beaches. Landing areas were mined and booby-trapped. Barbed wire and antitank ditches created an enormous gauntlet of fire that the attacking troops would have to cross—all this before the Allies even got to the Atlantic Wall.

"The war will be won or lost on the beaches," said German Field Marshal Erwin Rommel, who helped plan the French fortifications. "The first 24 hours of the invasion will be decisive." It would be, he added, "the longest day."

Bonk was there for every minute of it.

"Men were yelling and screaming ... they were dying everywhere," he remembered. "There was fire from all directions: the machine guns in front of us; German airplanes strafing the beach."

He turned to one soldier, saying they'd better move up. The next moment something spattered. That soldier had been shot in the head, his brain spraying all over Bonk.

He and his remaining men managed to hit the seawall, fighting for every single grain of sand they crossed.

The Allied air bombing that was to have knocked out German defense guns at Omaha Beach had not been accurate; the bombs had been laid down too far inland to do much good. As a result, the gunfire that met American troops was more murderous than anything that had been prepared for.

Initial losses at Omaha were ghastly; in some assault companies the casualties were at 90 percent within minutes of landing.

Bonk estimates that more than 50 percent of the men who were in his battalion were killed or wounded within those early minutes.

"It was a bloodbath," he said.

Was it anything like *Saving Private Ryan,* the 1998 Steven Spielberg movie?

Judging by his expression, Bonk becomes agitated at the mere mention of the film. Still seated, his body bends at the waist, as if the old soldier is preparing for an assault.

"Heard about it—didn't need to see the picture," Bonk said. "Unless you've been through that type of invasion, you cannot understand the experience. I don't want to sound harsh, but it's just a sore subject with me. I'm sorry."

Bonk need not apologize to anyone.

Not only is he a very courageous man, he walked in the company of others who were just as brave.

"It overwhelms me," he says. "I think of the price paid for our principles ... American ideals, you could say. No one should ever forget the young men who sacrificed their lives at Normandy. We weren't there to take over a country, but to make sure ours stayed safe. Hitler wanted the world. We wanted to stop him— nothing more, nothing less."

And stop him they did.

Allied landing craft covered the gamut, making runs not only onto Omaha Beach, but also Utah, Juno, Gold and Sword beaches.

Omaha was the bloodiest beach of all. Statistics show an estimated 3,000 casualties there on D-Day, more than the other beaches combined.

The total number of Allied casualties on D-Day has been estimated at 4,900. No exact figures were possible;

certain facts remain unknown, lost in the chaos and calamity of battle.

What was known centered on an absolute Allied commitment.

On the evening of June 6, 1944, President Roosevelt led America in prayer: "Almighty God: Our sons, pride of our Nation, this day have set upon a mighty endeavor; a struggle to preserve our Republic, our religion and our civilization and to set free a suffering humanity..."

Bonk believed in those words. He still does.

"I joined the Army in August 1940, before the war," he says. "I went in with a friend. We saw that poster, 'I Want You.' Well, we wanted to become soldiers."

Uncle Sam must have been elated.

One of seven children, Bonk was only 17 years old. By age 22, he was a master sergeant.

"Before D-Day, I was stationed in Iceland," says Bonk, who was born in 1922, married in 1946. "We were there to guard Reykjavik, an important port city. The Germans wanted Iceland, then they could control the North Atlantic. I was in the anti-aircraft battalion."

Bonk went from Iceland to England, where he prepared for the D-Day invasion.

Omaha Beach was going to be tough, but the Allies didn't know just how difficult and demanding the day would become.

"It was like a visit to hell," Bonk said.

The sand at Omaha Beach is golden in color, firm and fine, perfect for sunbathing, but not for fighting.

On both ends of Omaha, the cliffs were or more less perpendicular.

The beach itself is crescent-shaped, about six miles long overall. At low tide, Omaha stretches 300 to 400 feet in distance.

No tactician could have devised a better defensive situation. A narrow, enclosed battlefield, without the possibility of German troops getting outflanked.

Add to that, natural obstacles for the attackers to overcome, an ideal place to construct fixed fortifications and a trench system on the slope of a bluff.

It was a killing field dressed up as a beach. It became a no-man's land of death and despair.

The Germans had laid out gun positions at angles to the beach, giving them the advantage of covering an entire area with crossfire. Their trenches were set on high ground, then reinforced with concrete. Bunkers were almost unnoticeable from the front.

To attacking GIs, German firing openings looked like knitting needles stretched side-to-side.

Years after the war, one German soldier, Pfc. Hein Severloh, talked about crouching behind his machine gun during D-Day:

"My order was to get them when they were still in one line, one after the other, before they started spreading ... I did not have to swing my gun sideways."

Severloh estimates that he fired 12,000 rounds from his machine gun and another 400 from a carbine. At the end of that first day, he surrendered.

Earlier, face down in the sand, bullets whizzed over Bonk's head. He kept crawling forward, firing back when he could.

Omaha Beach turned boys into men, although a large number of them would soon be dead men. And those who survived would be frightened men. Some soldiers wet their pants, others vomited. Many of them cried unashamedly. Still, they found the inner strength to get things done.

Getting across the beach became an obsession, Bonk said.

Eisenhower hated the idea of assaulting Omaha Beach, but it had to be done. If not, the gap between Utah and the other landing areas would have been too great.

"There were nights after the war—well, I wondered how I ever survived," Bonk said. "The Germans had such an advantage in their position. You feel a certain humility. You thank God ... I couldn't help but feel proud—and it wasn't about anything I accomplished as an individual. Pride came from knowing that I had been among men. We were on the front line, defending our country."

The Allies were in France to stay.

War took Bonk to St. Lo, located in northwest France, 20 miles inland from the Normandy beachhead. After the D-Day breakout, the town's German defense base was attacked by the Allies. Severe fighting unhinged the entire west end of the enemy line and was followed by another Allied breakthrough.

St. Lo was almost completely destroyed in the battle.

"I remember being in the hedges, rows and rows of them, up higher than the enemy tanks," Bonk said. "Our bazooka men would fire at their tracks, stopping them and allowing us a chance to attack. We'd go after the Germans with our detonators and hand grenades, dropping them inside to blow up their tanks."

Bonk kept moving along a line. Ground troops aren't allowed to see the big picture. They are citizen-soldiers, not military planners or professionals.

"Here's something else to keep in mind," Bonk says, starting a new thought. "When you're fighting, you're fighting. It didn't matter if it was at Omaha Beach or St. Lo. When you're in it, you're in it. War was one continuous battle."

German strongholds were falling like dominos. Next came Paris.

The liberation of the city involved many troops and a large supply of fuel, which undoubtedly delayed the rush toward Hitler's Rhine defenses. The Allied offensive would have slowed in any event. As tanks, trucks and troops got closer to Germany, they moved farther and farther from Normandy, where supplies came ashore.

Bonk got a well-deserved day of rest in Paris, which was liberated in August 1944.

And when that liberation came, it was relatively peaceful.

As Americans approached Paris, a strong sense of excitement prevailed in the city. On August 20, Hitler sent an order to destroy Paris. He followed with a message demanding, "Is Paris burning?" The German commander in the city, General Dietrich von Choltitz, refused to go down in history as the man who burned Paris. He negotiated a surrender that allowed him to withdraw the occupying garrison while leaving the city intact. On August 25, General Jacques Leclerc, commanding the French Second Armored Division and equipped with American-built Sherman tanks, drove into Paris. He was followed by the U.S. Fourth Infantry Division.

Bonk was attached to the First Infantry Division, "the Big Red One."

He said that the Parisians were welcoming.

"They were very happy to see us," he said. "It was a day of victory for them. They were out from the tyranny of the German Army."

After Paris, Bonk saw action in the Netherlands and Belgium.

In December 1944, six months after he was part of the D-Day invasion force, Bonk became involved in the most challenging combat he had faced.

"That would be the Battle of the Bulge," Bonk said. "We were surrounded by the Germans. Things looked bleak—very, very bleak, in fact. Worse than at Omaha Beach. We were in frozen foxholes, with no food or winter-weather clothing. Ammunition was running out, too. Maintaining morale was extremely difficult. Mental fatigue was tearing us up."

At approximately 5:30 a.m. on December 16, the German Army launched the Battle of the Bulge, a no-holds-barred offensive against five American infantry divisions. Stretched thinly, they defended sixty miles of the Ardennes Front, a wooded plateau crossing Belgium that was pimpled with deep gorges and swift streams.

The battle's name came from the bulge the Germans created in the American line.

The German attack was a total surprise and at first achieved astonishing success. One U.S. division in the Ardennes was overrun and destroyed, others nearly so.

Hitler's objective was to break through the thinly held American line, then drive into Antwerp, severing Eisenhower's supply lines and splitting the British on the north from the Americans on the south. If the plan had worked, it would have been a devastating defeat for the Allies. The Germans could then turn their attention to the east, to fight the Soviets on a single front.

By December 1944, Allied intelligence thought that Hitler was fighting a strictly defensive campaign. A report released mid-month, just before the Battle of the Bulge, stated: "The enemy ... cannot stage major offensive operations."

That assessment changed in an instant.

A large number of the troops Hitler put into battle were fifteen or sixteen years old. In total, there were twenty-four divisions, many of them elite Panzer armored or Waffen SS units.

Conditions were miserable: deep snow and below-zero temperatures at night.

"As clearly as if it were yesterday, I can still see the frozen corpses ... my men, picked up and stacked one on top of the other in the trucks," Bonk said. "We were literally freezing to death. With some of my men, their feet were turning black and blue. If you wanted something to drink, you'd put snow in your helmet and try to melt it."

The pervasive fog added an unsettling element to the action.

"You'd see silhouettes, nothing else," Bonk said. "The Germans kept shelling us, firing their burp guns, too. We were trapped, there was no way out. If you lifted your head, you could catch a bullet, but we were going to hold our ground, that's all there was to it. At

Bastogne, where we were, you had to stay on tense alert, no matter how hungry or how cold you were."

Frostbite became an increasingly deadly enemy.

It was during the Battle of the Bulge that Bonk tried leading his men through their toughest times. Faith is the antidote to despair, he told them.

"I talked to the guys, telling them that we'd get through the days one at a time," Bonk said. "And even though I was doing the talking, I never pulled rank. There was little if any saluting."

Normandy notwithstanding, the longest days were when his men started committing suicide.

"Every so often, things would get quiet, then you'd hear a shot from one of the foxholes," Bonk said, adding that some soldiers saw dying as easier than living.

"As bad as things were, they weren't completely hopeless," Bonk said. "What happened, though, is that some of my men just gave up. They threw in the towel. That's tough to deal with. It broke my heart."

Weathering the storm meant hanging on when others were letting go.

A writer wonders why some survived and others didn't. So does an old soldier.

"I've asked myself millions of times: 'Could they have held on just a little longer ... Could I have done more?' " Bonk wonders out loud. He closes his eyes for a moment.

Eisenhower had General George Patton change the direction of his attack, from east to north, to relieve the troops positioned near and at Bastogne. Then, on Christmas Eve, the skies finally cleared. The Allies put

10,000 planes in the air, pounding the Germans. By early January 1945, it was the Allies on the offensive. And by the end of the month, they had driven the Germans back to their original position. Hitler's great gamble had failed.

Germany paid a terrible price for that failure: 30,000 killed, 40,000 wounded, 40,000 prisoners of war, thousands of tanks destroyed. On the U.S. side, of the 600,000 troops engaged—this was the biggest battle the American Army had ever fought—20,000 were killed, 40,000 wounded, 20,000 made prisoners of war.

Although the Battle of the Bulge ended close to where it started, it was a great victory for the Americans. Hitler had bet too much, and he had lost. It was a loss in men and material, occurring at a time when he could ill afford to lose anything at all.

Hitler was desperate. German soldiers were, too. They were involved in a number of murderous acts at the Battle of the Bulge. An officer lined up eight Americans and sprayed them with a burp gun.

Cruelty commanded enemy forces, especially those in the SS.

German troops disregarded a white flag displayed by five GIs and killed four, leaving one man alive. A tank then crushed the life out of his body. There were similar incidents. Some soldiers were used for target practice. Civilians were slaughtered as well.

The worst offense occurred at a small Belgian village, Malmedy. There, Battery B of the 285th Field Artillery Observation Battalion blundered into a Panzer spearhead. The tanks quickly overwhelmed the lightly armed specialists and more than 100 Americans were captured and lined up in a field. An orgy of murder erupted, first with pistols, then machine guns on tanks or set up along a road.

When it ended, eighty-six soldiers had been executed. Civilians who tried to come to their aid were killed, too.

For Bonk, World War II ended differently. He came home with medals and citations. His last act, however, concluded quietly.

"While making the push to Berlin, I got orders to bring 1,000 German prisoners to New York City, their port of embarkation," Bonk said. "From there, they'd be sent to POW camps. I had four men assigned to help me. The German officers were very cooperative. When we got into the harbor near New York, one German officer asked me, 'Can we see your lady?' His men wanted to see the Statue of Liberty. They cried, and we cried, too."

When Bonk checked the prisoners in, he was told that his military duties had come to an end.

"They sent me home before the war was over," Bonk said. "There wasn't any hero's welcome because Americans were still overseas."

After the war, Bonk became a successful businessman, working for General Electric Supply Company. He retired from there after 25 years because of a heart problem, stress-related and probably due to the war. Now in his eighties, he works part-time for one of his sons. He spends thirty minutes on a treadmill daily.

When he returned home in 1945, he was no longer a boy, but a World War II combat veteran. In the years since, he has lived by simple values—values his children could understand and emulate. He has been involved in countless community service events. Bonk has a way of breaking things down into irreducible truths.

"I keep things simple," he says, his smile at once sorrowful and sweet. "I've seen things that are better left alone, better left unsaid. They're too complicated."

While Bonk served his country well during World War II, he has had a lifetime of achievement after it. His quiet, unassuming nature and the helping hand he regularly extends shine as examples of the very best that the Fox Valley has to offer.

For more than three decades, Bonk has served as chaplain of American Legion Post 84 in Aurora. He comforts and consoles the families of deceased veterans, among other things.

"It's gratifying work," Bonk said. "I lost a lot of friends during World War II. My service as chaplain is a way of remembering them, of honoring what they did for our country."

Bonk also has dressed up as Santa Claus at holiday events in the area.

Men of his generation are not prone to tears, which makes an emotional interview particularly poignant.

Having been at Omaha Beach and at the Battle of the Bulge, boys became mature men overnight.

"I'm proud to have served this great country of ours," Bonk said. "But you wouldn't want your children to go through those things. The risks and the cost were much, much too great."

Bonk said he would not take a million dollars for his experiences, but he wouldn't want to go through those things again for a million dollars.

"People of my generation, we lived through some tough times—the Depression and then World War II," Bonk said. "Kids today don't know much about what we did for future generations, theirs included. That's understandable. Even so, we must never forget our dead soldiers, men who paid the ultimate price."

Their lost lives are a tribute to an American rule of action, a patriotic precept.

We must be ready to dare all for these United States, Bonk says.

History does not entrust the care of liberty to the timid.

America, if it is anything at all, is the uncrossed river and the unclimbed ridge. It is the star that is not reached and the harvest that's sleeping in the ground.

Only through service and sacrifice does America exist as an idea and as a reality.

At the end of every day, Gene Bonk honors the charge made at Omaha Beach, as well as at other places. He honors the toughness needed to hold an almost impossible position, which was the situation at Bastogne during the Battle of the Bulge.

"I pray for those fellows lost in World War II," Bonk says. "I pray for all veterans."

Guy Bodor

GUY BODOR

"We were there."

Truth is the thing that gives dignity and direction to history, which is little more than the essence of innumerable biographies.

His own biography becomes clearer in the telling.

He was at Pearl Harbor on December 7, 1941. So was about half of America's Pacific Fleet—ships of various size and shape.

In all, 185 United States Navy ships were in harbor that Sunday, "a date which will live in infamy," President Roosevelt said.

It was a date that America and the world would never forget.

The weather was warm. The gentle breeze was so slight it didn't disturb the water.

The territory of Hawaii was an ocean paradise. It had an estimated population of 460,000 in 1941, about one third of today's. One in three was ethnic Japanese, by far the largest of a varied demographic that included 65,000 indigenous Hawaiians and 112,000 Caucasians.

Then, as now, Oahu, though not the biggest, was the most heavily populated of the Hawaiian Islands, with about 275,000 people, most of them concentrated along the southern coastline in and around Pearl Harbor, Honolulu and the beach resort of Waikiki.

Guy Bodor joined the U.S. Navy before World War II.

"I enlisted in February 1940," says Bodor, who was born in 1922. "I had an affinity for the water."

A Californian by birth, Bodor grew up in the Midwest. He was the second of four boys.

"We were pretty typical kids," said Bodor, who has lived in Aurora for more than 50 years.

There was nothing typical of his experiences during World War II, however.

He spent 56 months in combat areas, including Guadalcanal.

But before that, Bodor was at Pearl Harbor.

He was an electronics repairman aboard the USS San Francisco.

At about 7:45 a.m. on December 7, he went to the mess hall, where he had pancakes for breakfast.

The pancakes were cold.

During breakfast, Bodor heard the sound of the ship's alarm.

Life would never be the same.

The world turned.

Americans instinctively understood that there had been a complete change, a passing of the old order.

Change occurred in two brief hours. Division gave way to unity, isolationism to engagement.

As a Japanese admiral had feared, the attack on Pearl Harbor awakened the sleeping giant that was America. A military, economic and cultural superpower was born in that raid.

The price was substantial—2,390 Americans were dead, nineteen warships were sunk or damaged, six airfields were bombed.

The United States was at war.

A heavy cruiser, the San Francisco was docked in a Navy repair yard at Pearl Harbor. It was there for renovations, anchored without guns, ammunition or fuel.

After hearing the ship's alarm, Bodor ran to the San Francisco's main deck. He saw six torpedo bombers, flying fast and low.

"If I would have had a 20-foot pole, I could've touched them," Bodor said of the enemy attack planes.

Other Americans saw the goggled faces of the Japanese pilots.

Smoke and flames were everywhere.

Three bombs struck just forward of the light cruiser St. Louis, moored between the Honolulu and the San Francisco. A fourth bomb landed on the pier, about fifteen feet from the Honolulu's side.

Despite losing its electrically operated guns, the Honolulu managed to shoot down one of the attacking airplanes.

Courage became the ladder on which all other American virtues mounted that day.

Across the pier from the San Francisco, the New Orleans also lost its electrical power. Despite disabled ammunition hoists, the ship continued as a fighting vessel. In the darkness below deck, crewmembers formed a human conveyor belt, passing powder and shells topside to keep American guns firing.

Japanese attackers had sunk several ships along Battleship Row, including the Arizona, California, Nevada, Oklahoma and West Virginia. Among ships significantly damaged were the Pennsylvania, Maryland and Tennessee.

The Utah capsized, as did the minelayer Oglala.

American aircraft losses, both on the ground and in the air, numbered 165 planes.

Assessed damage to Oahu's military installations ran well into the tens of millions of dollars, with damages to the Pearl Harbor navy yard alone estimated at $40 million, although some said that figure was inflated.

Despite death, destruction and widespread suffering at Pearl Harbor, the situation could have been much, much worse. Oil reserves at the navy yard, for example, were not harmed. In the opinion of many military leaders, those reserves were even more vital than the American warships. As Admiral Husband E. Kimmel pointed out:

"If they had destroyed the oil, which was all above ground at that time, it would have forced the withdrawal of the fleet to the [U.S. mainland] coast because there wasn't any oil anywhere else out there to keep the fleet operating."

Even so, Japanese attackers had all but demolished America's defensive stronghold in the Pacific Ocean.

That they had done so at an amazingly low cost of twenty-nine aircraft only added to America's anger.

Bodor doesn't discuss Pearl Harbor much anymore, at least not with writers.

Now in his eighties, he thinks that the past has been adequately explained. In some sense, he is a prophet in reverse, wanting to leave old war stories alone.

It is his right, something Bodor earned through decades of military service, both in and out of active duty.

"I ended up forty years in the U.S. Navy," he says, the words a bit slow, but as reliable as day following night.

A respectful writer should know when and where to stop. On this day, that isn't the case.

Like corks bobbing on a turbulent sea, questions come out of the blue, obviously bothering Bodor.

Could you sum up your World War II experience?

"With one sentence? That would be impossible," Bodor says matter-of-factly. "I will tell you this: We were sent to do a job. We did that job to the best of our ability."

In at least some small way, the grandeur of the American naval tradition is found in the quiet dignity displayed by Bodor. He is friendly, but firm. To grow old with class and courage cuts close to what it is to be a man.

He was young once, too.

"My dad emigrated from Hungary," Bodor says. "He was a skilled mechanic and cabinetmaker. He learned to fly in 1914 while working for an early aviation manufacturer."

Bodor's father died in 1928. He had taken the children for a rowboat ride. Jim Bodor, then two years old, decided to get his hair wet. When the toddler fell into the water, his father dove in immediately, thinking only of rescuing the boy.

Louis Bodor died of a massive heart attack after jumping in. His young son was pulled back into the rowboat, safe and sound.

The Bodor family moved to Chicago in 1938.

"After attending Senn High School, I enlisted in the Navy," Bodor says. "Not only was it a good job, but there were career opportunities. I was assigned to aviation radio school ... My monthly pay was $21."

World War II was a time of unprecedented growth for the U.S. Navy.

On the day of Japan's surrender in August 1945, the Navy had 105 aircraft carriers, 5,000 ships and submarines, and 82,000 vessels and landing craft deployed around the world, manned by experienced citizen-sailors and led by seasoned admirals. They and their allies had defeated Japan, liberated Europe and greatly reduced the German, Japanese and Italian navies. Thirty-nine months earlier, the American naval force had been a small, mediocre group, repeatedly overmatched in battle, nearly driven from the Pacific and unable to stop submarine devastation in the Atlantic.

America's naval turnaround in World War II remains one of the greatest sagas in military history.

Bodor was there for all of it, first aboard the San Francisco, then, after a transfer, as a radioman on a U.S. Navy bomber.

"I was a crewmember on a Privateer," Bodor says, referring to the naval airplane, which was similar to the B-24 Liberator.

As a Pearl Harbor veteran, Bodor was involved in the opening battle of World War II. In addition, he participated in one of the last.

After the dropping of two atomic bombs—August 6 and August 9, 1945—the war went on for almost a week.

As radioman on a Privateer, Bodor was involved in one of the last engagements of World War II.

"On the tenth of August, my squadron sank a Japanese freighter," Bodor said.

In an even later engagement, which Bodor wasn't part of, American airplanes swept over the Nagoya airfields.

The mission took place August 14, 1945, and included Privateers, as well as P-61s, B-24s and B-29s.

Nagoya took a beating. The mission was called a "milk run," meaning that there were no enemy fighters aloft and flak from the ground was light.

Nonetheless, a young flier named Phil Schlamberg was shot down and killed. He was one of the last American casualties of World War II.

Schlamberg got to fly a P-51 Mustang, but never even learned to drive an automobile.

The Japanese decision to surrender was reached at a final meeting of that country's Supreme War Council. Emperor Hirohito said: "I cannot bear to see my people suffer any longer."

On August 15, 1945, in a taped radio message—his first direct voice communication with the people he ruled—the emperor told them that the war was over and it was time to accept the terms of surrender, which would "pave the way for a grand peace for all generations to come," he said.

After World War II, Bodor came home to Chicago.

"I went into the Naval Air Reserves—the USNRR, the United States Naval Ready Reserves—and became a chief warrant officer," said Bodor, who rewrote the training manual for incoming reservists, among other things during his service time after World War II.

In addition, Bodor, a Purple Heart recipient, was employed as an advanced customer service representative with IBM, retiring in 1987 after forty years with that company.

He met his future wife at a church event.

"It was at the Bryn Mawr Community Church, on the South Side of Chicago," Bodor said. "I had an aunt and uncle who belonged to that church."

It was the proper setting for what would be an enduring relationship. Love, after all, is an act of faith.

Guy and Marilyn "Bobbi" Bodor were married in May 1949. They have three children and four grandchildren.

Bodor had come to the church to help out with an amateur theater production, which was to be staged at Bryn Mawr Community.

"I was there to install lights," Bodor said. "I also designed and manufactured a thunder machine ... a wind machine."

Bobbi Bodor was trying out for the lead in Thornton Wilder's *Our Town*.

"One day, he came to the house to pick up a sewing machine," Bobbi Bodor said, smiling, thinking back to her husband's earliest attempts at courtship. "We were going to make something for the play. My father said, 'Now that's the kind of young man you should marry.' Well, the thought had never crossed my mind. All these years later, we've been very, very happy together."

Love is proud of itself. It leaks out of people, even those with the tightest sense of security.

Bodor is not the type prone to overstatement. There are celebrated heroes and silent ones—men and women who readers have never heard of. But each one's story is essentially the same.

"When I enlisted in the Navy, I signed a contract with my country," Bodor said. "If I'm proud of anything, it's that I kept my end of the bargain. We had duties and responsibilities. We performed them without question or complaint."

Bodor is part of that generation of Americans— "our better angels," as Abraham Lincoln would certainly have said of them.

While he doesn't discuss it much, Bodor was wounded aboard the San Francisco during the fierce fighting involved in the taking of Guadalcanal, an island few Americans had ever heard of and none of the military planners knew much about in the early 1940s.

The Battle of Guadalcanal was much more than a battle. It was a six-month campaign marked by seven major naval engagements, as well as twenty or more clashes ashore, the almost daily cut and thrust of combat.

No campaign in World War II saw such sustained violence in all three dimensions—air, land and sea— where the issue hung in doubt so long.

If its intrinsic attributes made the battle at Guadalcanal special, it was its historical context that made it legend. World War II began for the United States at Pearl Harbor, a humbling of national pride. Bodor was right there, his ship docked not far from Battleship Row.

What followed was a succession of American defeats—Guam, Wake Island, Bataan and Corregidor, which rubbed salt into the original attack wound.

Beginning in 1942 and continuing into the next year, Guadalcanal gave America a much-needed shot in the arm.

It was a major American counterattack.

Guadalcanal is one of the southernmost of the Solomon Islands, east of New Guinea.

The Japanese were constructing an air base on Guadalcanal, which threatened Australia.

At dawn on the seventh of August, exactly eight months to the day that Bodor ate those cold pancakes at Pearl Harbor, the first Allied invasion armada of the war appeared off the coast of Guadalcanal. After an intensive three-hour bombardment, combat groups of the First Marines went ashore.

Throughout August and September, a beachhead was built up. Some 17,000 U.S. Marines occupied a seven-by-four-mile area of land, including Henderson Field, the renamed airstrip started by the Japanese.

The enemy decided that Guadalcanal had to be cleared, and they sent shiploads of reinforcements to the island. Japanese cruisers and destroyers hammered at the Marines and at American and Australian convoys trying to supply them.

On the night of November 13, 1942, the Imperial Japanese Fleet staged a dramatic sortie. This, the most furious sea encounter of the Solomons, became known as the Naval Battle of Guadalcanal. Led by two battleships, the Japanese force intended to land more troops on Guadalcanal, delivering a heavy shelling attack on a much smaller U.S. task force. But the more maneuverable U.S. ships pressed the attack, sometimes drawing so close that they had difficulty depressing their guns. The Americans lost two cruisers, including the Juneau, which carried the five Sullivan brothers. Two other cruisers were damaged, but the Japanese lost their first battleship of the war. The next night, a second Japanese flotilla was located by planes from an American aircraft carrier and was heavily punished.

The land campaign lasted until February 1943. It was the first Marine experience in the type of jungle warfare that they would become so intimately acquainted with during the next three years.

Not only was there malaria, but also intense heat and an enemy that came screaming out of the jungle at night in wild suicide charges.

The Army's Twenty-Fourth Division replaced the First Marine Division. On Guadalcanal, those GIs proved to be as adept at fighting the Japanese as the Marines.

Finally, having decided to pull out, the Japanese brought destroyers in at night and evacuated about 12,000 troops. By February 9, 1943, not a single living enemy was known to be on Guadalcanal.

The Japanese had suffered a critical land defeat. The first American offensive was deemed a success.

By the time the last enemy sniper was quieted, there were 24,000 dead Japanese; the dead Americans totaled 1,752.

But Tokyo was still 3,000 miles away.

Gray-haired and patriarchal today, Bodor is secure in himself. World War II is one of history's profound events. It's more than the momentous episodes written about in schoolbooks. More than battles won and lost.

161

More than costume dramas on television and in film. More than stories of the past.

Bodor remembers what the shouting was all about.

As of early 2004, he was putting his memories down on paper. In the latter stages of his life, Bodor is still learning about a dramatic part of his youth.

He came home a more serious person. He worked harder at everything, with a new sense of purpose.

He was not alone.

Professors have said that returning World War II veterans were among the best students they ever had.

In his decidedly understated way, Bodor speaks for all the men who were at Pearl Harbor, as well as for those who served in World War II.

His is a firsthand account. Sweeping, superfluous generalizations are best left to those who weren't there.

According to Bodor, most of what needs to be said has already been said.

Yet, all the historical dust has not settled. Personal perspectives are especially rewarding.

Bodor's words, although limited in this book, are truly valuable.

And anyone reading them should feel privileged.

He is an invaluable reference—even if offering only the briefest recollection of what war was like, of what it meant to be there at the beginning and at the end.

Lee Laz

LEE LAZ

"I was given a sector to fly and it was my duty to fly it."

Lee Laz always wanted to be a pilot.

As a young man, he had the type of confident manner that Tom Wolfe would highlight later in *The Right Stuff*: "A particular folksiness, a particular down-home calmness."

Regardless of the era, bravery never goes out of fashion.

Today, when Laz talks about World War II, it is with both feet firmly on the ground. He comes across as poised and polished—someone completely at ease; someone willing to answer questions on a variety of topics, including the combat missions he piloted.

"From as early as I can remember, I was nuts about aviation," said Laz, an Aurora resident who won the Navy Cross after dropping a bomb on one of Japan's super ships, the 72,000-ton Yamato.

The Navy Cross is given for "extraordinary heroism in the presence of great danger and personal risk."

Laz, who graduated from West Aurora High School, flew a dive-bomber for the U.S. Navy. He had enlisted in June 1942, six months after World War II began.

"Actually, I tried enlisting in 1941, a couple of weeks after Pearl Harbor, but I didn't have enough education in my field," Laz said. "I knew I wanted to fly for the Navy. I already had my private pilot's license, but they said I had to be nineteen years old, not eighteen. And I needed to have finished my second year of college. Anyway, the day I became eligible, I signed up."

Participating in flight training for the U.S. Navy was a "high honor," said Laz, who was born in January 1923. The dive-bomber he flew was a two-seater. A gunner sat behind him.

"We were well trained," Laz said. "We had outstanding airplanes and confidence in one another. Those things made a difference when you went out on a mission."

He was out in the wild blue, diving down and bombing Japanese ships through intense antiaircraft fire. Still, battle after battle, he returned to the American aircraft carrier on which he was based, the USS Wasp, CV-18.

It was dangerous duty.

Pilots were among America's last "loners," the flyboys of an apocalyptic era.

Take Laz, for example. From the time he was a boy, he wanted to get off the ground, fly like a bird, see the world from up high, travel faster than anyone could do while attached to the Earth. More than the electric light, more than the automobile and more than the telephone, the airplane separated past from future.

Horsepower meant more than the four legs of an earlier era.

In the blink of a collective eye, flying became the thing to do. American aviators epitomized masculine glamour. They wore bomber jackets and posed with their thumbs up. They were the ultimate in what would be called "cool" by a later generation.

By virtue of what they wanted out of life, Laz and others like him were wanderers. A sedentary existence left them unfilled. The frontier was everywhere. Adventure was something searched for. And those who went after it had an everlasting itch. Scratching that itch involved a certain craving, a dream of undiscovered lands and new worlds.

The entire Earth was but a single point.

It was the open sky calling Laz, who clearly remembers his first flight.

"My father was in the automobile business," he said. "A barnstormer came to Aurora in an old biplane. As a promotional gimmick, my dad rented the plane for a whole day. People were able to fly for free."

Years later and on another level entirely, Laz learned that freedom isn't free. It must be fought for and cultivated carefully. All things considered, it is the patriot's blood that feeds freedom's tree, which was a seedling when George Washington said: "Liberty, when it begins to take root, is a plant of rapid growth."

Never confuse free with free and easy, Laz says.

Nothing was easy at the Battle of Leyte Gulf.

As morning sunshine splashed from the waters of the Philippine Sea in late October 1944, the stage was set for the greatest naval battle in history.

The Battle of Leyte Gulf was, in fact, a three-part affair, the actions off Cape Engano and in the Surigao Strait complementing the action in Leyte Gulf itself. In reality, the battle was really only one part of an effort that had begun with the American carrier raids on Formosa and the Philippines two weeks before, and which continued for a full month after the main-force engagements and immediate follow-up operations.

American success at Leyte Gulf ensured eventual victory throughout the Philippines and exposed the Japanese home islands to direct Allied attack.

In the last days of October 1944, some 70 Japanese warships and 716 airplanes, split into three separate commands, opposed 166 U.S. warships and 1,280 airplanes, one of which was piloted by Laz.

"Every facet of naval warfare was in this battle," Laz said. "You had air combat, surface combat, submarine combat ... amphibious. Every weapon and gun imaginable was used, from the smallest to the biggest naval guns ever put on a battleship. There were 18-inch guns on the Yamato. Those were big suckers. The projectiles weighed about 3,500 pounds. Can you imagine that? Fortunately, they couldn't shoot those at our airplanes."

The battle was fought over 115,000 square miles between fleets that deployed across an area three times as large.

With the landing of General Douglas MacArthur's liberating army on Leyte, the Japanese Navy engaged in its last big bid for victory.

The Japanese strategy was to lure the U.S. Third Fleet away with a northern force made up of largely empty carriers; meanwhile Vice Admiral Takeo Kurita, whose fleet constituted 60 percent of Tokyo's major naval units, was to take his central force and come down into Leyte Gulf from the north. At the same time, a smaller southern force under Vice Admiral Shoji Nishimura was to enter Leyte Gulf from the south. The Allied beachhead with its unloading ships, caught between the two of them, would be wiped out. And so would Admiral Thomas Kinkaid's Seventh Fleet, which had no big carriers and no modern battleships. Then, when the U.S. Third Fleet returned, the Japanese would destroy it, too.

The U.S. Third Fleet was under the direction of Admiral William "Bull" Halsey.

As the central Japanese force entered Leyte Gulf in late October, the two U.S. fleets that could have protected the invasion beaches were far away. But the enemy had inadvertently charged into a group of escort aircraft carriers, which were small, slow and relatively defenseless. The battle should have been completely one-sided, but the Americans, though badly hurt—a carrier and three destroyers sunk—were able to sink three enemy cruisers and so confuse the Japanese that they withdrew without shelling the invasion beaches.

Halsey was chasing the decoy force far to the north. His planes sank a cruiser, two destroyers and four aircraft carriers—including the last surviving carrier that had participated in the Pearl Harbor attack almost three years before—but he finally had to answer urgent pleas from Allied escort carriers.

"They ordered us to get back there," Laz said. "We turned the task force around, 'flat out,'…'return right away,' we were told."

Regardless of how well the Japanese decoy strategy worked, the Allied victory ended up being as impressive as it was important.

Japan suffered immense naval losses, which it could ill afford. Furthermore, the naval power that the Japanese had first established in 1905 by sinking a mighty Russian fleet was finally and irreparably crushed.

From late October and through November of 1944, the Japanese Imperial Navy lost 50 warships in Philippine and immediately adjacent waters during American follow-up operations.

After Leyte Gulf, the Japanese Imperial Navy was never again able to offer battle with a balanced force: and after November 1944, the Imperial Navy was relegated and reduced to coastline defense status, barely able to perform that role, in fact.

As a sea people, the Japanese were instinctively aware of the maritime key to victory, and they had once boasted a massive fleet that included the world's two largest battleships, the Yamato and the Musashi.

In was at the Battle of Leyte Gulf that Laz dropped a bomb on the Yamato, valiant action that led to his Navy Cross.

Each of the Yamato's main turrets weighed more than a destroyer.

"To me, the ship looked big and black," Laz said. "It was overwhelming."

On an early approach, Laz turned too soon.

"I came in too shallow," Laz said. "I had to take a step up. That way I could get a really good bead on the ship, which was curving at the time. For a second or two, I thought the ship was on fire. But it wasn't burning; it was just antiaircraft gunfire—muzzle blasts shot from the Yamato itself. I thought, 'Wow, that's not something you see every day.' I went into a vertical dive and released my bomb at about 2,000 feet, leading it just enough to catch the Yamato. Then, I got out of there like a bat out of hell."

Laz did not sink the Yamato, but he did damage it.

The sinking of the Yamato came later in the war, when the Japanese ship was used in support of enemy forces on Okinawa.

On that day in April 1945, the Yamato was accompanied by one light cruiser and eight destroyers.

Caught 130 miles from Kagoshima with no air cover, the Yamato was overwhelmed by Allied aircraft from nine carriers, being hit by perhaps as many as eleven torpedoes and seven bombs.

The accompanying light cruiser and four destroyers were also sunk.

Japanese losses from the Yamato alone were 2,500 men. The Imperial Fleet was gone.

Laz himself sank a destroyer, for which he received the Distinguished Flying Cross, although that was before the action at Okinawa, an extremely important campaign contributing to the military defeat of Japan.

Okinawa provided the U.S. with airfields from which the campaign against Japan's home islands could be supplemented.

Okinawa also provided forward anchoring positions for U.S. ships. More importantly, the island's location astride Japan's supply line from Southeast Asia meant that no oil tanker reached enemy waters from the southern resource area after March 1945.

Okinawa, like Saipan, housed a substantial Japanese civilian population indoctrinated with tales of American brutality.

The Japanese 32nd Army, with some 131,000 troops, in effect ceded the central and northern part of the island in order to concentrate forces for a defensive campaign on the Shuri Line.

The Allied land conquest of Okinawa proceeded push by push, propelled by a combined force of 300,000 men—mostly Marines and GIs.

The fiercest fighting took place at Shuri, an ancient city and a center of pre-Japanese and pre-Chinese culture.

Japanese troops hid everywhere, but most of all in the caves that covered the area. It was not possible for the Marines and GIs to simply bypass the caves in a forward advance. Enemy attackers would emerge at their backs and fire on them from behind.

American flamethrowers proved to be the only weapon that could force the Japanese soldiers out of their caves or kill them.

Even with the flamethrowers, however, American losses were substantial. Altogether, the Army, Navy, Marines and Coast Guard suffered 49,200 casualties, the heaviest toll of the war in the Pacific. People back home shuddered, then wondered if there wasn't another way to bring the Japanese to the surrender table.

The Japanese suffered even more losses on Okinawa than the Americans did.

When the last stronghold on Kiiyama Peninsula fell, more than 110,000 Japanese were dead—nine for every American killed on land.

Okinawa marked an increased fanaticism among the Japanese military. They had fought on in a hopeless situation, dooming tens of thousands of young men to a senseless death. Both sides suffered. By all accounts, morality was held hostage by the enemy.

Japanese leaders tried to absolve themselves through suicide.

Before dawn on June 22, 1945, for example, Japanese General Mitsuru Ushijima and his principal subordinate, Lieutenant General Cho, knelt in full-dress uniform before their headquarters cave and cut out their own insides.

Likewise, rather than surrender, Japan's leaders were willing to commit national suicide.

Kamikaze activity was heavy at Okinawa, but the suicide missions started at the Battle of Leyte Gulf, where Laz distinguished himself most. It was after hitting the Yamato that the Fox Valley aviator met Admiral John S. McCain Sr., grandfather to Arizona Senator John McCain III, himself a Naval aviator.

"He was an old salt ... U.S. Navy through and through," Laz said of the admiral, who was born in 1884.

It was a Japanese admiral, Takijiro Ohnishi, who announced the initial appearance of the Kamikaze in October 1944:

"With so few planes we can assure success only through suicide attack," Ohnishi told senior Japanese commanders. "Each fighter must be armed with a 550-pound bomb and crash-land on a carrier deck."

This was the origin of the Kamikaze, which is Japanese for "divine wind." The word refers to the typhoon that blew away a Mongol fleet that had tried to invade Japan in the Middle Ages.

Many Kamikaze pilots pressed their attack with passion, persistence and resolve. It was considered a great privilege among some Japanese airmen to volunteer for the one-way missions, which were wrapped in a sort of religious fervor.

Almost all the pilots were in their early twenties.

In many instances, Kamikaze pilots drank alcohol before flying off to their deaths. Not all of the pilots died, however. Some returned to their base, reporting that they could not get through the screen of U.S. fighter planes protecting a given group of ships.

Very few Kamikaze pilots, in fact, got through to their prize targets—the American aircraft carrier. Even so, they did considerable damage to U.S. ships, causing destruction and loss of life.

Admiral Halsey said that the Japanese suicide aircraft was "the only weapon I feared in the war." During the battles for the Philippines, Iwo Jima and Okinawa, the Japanese sent 2,257 aircraft on organized Kamikaze attacks, of which 936 returned to base, unsuccessful.

Kamikaze attacks still sank 30 combat ships, damaged some 300 others and killed an estimated 4,000 men on board ships and injured about twice that number.

More U.S. sailors were killed or injured and many more U.S. vessels were sunk or damaged by Kamikazes off Okinawa, for example, than in the Japanese attack on Pearl Harbor.

Laz left the Pacific Theater in one piece. His best friend, Jud Doane, did not.

"That was a hard loss," Laz said. "Jud was on a search and destroy mission ... a sector search, and he got separated somehow. He called once, then we didn't hear anything again."

Although the two grew up in the same town, they never met until each enlisted in the U.S. Navy. Doane lived on the East Side of Aurora; Laz lived on the West Side.

"We were introduced to one another during advanced flight training—Corpus Christi, Texas," Laz said.

Doane also was a Naval aviator.

"He was a very, very good pilot," Laz said of his friend, who disappeared at the conclusion of the Leyte Gulf campaign.

The two were part of the same squadron and served together through the war. After Doane's disappearance, the Navy declared him missing.

Home on a 30-day combat leave in December 1944, Laz stopped at the Doane residence, where he had visited months earlier.

Jud Doane was with him then. That initial visit came before the two were originally ordered overseas.

Things were different when Laz returned to Aurora alone.

"They prayed Jud would find his way home ... he never did," Laz said. "Anyway, I had called and asked about coming over. I brought some charts and maps, showed Jud's parents where he could conceivably be. We were always hoping that he might be with friendlies on an island somewhere."

On his first visit to the Doane residence, Laz met one of Jud's sisters, Bette, who was several years younger than her brother, and two years younger than Laz.

Bette began writing to Laz when he returned to the Navy.

Around the time of his discharge in September 1945, the two started dating.

"Our first date was for dinner and dancing at the Sherman Hotel, downtown Chicago," Laz said. "On the way to the city, I told her to open the glove compartment. I had bought this bottle of Chanel No. 5, which was hard to find then. And that's what got her, I think. We've had a terrific time together ever since."

The two were married in June 1946.

Lee and Bette Laz have four daughters, as well as thirteen grandchildren and three great-grandchildren.

Laz went to the University of Illinois on the GI Bill, majoring in aeronautical engineering. After graduation, Lockheed offered him a job, but Laz would have had to relocate to California.

"The money was decent, but not enough to really induce us to leave Aurora," Laz said.

He and Bette built their own home. Laz worked for his father, who managed a Dodge dealership and also received a small percentage of the business through the years.

In the 1950s, Laz bought the dealership. Things didn't work well financially, however.

In January 1957, Chrysler Corporation purchased his stock. They paid $1 for Laz's business.

"I never did cash their check," Laz says, smiling. "Guess I showed them."

Either way, he showed the Japanese quite a bit. Listening to Laz is a reminder that life shrinks or expands in proportion to a person's courage.

For Laz, the sky was the limit.

He talks calmly and casually about his airplane being hit with antiaircraft fire or bullets from an enemy fighter.

"Sure, the plane took some hits, but I never got a scratch," he says. "You kept your wits under fire, no matter how much flak was coming."

Along with the battles of Leyte Gulf and Okinawa, Laz saw action at Saipan, Wake Island and the Mariana Islands, among other places.

During one engagement, the wing of Laz's airplane caught fire.

"My gunner wanted to bail out," Laz said. "Turns out, the hydraulics were on fire. A line had been hit. We were able to shut down a valve and land our airplane. Everything turned out just fine."

After the automobile dealership failed in the 1950s, Laz went to work for Inland Steel—first as an inside salesman, then as a product manager.

He retired in 1988.

Thinking back to the years before World War II, Laz describes himself as a fairly typical young man. One of his brothers, Don Laz, was a highly regarded athlete who went on to win a silver medal as a pole-vaulter in the 1952 Summer Olympics, which were held in Helsinki, Finland.

Laz's own accomplishments represent the very best of an American spirit that is the sum of its people. The primary principle of democracy is the worth and dignity of the individual.

"I'm proud of my time in the Navy," Laz said.

He thinks back to the time when all layers of society were absorbed in a monumental challenge. Everyone had a role in World War II. Everyone understood that the successful outcome of the war was critical to the continuing evolution of mankind.

The United States was infused with a sense of purpose and patriotism. Laz was part of that culture. He came home with hard-fought, fundamental lessons on the nature of humanity. He entered into a common effort for the greater good. Like others of his age, he matured quickly and quietly, without any fuss.

American author James Thurber advised: "Don't look back in anger. Don't look forward with fear. Look around you with awareness."

Today, nearly two generations after World War II, Laz likes what he sees.

"When World War II started, I thought that America was the last great hope of mankind," he says. "To me, it still is ... always will be."

Dick Young

DICK YOUNG

"The Japanese were everywhere."

And they were almost invisible, hidden in pillboxes and concrete huts.

He kept advancing.

Discipline held, even under a sheet of deadly fire.

"Iwo Jima was a fight for survival," said Dick Young, a lifelong Oswego resident. "As a Marine, you held yourself to strict standards of discipline, duty and physical endurance."

For Young, it was a special attitude, part of the Marine tradition, an inheritance involving combat excellence and an unbending code of honor. It centered on an *esprit de corps*.

Starting with the American Revolutionary War, U.S. Marines have developed a reputation for "getting the job done," making them one of the most famous fighting forces in history.

"*Semper Fidelis*—always faithful," says Young, who was born in October 1924. "You believed in the men who were around you. It's part of the fabric of the Marine Corps. As long as they were there, you knew you had a chance, no matter how bad the odds."

Courage can be contagious.

But being bold doesn't mean an absence of fear—just a mastery of it.

"Sure you were scared, but you honored the brotherhood of the Marine Corps," Young said. "We were fighting for one another on Iwo Jima."

The very name of that island evokes the Greek myth of Sisyphus, where a man keeps pushing the boulder up a mountain, only to have it roll back again and again and again.

It took monumental effort to get to the top of Mount Suribachi, the extinct volcano on the southern tip of Iwo Jima. When viewed from the air, the island resembles a pork chop, with the shank extending into the Pacific Ocean.

It was atop Suribachi, the island's highest point, that the famous flag-raising photograph was taken. To millions of Americans at home, that image became the ultimate symbol of valor and victory.

Now in the twilight of his life, Young comes across as genteel and gracious. He is soft-spoken and studious, characteristics not generally associated with a retired Marine.

Retired?

Young's smile looks like the first scratch on a new car.

"Once a Marine, always a Marine," he says.

It's that way with certain callings. For more than two decades, Young was the Kane County environmental director.

He lives in a marvelous multilevel home along the Fox River in Oswego, just steps from where he grew up.

The area was called "Poverty Point," Young said, adding that his family ate fish from the river during the Depression. Money was pretty tight.

"I've always been close to the land here," he says.

His house has a sod roof, reinforced by concrete. Young designed the environmentally friendly home himself.

Young is educated and articulate. The protection of

Kane County's natural resources is his ongoing passion. Nature, he says, is like a great poet. It knows how to produce the greatest effects with the most limited means. And it is as delightfully and as truly known at a certain distance as upon a closer view.

People who know Young almost always bring up his inherent decency. He is said to be honest and hardworking. Years ago, for example, an area policeman pulled him over for speeding.

Young was driving slightly above the posted limit.

When the officer realized that Young was a Kane County official, he came close to not handing him the ticket.

Young insisted, then paid the ticket, even after a judge told him he didn't have to.

Young received a national environmental award from President George H. Bush.

Earlier, in 1948, Young married his childhood sweetheart. She died more than fifteen years ago.

Dick and Charlene Young had four children—two boys and two girls, one of whom lives in a home alongside her father.

His children have families of their own.

Poverty Point went upscale decades ago.

Young graduated from Oswego High School.

When World War II began, he was accepted as a U.S. Navy pilot. He was told that there would be a wait, however, due to overstaffing in the training program.

"I wanted to get in the service, do my share for our country," Young said. "I told my father I was going to join the Marines."

Young enlisted in February 1943.

Two years later, in February 1945, he was on Iwo Jima, located in the Nanpo Shoto, a chain of island groups starting at the entrance of Tokyo Bay and stretching south for 750 miles.

Composed chiefly of rocks, gray sand, sulfur and areas of scraggy vegetation, Iwo Jima held two strategic airfields and the beginning of a third.

Long before the American invasion, Japan marked Iwo Jima for a major military buildup.

America did its best to hinder Iwo Jima's development as an island fortress. Submarines stalked supply ships coming down from Tokyo Bay. Carrier planes and Army bombers from other islands attacked Iwo Jima, blowing up buildings, destroying Japanese planes and pocking the airstrips.

Nonetheless, the buildup continued. By September 1944, Iwo Jima held 15,000 enemy soldiers. More would come, bringing the Japanese fighting force to more than 20,000.

The basic Japanese army unit was the 109th Infantry Division, and its chief components were the 2nd Mixed Brigade, the 145th Infantry Regiment, and the 3rd Battalion, 17th Mixed Infantry Regiment. Attached to them were several independent tank units and an air group. Navy personnel consisted of air groups, a Naval Guard force and the 204th Naval Construction Battalion, which included Koreans.

Among the island's heavier armaments, in addition to the coast defense pieces, were artillery, antiaircraft guns, rockets and mortars.

Built close to the surface, with sand piled over them, were the pillboxes, bunkers and blockhouses. Many of those in clusters were connected by trench systems. Under the ground were living quarters, some of the chambers capable of holding only a few men, and others large enough to accommodate three or four hundred of the enemy. Included were hospital wards with surgical instruments and operating tables. There was room for storage of food, water cans, ammunition and other supplies. The lighting ranged from electricity to oil lamps and candles. To guard against entrapment, the chambers were provided with multiple entrances and exits. Those on levels one above the other were linked by stairways. Some of the chambers were made of building blocks cut from the volcanic rock, while others made use of the island's caves. This network was augmented with miles of tunnels, much of the system interconnected. The surface openings were designed as fighting positions.

There would be no turning around. Iwo Jima was going to be an assault—war without quarter, a battle of heart and hardware.

The American bombardment had not damaged the subterranean shelter. Enemy soldiers would have to be killed individually, up close, at a tremendous cost.

For a Japanese soldier, death was the only way home.

When Young hit the beach, he was among the first Marines on the island.

Young was with the 28th Regiment of the Fifth Marine Division.

While the Japanese were willing to fight for the Emperor, the Marines were willing to fight for one another—fight to the death if necessary.

That motive made them almost invincible as a fighting force. It personalized their battle experience.

Robert Leader was a U.S. Marine, one of an estimated 80,000 on Iwo Jima. Years later, as a full professor of fine arts at Notre Dame University, he wrote about the island:

"It was like being on a winning athletic team and everyone was playing over his head. Can you possibly imagine the unspoken affection we felt for each other? An affection that allowed men to offer their lives daily for each other without hesitation and, I suppose, without understanding. And yet, to place oneself between danger and one's people is the ultimate act of love."

Uncommon valor was a common virtue on Iwo Jima.

Young stepped ashore at about 9 a.m. on that first fighting day, part of the invasion's initial wave.

"It was all very quiet at first," Young said. "Everyone was milling around."

Within thirty minutes, the slaughter began.

Only 660 nautical miles from Tokyo, Iwo Jima became the setting for one of the bloodiest battles of World War II.

Earsplitting noise and smoke suddenly filled the air. The almost unnoticed blockhouses, situated on flat ground, exploded with gunfire, raking exposed Americans with machine-gun attacks. But the heaviest hailstorm came from above, from Suribachi. Hidden inside the mountain, two thousand Japanese troops started hitting the stunned Marines with everything they had, including heavy artillery shells, mortars and machine-gun rounds.

By day's end, half of those in Young's platoon were wounded or dead.

Young was a Marine PFC. He carried the walkie-talkie for a Marine lieutenant.

"I also got to carry a carbine, something that I really liked," Young said, referring to his rifle, which was smaller than the American M1. "With the carbine, you could get it up quicker and shoot. Japanese rifles were heavier ... not as fast to the trigger."

Young carried a carbine because he also carried the walkie-talkie radio, which was big and bulky, the size of a whole knapsack, thus necessitating the smaller rifle.

There were 39 men in Young's original platoon on Iwo Jima. Before the Americans left the island, 38 of the 39 were wounded or killed.

The one Marine who wasn't wounded or killed suffered a compound leg fracture, which occurred as he jumped away from a Japanese hand grenade. It landed near him. He had been standing at the edge of a cliff.

In another branch of the military, he might have qualified for the Purple Heart.

"Not in the Marines," Young said. "You have to bleed in order to receive the Purple Heart."

Anyone who was on Iwo Jima need only close his eyes to remember that island hell, Young said.

On D-Day morning, its silhouette was overwhelmingly Japanese. A well-known war correspondent said that the island looked like a sea monster, with the dead volcano for the head, and the beach area for the neck, and all the rest of it with its scrubby, brown cliffs for the body.

The monster roared that entire day.

Marine injuries were traumatic. So was the experience. Bodies were cut in half. Arms and legs littered the beach area.

"It was like stepping through the gates of hell," Young said.

In the haunted house that was Iwo Jima, this hell was worse than anything he had imagined.

With overcast conditions, the island was a darkened land of phantoms. The interior of Suribachi had been hollowed out, making it a seven-story subterranean world, fortified with concrete and finished off with a sewer system and conduits for fresh air, electricity and water.

After the Marines landed on the island, that subterranean world exploded, almost as if Suribachi suddenly were an active volcano again.

The area from the beach to the mountain made for one of the worst killing fields in World War II.

Young remembers seeing his first enemy soldier.

"We were trying to cross the island," he said. "A pillbox had been bombarded. I saw a Japanese soldier, who was still shocked from the blast, looking out at us through a hole. I had a good shot at him, but at the last minute I drew my aim away. The whole thought of it, of killing another human being, was outrageous to me."

The Japanese soldier ducked down into the pillbox or ran to another area; Young couldn't say which with any certainty.

But before long he was certain about something else. He would never pull his aim away from another enemy soldier.

"I learned," he said. "When you saw your buddies blown apart, you learned that this was for real."

Marines crumpled together, raked again and again by machine-gun fire. They crouched shoulder-to-shoulder, one popping up to shoot while the other reloaded.

Some were blown to bits by mortar shells; others were sliced open by shards of hot lead.

The dead died with the greatest possible violence. The Japanese had constructed a lethal gauntlet of concrete. American steel, however, would allow the Marines to overtake the most fortified mountain in history.

That type of steel was found in more than their weaponry. It also stiffened the backbone of most Marines on the island.

But not all of them could take the emotional onslaught associated with so much death and destruction.

"During one mortar attack, a group of us sought cover in a large shell crater," Young remembered. "As we crouched in the bottom of the hole, one man reached down and picked up an object protruding from the ash. The sight of a detached hand destroyed the last of his fragile sanity. He dropped the hand and ran screaming down the beach, disappearing out of our sight."

Being a radioman with a backpack and antenna, Young was a coveted sniper target. Marines on Iwo Jima wore no insignia. The Japanese looked for things that might be important, particularly leaders giving directions.

While on Iwo Jima, Young's platoon had four lieutenants, all of them wounded or killed. In the later stages of battle, the Oswego Marine often became a PFC platoon leader.

On that first invasion night, darkness came early, around 6:45 p.m., Young said.

The Marine command warned that the first night would be critical to the overall success of the operation.

To the Americans ashore, the blanketing darkness almost seemed to have a physical weight. Its effect on their vision increased the threat to their lives. The ground they occupied was completely unfamiliar to them, while the Japanese knew it intimately.

"It was obvious that a bad day was going to be followed by an even worse night," Young said.

His blue eyes become as round as quarters. His voice rises slightly, becoming crystal clear, like running water over a settled streambed.

"During the first night, they kept coming at us," Young says. "They tried to go right through us and around us at the same time. Occasionally, the Japanese would throw hand grenades at us. We were wide-awake, not a wink of sleep. We had just a perimeter defense, not a frontline. The Japanese didn't get inside our shell hole, but they were very, very close. We even saw them coming back the other way."

Although daylight had ended, the fighting did not.

Shelling filled the night sky. American destroyers fired more than 10,000 rounds that first evening. Phosphorous "star shells" were used to keep Suribachi illuminated.

Tracers were fired, too.

To a Marine lying on his back in a foxhole, the night must have looked like a mesh of hot light, a net of crisscrossing fire.

The first day's fighting had claimed more than half as many casualties as the entire Guadalcanal campaign: 556 men killed ashore and afloat, and 1,755 wounded. Nearly 100 Marines suffered combat fatigue.

Thousands more would die during the subsequent weeks on Iwo Jima.

On that first night, the remaining American troops lay as still as they could. Shadows darted here and there.

Finally, the first day of the Battle of Iwo Jima had come to an end. There were thirty-five left to go. Young was there for every one of them.

He was wounded twice. Later that year, at a hospital off Iwo Jima, a Marine officer told Young he would be nominated for the Purple Heart and Silver Star.

Any awards would come later. The war went on.

After four days of fierce fighting, the Japanese were beginning to crack. Still, for the Americans, ongoing operations were hampered by bad weather and poor visibility.

February 23, 1945 dawned cold and stormy. But rain would give way to a midmorning clearing. Navy airplanes ignited Suribachi, showering it with napalm.

Was the monstrous mountain fortress finally dead? Or was it ready to spew its venom again?

A group of Marines would attempt to answer those two questions, which were tied together as one. The Americans were going to feel their way upward amid the smoking rubble. Climbing to the top of Suribachi was daunting. No one believed that the Japanese were finished fighting.

Young was with that first group of Americans. Just before the 40-man patrol began its climb, Lieutenant Colonel Chandler Johnson turned to his adjutant, Lieutenant Greeley Wells, and asked for something from a map case.

Johnson was handed an American flag, which had been brought ashore from the USS Missoula. The flag was a relatively small one, measuring fifty-four by twenty-eight inches.

Johnson, in turn, gave the flag to a combat lieutenant, an officer who was leading the group to the top of Suribachi.

"If you get to the top, put it up," the colonel told the lieutenant.

The wording of the command was not typical to the Marines. The colonel didn't say, "When you get to the top." He used "if" instead.

There were two flag-raisings atop Suribachi. It was the second that was immortalized by the famous photograph.

The first flag was taken down for two reasons: first, Johnson wanted to safeguard the flag from souvenir seekers. More important than that, he wanted a bigger flag, something that would be even more visible, "... so every son of a bitch on this cruddy island can see it," the commanding colonel said.

At 10:20 a.m. on February 23, 1945, Marines thrust a makeshift flagpole upright into a gusty wind. It was the first foreign flag ever to fly over Japanese soil. Japan's history stretched back four millennia.

"I was with the group that went up there and raised the first flag," Young said. "Lieutenant [George] Schrier was trying to get a platoon organized to go to the top of Suribachi. Some of us just joined him. Nobody told us to go. We just did it."

What they did was bold, brave and inspired.

When the small swatch of red, white and blue began to flutter in the wind, Iwo Jima was temporarily transformed into Times Square on New Year's Eve. Infantrymen cheered, whistled and waved their helmets. Ships offshore opened up their deep whistles.

The first flag-raising was the symbol of an impossible dream realized. That dream was the meat and potatoes of an extremely tough time.

Of the five Marines in Young's platoon who went to the top of Suribachi as part of the larger group, two would later be wounded and three would die on Iwo Jima.

While he was right there, Young wasn't part of the first flag-raising. He had seen a Japanese sniper, then tossed a hand grenade down the hole he was hiding in, undoubtedly saving American lives.

"When I turned back around, the flag was going up," Young said.

General Holland "Howlin' Mad" Smith spoke of that important Marine moment:

"The raising of the flag high atop Suribachi was one of the proudest moments of my life," Smith said. "No American could view this symbol of heroism and suffering without a lump in his throat. By a happy circumstance, I was standing beside [Secretary of the Navy James] Forrestal when the tiny speck of red, white and blue broke and fluttered on the gaunt crest of the volcano. Turning to me, the secretary said, 'Holland, the raising of that flag means a Marine Corps for the next 500 years.'"

The second flag, made famous in the Associated Press photograph, was much larger than the first. The second flag measured ninety-six by fifty-six inches. It had been found in a salvage yard at Pearl Harbor, rescued from a sinking ship on that date which will live in infamy.

The fighting did not stop with the two flag-raisings atop Suribachi. It would continue for weeks, with the Marines taking terrible casualties.

The Japanese were desperate. They were determined to maintain their territory, at least what was left of it.

Young's platoon captured Iwo Jima's first Japanese prisoner.

"He was buried in the sand up to his neck," Young said of the enemy soldier. "A shell had hit him and buried him. He wanted to kill himself. He didn't want to be captured. The higher-ups were very glad to have him."

Coming down from the first flag-raising, the Marines moved to the other side of the mountain. It was there that Young saw one of the most horrible sights of the battle.

"It has stayed with me," Young said. "We were going down to the narrow beach on the west side of Suribachi, where there was a lot of hidden artillery. If we had landed on that side, we would have been blown apart. I remember there was this dead Marine. He had his legs shot up and his clothes were blown off of him. He was sitting upright. We wondered how he got to that side of the mountain."

Like the Japanese, the Marines were prepared to fight to the end. They would do whatever was necessary to take Iwo Jima.

The cost was staggering.

By mid-March, the average battalion, which had landed with thirty-six officers and 885 enlisted men, was down to about sixteen officers and 300 enlisted men, including replacements brought up from the rear. In addition, numerous men had been hurt but were still in action.

Young was one of those.

Having stayed alive and having remained in action on Iwo Jima, he was an exception to the rule. The majority of American men connected with the two flag-raisings were either dead or had been evacuated with wounds.

On Iwo Jima for weeks and with only a few days of island duty remaining, Young was wounded the first time.

"We had cleared some ground," Young said. "I went to see our major, trying to find out if we should move up ahead. So I worked my way back. The major said, 'God yes, get up as far as you can.' I was gone from the platoon for maybe 45 minutes."

When Young returned, the platoon had moved back from its original position.

"I asked, 'What are you guys doing back here?'" Young said. "They said they were pinned down. I told them, 'Well, hell, there's nothing here.' At that moment ... blurrrpt, a shot caught me. It drove my knife into my right leg and threw me into a foxhole. The men saw where the shots came from. They blew the enemy position apart."

Someone asked Young if he wanted a stretcher.

"I said no, I could go to the aid station on my own," Young said. "My whole leg was soaked in blood. The aid station was about a quarter of a mile away. It was just a tent with cots and an operating table. That's where they dug some shrapnel out of my thigh. The doctor cut into my leg, digging out pieces of the knife for a couple of hours. Finally, he said, 'Son, the war is over for you.'"

Well, not quite.

That night, while waiting to be evacuated off Iwo Jima, the Oswego Marine was approached by a wounded lieutenant, who was with several members of Young's platoon—men who had seen significant action. They were wounded, too, and had been carried to the aid station.

"They told me that the platoon had lost all the ground we'd gained earlier," Young said. "The lieutenant asked me to go back and help retake the position. I guess a lot of the guys looked up to me. So I asked if they still had any phosphorous grenades, which they did. I told the lieutenant I'd go back."

The doctor had other ideas, however.

"He said, 'I don't think you should, but I won't stop you,'" said Young, who had lost about one-third of his body weight on Iwo Jima. "You didn't eat too much on the island. I was really weak, but I was a Marine. I had a responsibility to the others. I went back to the front."

Young limped back to the fighting.

He would be wounded again, this time from a Japanese grenade, which blew off one of his shoes, broke bones in his foot and peppered his backside with shrapnel.

"I was organizing a move forward when the Japanese attacked," Young said. "We started fighting at 9 a.m., and I think it was 3:30 in the afternoon by the time we got the last one."

Young tried walking barefoot back to the aid station. He had helped carry stretchers on Iwo Jima, but now didn't want to take anyone away from other wounded Marines.

He collapsed from a loss of blood.

"I woke up in the aid station," he said. "A lot of time had passed."

For Young, life as a combat Marine was over.

He had two brothers still serving overseas.

Young's father, although out of work during part of the Depression, was a carpenter, as well as an amateur inventor and a self-taught physicist. He had no formal training or experience. He had only a high school education, but was said to be very "intelligent."

Apparently so.

Through an acquaintance who was also an area inventor, Young's father entered the Manhattan Project. He worked with internationally known scientists at the University of Chicago, including Enrico Fermi.

Later, Dwight Young would work at Los Alamos, New Mexico, where America's first atomic bombs were developed.

He witnessed the first atomic bomb blast, called the Trinity Shot.

A 1974 story in The Beacon News called Dwight Young "the Horatio Alger of atomic energy."

Dwight Young died in 1975.

"His main virtue was knowing what to do to photograph experiments," Young said. "He would photographically measure what was going on with various experiments. He had read enough and experimented enough to know what was taking place atomically. He was putting things together with prodigious amounts of energy, thought and study. I don't remember how he did it, and wouldn't have understood if he had told me. His letters from Los Alamos were mostly newsy things about climbing the mountains and looking for Indian artifacts."

Young grew up with an appreciation for the land along Poverty Point. He has seen the Fox River change and change again. He enjoys the mornings most, when the river is wrinkled with light. And he enjoys the river's constant flow, which rolls and ripples like stretched silk in the wind.

It is a long way from the horrors of Iwo Jima.

Young has spent the better part of his life protecting the environment for future generations.

He did the same for America.

There are two area forest preserves named in Young's honor. One is in Kane County; the other is in Kendall County.

After the war, he went on to earn a master's degree at Northern Illinois University. Now formally retired, Young still serves as an environmental consultant.

"There was no substitute for luck," he says of his time

on Iwo Jima.

And in America, there was no substitute for hope, which was the thing with feathers that perched in the soul of a country. It was able to see the invisible, feel the intangible and achieve the impossible.

As a combat Marine and as an environmentalist, Young has helped both his country and his community.

In an analogy about the river, he says that the simplest acts of kindness can become something symbolic.

Like a widening ripple, they may reach across a long eternity, eventually touching tomorrow's shore.

Just as true patriotism has no party affiliation, heroes give their lives to something bigger than themselves.

Young qualifies.

Yes—yes, indeed. In that, he certainly does qualify.

He was called to duty. He went without hesitation.

It's as simple as that.

It's as simple as never giving in, except to a higher hope—the heart and humanity of America, which is a process as much as it is a country or condition.

Jack Richardson

JACK RICHARDSON

"Do you know where my wife went?"

For the most part, he has lost himself.

A war hero, longtime local business owner and accomplished amateur musician, John "Jack" Richardson struggles with Alzheimer's disease.

"Have I really led an interesting life?" the Geneva resident asks, vaguely rephrasing the question he has just heard.

The interview is conducted over cake and coffee on a bright blue Saturday morning.

Richardson's home is stately and upscale, but without all the glossy undulations and shining declivities that are located in others nearby

Memories slip out of his mind like a newspaper dropping from the hands of a sleepy senior citizen.

"I just don't recall ... I'm so sorry," Richardson says, his voice sounding sad, almost as if it were a ship lost at sea.

Decades earlier, it was at sea that Richardson distinguished himself during World War II.

Born in October 1917, he was a lieutenant and chief engineer aboard the USS Balao, an American submarine, which was officially credited with having sunk seven Japanese ships totaling 32,108 tons, in addition to sinking

1,100 tons of miscellaneous enemy craft by gunfire.

The Balao received nine battle stars for its World War II missions.

After being decommissioned in 1946, the Balao became a Hollywood prop, according to Richardson's wife, Margaret, who's called "Marty."

She said that the submarine was painted pink and used in the 1959 feature film *Operation Petticoat*. The comedy concerns the interplay between a no-nonsense naval officer (Cary Grant) and his con artist subordinate (Tony Curtis), both of whom want to get the ship seaworthy, although their motives vary greatly.

"It's a very funny situation, but nothing like that happened to Jack," says Marty Richardson, her husband's full-time caregiver.

They met before World War II. Richardson was pursuing a master's degree at the University of Cincinnati. He received the advanced degree and was working for Dow Chemical Company when World War II started.

His wife is an Ohio native.

Jack and Marty Richardson have children, grandchildren and one great-grandchild.

Before attending graduate school in Ohio, Richardson received an undergraduate degree at the University of Illinois. He grew up in Geneva, having come to town in the early 1920s.

Richardson was born in Beaver Falls, Pennsylvania.

By all accounts, he was as pragmatic as he was patriotic.

"Jack wanted to enlist in the submarine program because the pay was better," Marty Richardson said, smiling. "In any event, he was very, very proud of his time in the military."

According to the Chicago Sun-Times, Tom Brokaw failed to interview a single submarine veteran in his best-selling book about World War II, *The Greatest Generation.*

A resourceful reader might wonder why.

Dubbed "The Silent Service," due to the U.S. Navy's almost total blackout of information about submarines and submarine operations during World War II, the full force consisted of more than 300 submarines. Of those, 258 conducted one or more offensive patrols against the enemy, while the others served in support and training activities or were commissioned too late in the war to join their sister subs already on patrol.

The record of those that did patrol, however, is indisputable.

According to official statistics, combined U.S. military forces sank about 10 million tons of Japanese shipping, of which approximately 8 million tons were merchant vessels, the rest warships.

U.S. submarines sank more than half that total—54.6 percent to be precise, amounting to 1,314 enemy vessels, or 5.3 million tons of shipping.

Military historians say that the achievements of the submarine service were considerable. This silent service, which in 1,690 separate war patrols caused more than half of Japan's sea losses, numbered less than 1.6 percent of the total U.S. naval strength during World War II.

These were not easy victories.

Submarine sinkings were made at the heaviest relative cost of American lives in any branch of the U.S. Armed Services, including the Marines. One out of every seven submariners died: 3,516 officers and enlisted men.

According to BattleBelow.com, an Internet source, the silent service lost fifty-two submarines: forty-two were sunk while out on patrol, one was bombed while under overhaul and nine were lost to various operational accidents.

"By my recollection, I wasn't too scared about any mission," Richardson said. "We just did our job. What else can I tell you?"

Before serving on the Balao, Richardson had been assigned to the Flying Fish, another American submarine.

"Among other things, they rescued nurses off islands and saved a number of downed pilots," Marty Richardson said, referring to her husband's time on the Flying Fish.

Total pilot rescues of the submarine service grew yearly. In 1943, there were seven rescues; 117 in 1944. In 1945, submariners saved 380 pilots and crewmen from the sea.

One such rescue has special significance in its impact on history.

The USS Finback was on lifeguard patrol off Chichi Jima during air operations in September 1944. A plane was reported to have splashed down. The pilot was rescued and the navigator was seen to be near an island held by the Japanese, who were firing at the small rubber raft close inshore. The Finback dove and came to periscope depth alongside the navigator, who held on to the periscope and after some difficulty was gradually pulled out to sea and out of range of the enemy gunfire. The submarine surfaced and took the crewman on board. The pilot rescued earlier was a lieutenant named George H. Bush, who was elected president of the United States in 1988.

American submarines also rescued and captured Japanese seamen.

On the Balao, one such prisoner was transformed into a quasi kitchen helper.

"He would go around saying, 'Chow down, chow down, chow down,'" Richardson said, laughing slightly at his own impression. "We got a kick out of that."

Other kicks came by way of Japanese depth charges,

although no one was laughing then.

The Balao, the first and namesake boat of a new "class" of U.S. submarine, had a superthick hull. Its test depth was 400 feet. In an extreme emergency, it might survive at 800 feet, the first American sub capable of withstanding such pressure.

It would prove fortuitous.

On one of the Balao's most successful missions, the submarine encountered four enemy ships off the coast of an island controlled by the Japanese. A torpedo attack set three of the vessels ablaze before sub-chasers could react.

Richardson remembered diving to a depth of 600 feet. After the enemy passed overhead, the Balao made a 180-degree turn and disappeared, leaving the immediate area. Depth charges had harmlessly exploded at the conventional setting of 300 feet.

Both the submarine captain and Richardson were awarded citations for the event, which the Geneva grandfather jokingly referred to as "running away."

But there is no running away from Alzheimer's, a disease named for Alois Alzheimer, who was a German scientist born in the 1800s.

Alzheimer studied dementia associated with old age.

The disease robs people of their own history. It affects an estimated fourteen million people. As the world's population continues to grow and people live longer, that figure is expected to rise rapidly. Some scientists say that within twenty-five years, there may be as many Alzheimer's patients as cancer patients.

More than four million Americans develop Alzheimer's every year.

Its particular terror is that it gradually eradicates the memory and the mind.

A healthy human brain is roughly the size and shape of

two adult fists, closed and pressed together at the knuckles. Typically weighing three pounds, it consists of about a hundred billion nerve cells, linked to one another in about one hundred trillion separate pathways. It is without question the most complicated system known to exist in nature or civilization.

The brain is the control center for the coordination of breathing, swallowing, pressure, pain, muscular movement, mood, thought, identity and a symphonic score of memory that is partly predetermined and partly written on the fly.

The brain is so incomparably complex, in fact, that in considering it at any length leads to wondering why it works at all.

Mostly, people don't think about it. They take the brain for granted. Richardson did, but that changed one day several years ago.

He had gone to visit a friend who lived at an area senior center, someone who collected stamps, as Richardson did himself. The visits were intended to lift the other man's spirits, giving him someone to talk to.

Marty Richardson remembers the last time her husband drove a car.

"Jack had gone to visit Charlie [the stamp collector]," she said, starting to tell the story, which was like a bad dream at the outset. "When he returned home, he said he hadn't made it as far as Charlie's place. Hard as he tried, Jack just couldn't remember how to get there ... He set his car keys on our kitchen table. And that was the end of his driving."

In Richardson's case, old age became more than the home of forgetfulness.

A slight deterioration of memory is so common among the elderly that even today it is considered to be a natural consequence of aging. About a third to a half of all human beings experience some mild deterioration in memory as they get older, taking longer to learn directions, for example, or having some difficulty recalling names and numbers.

"I'll try to help you as best I can," Richardson says, straining to remember much about his own life, which included running a successful business partnership in Geneva.

Smith and Richardson employed more than 30 people in the decades that the submarine veteran ran the company.

They manufactured small components for fuel systems, the type used in automobiles. Home ovens also used the same sort of device.

Richardson sold the company in the 1980s. It still carries the same name, however.

Regardless of his illness, Richardson is said to be someone special.

His wife says that he has a gentle soul.

Even while under the sea in the Balao, everything he did was above board, so to speak.

"Jack was involved in the church and community," his wife said. "He was a scout leader and truly enjoyed working with young people."

In addition, during the twelve years Richardson served as a member of the Geneva Public Library Board, the library converted its heating system to gas. To accommodate a lean and limited budget, he helped shovel tons of coal up and out of a basement bin.

He also served on Geneva's Police and Fire Commission, logging twelve years there, too.

"What can I tell you about my feelings for Geneva?" Richardson asks, again answering a question with a question. "It's home. We've enjoyed our time here."

Jack and Marty Richardson were married in 1944.

"Jack came home on a short leave," his wife said. "Everything was done in a big hurry."

The undying affection she has for her husband is obvious.

Love, she says, is what you've been through with somebody. It is an act of faith, and whoever is of little faith is also of little love.

But then there's the reality of her husband's condition. Not only does he have Alzheimer's, Richardson also is a diabetic.

"I'm going to take care of Jack for as long as I possibly can," says Marty Richardson, who is younger than her husband and in very good health, she said.

More often than not, people who think that marriage is a 50-50 proposition don't know the half of it.

Right now, their scales are not balanced. Nonetheless, Marty Richardson remains at her husband's side.

"Jack was always a good husband and father," she says.

She speaks admiringly of the time he attended a Navy dinner and sat with the enlisted men, a move that had him in front of his superiors shortly thereafter.

"It was a formal affair," Marty Richardson said of the dinner. "When Jack got called on the carpet, he told them, 'Without those enlisted men, none of us would be here today.'"

With Richardson, who was a naval officer, what was right was not forgotten by what was convenient.

Morality was its own advocate, and it was never necessary to apologize for it.

The conversation comes back to Alzheimer's.

Marty Richardson says her husband is fragmented

within himself. Like the wake of a great ship, that fragmentation is his memory—wide and vast, but diffuse and fading fast, mile after mile.

In a sad sense, Alzheimer's is the perfect disease for this modern age. It is an affliction of averted eyes and passing strangers who don't pay attention to one another.

As with almost every Alzheimer's patient, those strangers are just trying to get home.

The disease usually begins in the hippocampus, the area of the brain that controls recent memory. The plaques and tangles that define Alzheimer's attach themselves there first. Yesterday vanishes. A life disappears in an order reverse to that in which it was lived.

Old age becomes the last childhood.

To an outsider looking in, it's surprising that Richardson remembers anything from his World War II years. At the same time, he can't recall what he had for lunch the day before.

There is no cure for Alzheimer's at the present time, and not too much in the way of progressive treatment. In the past, the one saving grace of the disease had been that many, if not most, of the people who acquired it did not comprehend what was about to happen to them and their families. Now, for better or worse, that has changed. More and more people are learning at the earliest possible opportunity what they have, and what that means.

Richardson's wife tries to keep his mind active. She still drives, and takes him out almost daily—sometimes to visit an old friend, other times to eat at an area restaurant.

"I read to Jack every night," she says. "But by the time I get to Chapter 2, he has forgotten Chapter 1."

Jack and Marty Richardson share a love of music. For more than 40 years, he was a member of the Fox Valley Symphony and the Naperville Band.

Richardson's musical career began with a violin tucked under his chin, but a lawnmower accident shortened one of his fingers. Not yet an adult, he switched to the oboe and the English horn.

Marty Richardson, an accomplished cellist, said that her husband performed with more than a dozen area orchestras through the years.

In their time together, music has become the shorthand of emotion.

They have always drawn strength from one another.

And they continue to.

Health issues aside, the gift they offer one another is so simple a thing as hope.

American author F. Scott Fitzgerald wrote of that same sentiment in the conclusion of *The Great Gatsby:*

"Gatsby believed in the green light, the orgiastic future that year by year recedes before us. It eluded us then, but that's no matter—tomorrow we will run faster, stretch out our arms farther...

And one fine morning—

So we beat on, boats against the current, borne back ceaselessly into the past."

While he can't remember much, Richardson will be hard to forget.

He waves goodbye from the front door.

His wife waves, too.

Stepping back into their home, Jack and Marty Richardson turn toward one another like the arms of a parenthesis.

It seems so fitting—that their togetherness has some space.

That space is a campaign promise of the heart; it is another act of faith.

And, along with friendship, perhaps the best proof of love.

Johnny Vargas

JOHNNY VARGAS

"The newspapers said we were fighting for an idea."

This one wasn't about national survival or manifest destiny.

Korea was America's first ideological war.

In the aftermath of World War II, the Korean peninsula was an unholy mess.

A Japanese colony since 1910, Korea had been divided into two nations after the war. Those two nations were separated by the 38th parallel, an almost arbitrary geographic calculation.

Its original purpose was to stretch an imaginary line between forces from the United States and forces from the Soviet Union, which were moving into Korea to accept the surrender of Japanese troops there.

Prior to 1910, Korea had nearly two thousand years of independence, much of it under the protection of Imperial China.

"I don't know much about the politics, but I can tell you that we froze, starved, suffered and survived," said Amador "Johnny" Vargas, a Korean War combat veteran and Elgin resident.

On June 25, 1950, nearly 100,000 North Koreans smashed across the border and overran Seoul, the South Korean capital.

War was back in the American vocabulary.

President Truman saw the invasion as a Soviet test of American resolve. What followed was the first armed conflict of the Cold War era.

"There's no telling what they'll do if we don't put up a fight right now," Truman said, referring to the communist-backed invasion of South Korea.

At that particular point in time, the Soviet Union was boycotting the United Nations Security Council. Consequently, it did not have a representative there to veto the decision to send in a multinational force to defend South Korea.

Multinational or not, U.S. and South Korean troops made up about 90 percent of the fighting force at its peak. General MacArthur, the fabled American hero of World War II, was appointed commander.

At first, only overwhelming air superiority prevented U.N. forces from being driven into the sea. But by September 1950, MacArthur was ready to take the offensive.

American Marines mounted an assault behind enemy lines at Inchon, 30 miles west of Seoul. It was a bold stroke, cutting off thousands of the enemy.

Other U.N. troops pushed northward, reaching the 38th parallel by early October.

MacArthur wanted more. He slashed toward the Yalu River, the border with Communist China.

The Chinese reacted immediately.

Like lightning striking, about one million enemy assault troops swarmed across the Yalu, stunning U.N. forces.

In some of the most ferocious fighting ever endured by Americans, the Chinese drove them back into South Korea. By early 1951, resistance stiffened, and the opposing fronts stabilized near the 38th parallel.

Three years and more than five million casualties later, an armistice was signed, ending the war within miles of where it started.

The date was July 27, 1953.

According to statistics, the fighting took the lives of more than half a million North Korean and Chinese soldiers.

More than 50,000 Americans died.

"When we came home, you sometimes had the feeling that we were pushed into the background," said Vargas, who was born in January 1928. "Maybe what we did was on a smaller scale than World War II, but having been in Korea, I can tell you that we gave everything we had ...You did it. You didn't make a big deal about it. You were scared almost all the time, but you kept it to yourself. To my thinking, we did as much for our country as the guys who were in the European and Pacific campaigns."

In mentioning World War II, Vargas said he intends no disrespect to those who served during the 1940s. His oldest brother, Frank Vargas, was a U.S. Marine and was wounded while fighting against the Japanese in that decade before Korea.

But at the same time, Vargas thinks that while the Korean War was one of America's most important, it is also the least remembered.

"When we came home, there was no 'heroes welcome,' " Vargas said. "And to young people today, what we did is little more than a footnote in their history books."

It should be much more than that.

For those involved, the war was a terribly traumatic event. It was a long war, too, during which 6 million men and women served in the armed forces. Americans fought in Korea nearly three times as long as they had fought in World War I and almost as long as they had fought in World War II. The first year of combat was especially brutal and bloody, often surpassing the toughest battles of any war in American history.

Contrary to ongoing public opinion, the Korean Conflict was not the first American war that had not been fought through to victory. Certainly, the War of 1812 was a draw. Yet twentieth-century Americans had become habituated to victory. For those who remembered the wild celebrations of November 11, 1918, or V-E and V-J Days, the 1953 armistice was acknowledged as a "poor substitute for victory" and was generally greeted with sullen indifference. Ask anyone. How many Americans can, within a year, correctly date the end of the Korean War? A half-century ago, it was difficult for U.S. citizens to get excited about an armistice that ended a three-year war with the status quo.

Nonetheless, as historians have noted, the impact of the war on the United States government and society was profound.

The war:

• Greatly intensified hostilities between the West and Communist-bloc nations, especially the newly founded People's Republic of China, delaying for decades a normalization of relations between Washington and Peking, now named Beijing.

• Gave powerful impetus to a massive nuclear and conventional arms race between the United States and the Soviet Union, which helped transform America into the modern military force it is today.

• Gave root to the notion that the "spread of communism" in the Far East could be contained by "limited" American military power, which led to American military intervention in Vietnam.

• Fostered a national climate that strengthened the appeal of McCarthyism and similar repressive ideologies and unseated the Democratic party, which had held the White House for twenty years.

Vargas doesn't claim to be a politician or historian.

"I was a soldier, drafted into the Army in 1951," he says. "My two younger brothers, Rudy and Joe, were already in Korea at the time. I spent eleven months in combat, and was involved in five major engagements."

Vargas grew up on the Near West Side of Chicago, one of the only Mexican kids in an almost all-Italian neighborhood.

"My parents came from Mexico, but I was born here," Vargas said. "We lived all around the Taylor Street area."

While there were problems being Hispanic in that neighborhood, Vargas said he enjoyed his childhood.

"Once you got to know people, things were all right," he said. "Early on, though, it wasn't that easy. I'll give you an example. As a young boy, I had really curly hair. And when we first moved to Taylor Street, the older Italian guys didn't like the way I looked. They grabbed me one day, brought me to someone's house. They cut all my hair off. Having a crew cut was very embarrassing."

Vargas' father worked in a steel mill.

"We had a tough time financially," Vargas said. "I was one of eleven kids. There weren't many second helpings at the dinner table."

Vargas started playing trumpet as a high school underclassman. He quit attending class after his third year.

"I needed a job," he said. "It was time to help out at home."

Playing the trumpet became his passion, something that continues today.

"After the war, I made my living playing the trumpet, though that didn't last too long," Vargas said. "I did the 'Vegas thing' for a while, but that wasn't such a good gig, not for someone with a family."

He ended up working a series of day jobs, playing music

mostly at night.

"I always had a job," Vargas said, adding that he eventually worked in an area machine shop, staying there more than twenty years.

Vargas' first wife died of cancer. They had two children, a son and a daughter.

The Chicago native remarried more than a decade ago.

His second wife was living in Elgin at the time. Vargas said he enjoys his adopted hometown.

Johnny and Mary Jo Vargas are currently involved in a major restoration project.

"We're renovating our home, which is in one of the historic districts," he said. "We love Elgin. It's my final stop."

Decades earlier, Korea came close to being his final stop.

Vargas, a combat engineer and infantryman, was awarded the Purple Heart when wounded by shrapnel. He was wounded a second time in Korea.

Along with the Purple Heart, there were additional citations and commendations.

After helping save the lives of four GIs, Vargas was told that he would be recommended for the Bronze Star.

"They were trapped in a minefield," Vargas said. "I helped get them out of there alive."

Given his combat engineering training, Vargas knew the probable configuration of the minefield, which he crawled through to lead the others out.

During his tour of duty in Korea, he was at Hill 1179 and Bloody Ridge, which was one of the roughest ridgeline battles of the war. It was seized after three weeks of fighting and 2,700 U.N. casualties, most of them American and South Korean.

"That was a tough one," Vargas said. "We were moving up, the enemy was shooting down at us. And that gave them a big, big advantage."

Vargas was with the 2nd Infantry Division, Charlie Company.

"When we reached our first position at Bloody Ridge, we dug in," he remembered. "There was this terrible smell, like blood and guts mixed in with the dirt. We were under mortar and artillery attack. Little by little, we kept moving up and up, but it wasn't easy. I lost a lot of buddies out there."

On September 4, 1951, the North Koreans—weakened by an estimated 15,000 casualties—withdrew suddenly. The next day, the U.S. 2nd Division finally seized Bloody Ridge, a two-mile wide and three-mile-deep mountain mass.

The preliminary to the assault on Bloody Ridge was a days-long concentration of artillery fire. It gradually eliminated practically every trace of vegetation upon the ridgeline, turning it into a brown landscape with tree-like skeletons clawing the air, Vargas remembered.

An army unit from the Republic of Korea (ROK) attacked the fingers leading to the peak, quickly establishing the pattern of battle that was to predominate in Korea over the next two years through hundreds of battles, engagements and sorties on mountains and ridges all across the front. The heavy bombardments and air strikes had removed trees and underbrush, but had not destroyed the communist bunkers or all the thick minefields protecting the encampments. For the most part, the bunkers—constructed of heavy timbers and usually covered with deep layers of rock and earth— were so massive that only a direct hit by heavy artillery was able to destroy them.

And direct hits were difficult, given that the surrounding ground was torn up, making the bunkers hard to find.

Early frontal attacks on Bloody Ridge were led by the ROK. They gained ground, but withdrew because of concentrated counterattacks by the enemy. The ROK's 36th

217

Regiment suffered heavy casualties, which led to a sharp decline in morale.

Some groups broke and ran away. Panic spread among parts of another ROK regiment, also attacking Bloody Ridge.

Meanwhile, the U.S. 2nd Division got the assignment to take the ridge.

"I wanted to be a musician, but you had to think like a soldier ... fight like one, too," Vargas said.

At night when he closes his eyes, Vargas still sees the mountains of Korea. They were jagged, he said, almost as if pages ripped out of a book—the edges looking like the teeth of a handsaw.

"You know, we were always hearing about taking this hill or that hill, but believe me, those were mountains, not hills," Vargas said, smiling.

Mountain, hill or otherwise, the fighting was extremely tough.

"When the weather was warm, you were sweating and your heart was pounding," Vargas said. "Your legs were sore, but we were always moving, always climbing. The enemy threw grenades at us, and bullets were whizzing by. It was murder, man, I'll tell you that."

At Bloody Ridge, American soldiers slid and suffered. They tried to regain their position, circling and climbing while under relentless fire.

Minutes seemed like hours, hours like days, and days like one long nightmare, Vargas said.

Bloody Ridge led to fighting at Heartbreak Ridge, the site of the last major U.N. offensive of the Korean War.

There were 3,700 American casualties at Heartbreak Ridge. Concluding that it was "unprofitable to continue the bitter operation," General James Van Fleet, commanding the U.S. Eighth Army, told General Clovis Byers to "firm up the line" and "plan no further offensives."

Van Fleet had replaced General Matthew Ridgway, who replaced General MacArthur as commander of the U.N. forces in Korea.

Less than a year after the dramatic Inchon invasion, MacArthur was unceremoniously dismissed—not for military failures, but for political ineptitude. When the Chinese forces began fighting alongside the North Koreans in November 1950, he advocated an extension of the war into China.

President Truman thought that moving into China could lead to World War III. He relieved MacArthur of his command in April 1951.

Fast forward to Heartbreak Ridge, where in September and October of 1951, the enemy was well entrenched, explaining why the battle continued for as long as it did and why it resulted in such heavy bloodshed.

Heartbreak Ridge was a month-long fight.

Months earlier, in July 1951, negotiators from the U.N. command met with their counterparts from Communist China and North Korea for the first time. They met in the communist-controlled city of Kaesong, located in western South Korea. At issue were truce talks.

"Out on the line, we didn't know much about that," said Vargas, whose Army nickname was "Cat Man," owing to the smooth sensibility associated with being a musician.

"The guys thought that musicians were pretty 'hep,' " he said. "They figured I was in the know because I played trumpet. Back home, yeah, I knew what was what. But in Korea? Forget about it."

The truce talks were in continuous danger of collapse. The communists broke off all negotiations in August 1951. Then, with Heartbreak Ridge almost over, they were resumed in late October of that year in a new location, the village of Panmunjom in southern North Korea.

When no substantial progress had been made by

October 1952, the U.N. negotiators walked out. It wasn't until April 1953 that the first real breakthrough was made in negotiating an end to the war. In the meantime, fierce fighting continued on the ground and in the air, hundreds of thousands of soldiers and civilians would lose their lives and a new administration would take office in Washington with the promise of ending the war.

Truman left the Oval Office after his presidential term, which began with the death of President Roosevelt in 1945.

The 1952 presidential election pitted World War II hero Dwight David Eisenhower against Democratic rival Adlai Stevenson.

Ike won in a landslide and pledged to end the war in Korea.

By winning Heartbreak Ridge, U.N. troops secured a portion of the 38th parallel that defined the final demarcation line when the armistice was signed in 1953.

Vargas returned to Korea in 2001.

"You hardly recognized anything," he said, adding that he visited several Korean War battle sites.

"This time, we drove up those so-called hills," Vargas said. "I'm a little too old for that type of walking."

But not too old to remember the sights and sounds of war.

The world would be so different if people could consult veterans instead of politicians, Vargas said.

In Korea, among other things, he had been awarded a Combat Infantry Badge, which was designed by internationally known Elgin resident Trygve Rovelstad.

One of Rovelstad's most famous works of sculpture is the Pioneer Family Memorial, which celebrates the 1935 centennial of Elgin. It is situated along the Fox River near the Kimball Street Dam.

Rovelstad was inducted into the Fox Valley Arts Hall of

Fame in April 2004.

The infantry badge Rovelstad designed almost certainly saved Vargas' life, decades before the soldier moved to Elgin, where the artist went to high school, graduating in 1922.

"One day, I was in the front of this particular charge up a hill in Korea," Vargas said. "Earlier, our officers had warned us about not wearing the badges during combat. They could shine and become an easy target for the enemy. I put mine away, tucked it into my breast pocket ... I was a scout up Old Baldy [Hill], another tough battle. Anyway, the badge caught a piece of shrapnel and curled up, almost like a catcher's mitt. If I didn't have the badge in my breast pocket, that shrapnel might have gone right into my heart. And you know what? I wouldn't be here today. I wouldn't be here talking."

Talking comes effortlessly to Vargas. Words flow freely, gushing and tumbling as if a garden hose had been turned on.

His easygoing manner seems suitable, a likely offshoot of time spent in front of an audience.

"For me, trumpet was 'the thing,' " Vargas says.

His son, Dale Vargas, is a professional musician.

"We're very close," Vargas said of the relationship he has with his son. "Dale and I are working on a father-and-son CD. He is a singer/songwriter. Also a piano player and guitarist."

Vargas began playing trumpet while working with the milkman, whose delivery route started at 3 a.m.

"I did it before school—when I went to school," Vargas said. "The money helped our family."

What does a country owe to the men and women who defended it? People such as Vargas, who went where they were told and put their lives on the line, whether it was in Europe, the Pacific or Korea. And in the wars that came later, others put their lives on the line, too.

Doing so wasn't always popular. While veterans served, many Americans went about their ordinary lives. They were untouched.

The Korean War, for example, made few real demands on people at home. The draft interrupted only the lives of the young. There was no rationing, and material shortages seemed to have mostly affected the quality of chrome on 1952-1953 automobiles. The fierce inflation of the first year of the war was more than countered by the wartime industrial and employment boom that delayed an expected recession until 1954—after the armistice.

Korea aside, for many, the 1950s represented the culmination of the American dream. The United States was nearing the peak of that most prolific period in the nation's history known as the baby boom.

But there was a dark side—conformity and racial discrimination perhaps topping the list.

Like perfection itself, defending the notion of freedom is a moving target.

A country owes its veterans respect and remembrance.

That sounds simple enough, doesn't it?

Joe Gatz

JOE GATZ

"We were surrounded, not intimidated."

Courage can be a kind of salvation.

And in Korea, salvation was well worth remembering, even if America had forgotten the men who were there.

He was one of those men—someone who was there, someone who was part of an elite reconnaissance group.

Just three years after World War II, Joe Gatz enlisted in the U.S. Marines.

The year was 1948, a time when permanent prosperity became a given in American life. Slowly but surely, people began to realize that the Great Depression was not coming back.

Cultural commentators called it a "revolution of rising expectations." Young men and women began betting on the promise of a brighter tomorrow.

The youngest of eight children, Gatz wasn't interested.

He was a street-smart kid, quick-tempered and tough, ready to fight at the slightest challenge.

Smaller kids paid protection money at school. Gatz gladly took their "donations."

Most of the time, he'd wear Levi's with a T-shirt—or Levi's with a sweatshirt and leather coat when winter came.

His shoes had steel-tipped toes.

Born to Polish parents, he grew up in an Italian neighborhood on Chicago's North Side.

"As a teenager, I thought that I had all the answers," said Gatz, a longtime Carpentersville resident. "I thought that I was really, really rough. But in the Marines, I met some guys who were rougher than anyone I ever knew. There was this one 'stump-jumper' from Alabama. I pushed him into a fight, which was a big, big mistake. And I hit him hard, landing a first punch that would've knocked out Joe Louis. He just flicked it away. And then, when he hit me, it was like getting kicked by a mule. But he wasn't out to really hurt me. He only wanted to teach me a lesson. He even ended up shaking my hand. I'll tell you something— you have to watch out for those unassuming types. It ended up being an 'eye-opening' experience."

So was the Chosin Reservoir, one of the most profound defeats in American military history.

One by one, neatly, like computer cards out of a machine, the questions drop into order.

How could one of the most brutal battles in modern history also be one of the least spoken about?

How could American Armed Forces get themselves trapped in one of the coldest places on Earth?

How could so many have died during a war without changing the overall outcome?

In some sense, the Korean War bore out the judgment of ancient Chinese strategist Sun Tzu, who wrote in 500 B.C.:

"In all history, there is no instance of a country having benefited from prolonged warfare," the strategist said.

For the United States, the Korean War was as painful as it was prolonged, and certainly of little or no benefit to its global situation.

"In itself, Chosin was an absolute nightmare," said

Gatz, who was born in 1930.

It was much more than that.

Chosin was the first of its kind—an American defeat that wasn't reversed, as were battles at Bunker Hill, the siege of Washington, the Alamo, Pearl Harbor, Guam and Wake Island.

Unlike those earlier battles, Chosin was never turned to ultimate victory.

"It was a real struggle," Gatz said of the battle, which began in late November 1950 and continued through the middle of December. "We had a decent meal on Thanksgiving Day, then all hell broke loose. Sometimes you thought that all of China was on the attack. We had heavy casualties. We were greatly outnumbered. That we survived at all is an extraordinary thing. More than once during the fighting, you figured that your time was up. But if we were going down, we were going down as Marines."

While Gatz survived, America's fighting tradition didn't, at least not in terms of its apparent invincibility. U.S. soldiers lived through the defeat, even achieving "military" victories after Chosin. But a political victory would be something else entirely.

Some say that America's fighting forces were defeated by the administrative maneuvers that their highest commanders chose to play against one another in Korea, a scenario that repeated itself a decade later in Vietnam.

According to several sources, while American forces were overwhelmingly outnumbered at Chosin and had to face incredibly bad weather, their utterly unpardonable enemies were the generals and statesmen of the world.

In Korea, the war was fought with restraint—a quality that is unsuited both to victory and to the American character.

Korea ended in ambiguity. The Communists were

denied their wartime goals, though they had come close to achieving at least some of them. America's lasting legacy was of uncertainty.

Not that those things had a place on the battlefield.

Still, weapons of mass destruction had been used only five years earlier. In the aftermath of World War II, American military muscle lacked definition. And fully flexing it in Korea was a constant concern. Anticommunist containment was still seen as a viable policy.

"Being a Marine, you never wanted to take a step back or stay in a holding pattern," Gatz said. "But our hands were tied, too. We were following orders, even if they were against our better judgment."

Gatz was in Korea from September 1950 to October 1951.

He was with a reconnaissance company attached to the First Marines, then the Fifth Marines.

"The enemy hated us," Gatz said. "We were told that they didn't take Marine prisoners. That's what happens when you're the best."

Chosin was an important target because its generating system supplied a great deal of North Korea's electrical power. Transmission of electrical power on the eastern side of the country was achieved through an elaborate array of sub-stations.

The sub-stations at Chosin fed others in the region.

U.S. airplanes had hit the generators repeatedly, causing Chosin's electrical production to stop for an extended time.

Be that as it may, U.S. commanders wanted to take the territory. They sent 25,000 American men in, deciding to string out a Marine division for 120 miles along a single mountain road.

Considering the bitter cold, formidable terrain and the possibility of Chinese attack, America's decision to take the offensive proved extremely ill-advised.

Chosin was not the right place.

On November 27, 1950, Communist forces attacked. There were more than 120,000 Chinese infantrymen hidden in the mountain country around Chosin, nearly 500,000 in North Korea or immediately across the Yalu River.

Earlier in the month, the Fifth and Seventh Marines had been assigned parallel tracks along either shore of the Chosin Reservoir, which is extremely scenic, the landscape looming absolute, as an ancient world would.

But when war hit, silence settled elsewhere.

Unable to support each other across the wide stretch of intervening water, the two Marine regiments were on roads leading nowhere, though both were vaguely bound for the Yalu.

The Third Infantry Regiment of the 1ˢᵗ Marine Division was just then being ordered up from duties nearer the Korean coast, called to act as a reserve force and to guard the Main Supply Route (MSR), a vulnerable one-lane road linking the Marines to their base at Hamhung.

In addition, the offensive called for a Marine contingent to link up with the 8ᵗʰ Army.

Organizational confusion was the order of the day, but not with one dynamic American leader.

And Gatz got to know the legendary Marine at Chosin.

"That would be 'Chesty' Puller," Gatz says, his tone almost reverential, referring to Colonel Lewis B. Puller. "He was a 'Marine's Marine.' "

It was Puller's barrel chest that inspired the notable nickname.

At the outbreak of the Korean Conflict, Puller was assigned as commander of the 1ˢᵗ Marine Regiment.

As always, he was said to be an unusually aggressive combatant, who never relished being behind anyone when there was fighting up ahead.

Puller had been a legend for decades. He was an authentic character. And the aging lion clearly wanted to turn Chosin into a legacy. On some sort of mythical Marine level, he hoped that the mere mention of his name would roar forever.

"During our toughest time at Chosin, I stepped out of a warming tent and ran right into Chesty Puller," Gatz remembered. "He said that there was nothing to worry about. He was totally fearless."

Gatz smiles, then repeats perhaps the perfect Puller story, cleaned up a bit for this book.

"It goes like this," Gatz begins. "A regiment reporter said, 'Colonel, you've got Chinese to your front, to your rear, to your left and to your right. What are you going to do now?'"

Puller's reported reply remains part of Marine lore.

"Well, they aren't going to get away this time!" Puller said, according to the story.

Puller, who was born in 1898, enlisted as a private in the Marine Corps in 1918. America was involved in World War I at the time.

According to biographical material, Puller's logic for enlisting was quite simple.

"I want to go where the guns are," he said.

He remained on active duty for the next thirty-seven years, serving at Guadalcanal during World War II, as well as in other battles.

During the Korean War but after Chosin, Puller was promoted to brigadier general.

He subsequently achieved promotions to major general and lieutenant general, and served in various command capacities until his retirement due to health issues in 1955.

A decade later, he requested to be reinstated in the

Corps in order to see action in Vietnam. The request was denied.

Puller died in 1971.

He was the most decorated U.S. Marine in history, and the only one to be awarded five Navy Crosses. His other decorations included the Silver Star, Bronze Star and Purple Heart.

His son, Lewis B. Puller Jr., followed him into the Marines, but fared much differently, losing both legs and a hand in Vietnam, running for Congress as an antiwar candidate and losing, then writing an autobiography that won the prestigious Pulitzer Prize in 1992. Two years later, he committed suicide.

His wife said that some sorrow can't be shared.

"To the list of names of victims of the Vietnam War, add the name of Lewis Puller," she said at the time. "He suffered terrible wounds ... [they] never really healed."

Gatz was wounded in Korea, taking shrapnel in his leg.

He received the Purple Heart.

"I'm very proud of the time I spent in the Marines," Gatz said. "It changed my life. God knows what would have become of me if I stayed in the neighborhood."

Gatz was in his barracks, listening to the radio, when he heard about the invasion of Korea.

"My first thought was, 'Where the hell is Korea?' " said Gatz, who was certified as an intelligence scout. "We engaged in 'snatch' missions, which means we went into an enemy camp and brought out a prisoner. We were swift, silent and deadly."

There are missions he still doesn't discuss much, but Gatz did say that he was trained in underwater demolition, among other things.

Before the Korean War, he was sent to an area close to the North Pole. Gatz was assigned to a submarine and participated in testing for cold-water suits, which turned out to be rather ominous.

Gatz suffered severe frostbite at Chosin.

So did thousands of other Americans, many of whom had to fight through the encircling Chinese army.

"We faced flanking fire and enemy ambush," Gatz said. "We were the rear guard, part of the last regiment out of Chosin."

By December 7, all U.N. forces were out of Hagaru, a Marine stronghold on the reservoir's southern tip. The rear guard then blew up the bridge over the Changjun River, slowing the Chinese.

Still, the road out was full of peril, Gatz said.

"It was tough and treacherous every step of the way," he said.

Riding down the narrow, twisting and icy road, trucks and tanks skidded off onto the rocks below.

General Oliver P. Smith, a Marine commander, resisted suggestions that the men abandon their vehicles and be evacuated by airplane. Smith reasoned that even if some of the Marines could be evacuated that way, Chinese troops would eventually overrun those guarding a shrinking perimeter. In the end, the only Americans flown out of Chosin were wounded—about 4,000 of them total. The rest of the men would walk out on their own.

"We were not retreating, just advancing in a different direction," Gatz said, remembering the words attributed to General Smith.

To a certain extent, however, air superiority did help the Marines. Supplies were parachuted in, providing provisions to the long line of marching men.

In addition, air strikes helped beat back the Chinese attackers.

But nothing could protect the Americans from the

freezing cold, which was worse than anyone anticipated. At night, temperatures dropped to 25 degrees below zero, with wind and snow intensifying already arctic conditions.

"Frozen Chosin" became part of the Marine vernacular.

And a frozen weapon could cost a Marine his life. Like others in his regiment, Gatz slept with his rifle pressed against his body.

Cans of rations and canteens of water had to be thawed over open fires so that the men could eat and drink. The fires, however, gave the Chinese a target to attack.

Gatz knew many men who were suffering—one Marine, for example, whose feet froze.

When he pulled his socks off, the skin came off, too, Gatz said.

The Chinese also suffered in the intense cold. Gatz saw several soldiers who had been captured. They were wearing lightweight tennis shoes. Their frozen feet had swollen to the size of footballs.

Some of the Chinese had to have their fingers broken in order to take the rifles from their frozen hands.

Gatz made it out of Chosin before Christmas 1950. Others didn't.

There were 6,000 American casualties at Chosin. Another 6,000 men suffered frostbite.

Marine officials estimated that 25,000 Chinese were killed. Another 12,500 were wounded. In addition, an estimated 30,000 were frostbitten.

After the Korean War, Gatz returned home to Chicago.

Irony of all ironies, the onetime street tough had an opportunity to take a job with the Chicago Police Department.

He had had his fill of carrying a gun, however. Gatz

again became a federal employee, this time with the U.S. Postal Service.

"I was a letter carrier for more than thirty years," said Gatz, who retired in 1992.

He was married in 1956. His wife, Lolita, also worked as a letter carrier. They have no children. The couple came to Carpentersville in 1964.

"We're happy here," Gatz said.

Lolita Gatz was diagnosed with multiple sclerosis years ago. Her husband takes care of her on a day-to-day basis.

"When you love someone, you don't look for anything in return," said Gatz, who remains relatively active in several veterans' organizations.

He has been a member of VFW Post 2298 in West Dundee and a member of American Legion Post 57 in Elgin. In addition, he has served as the state president for the Illinois Chosin Few. He turned down national office to stay home with Lolita.

Among additional groups, Gatz also is active with the Marine Corps League. He is junior vice commandant of the Elgin detachment.

"Once a Marine, always a Marine," he says.

And once a veteran, always a veteran.

They have done so much for so many.

Gatz thinks about the young military men and women currently serving, especially those stationed in the Middle East.

"You know, we've enjoyed our freedom for so long that we sometimes forget how much blood brought us to where we are today," he says.

Freedom has always been costly. And Americans have always paid the price. They paid dearly in Korea, among many other places. For all that and more, they deserve to be remembered, respected and recognized as patriots.

It is because of veterans, not reporters, that Americans enjoy freedom of the press.

It is because of veterans, not writers, that Americans enjoy freedom of speech.

And it is because of veterans that America remains a land of unlimited possibilities.

For Gatz, America is a blessing.

"And I learned long ago, you must earn every blessing," he said.

Willie Lewis

WILLIE LEWIS

"No one wanted war, but there we were."

The geopolitical face of the world had changed. In 1946, Winston Churchill announced that an "iron curtain" was descending over Eastern Europe.

The Cold War was swirling worldwide.

At home, a different type of Cold War was swirling, this one denying equal rights to African-Americans.

Southern states, for example, continued their traditional public practices. Supporting segregation was at the top of a dirty laundry list.

Several states, in fact, became battleground areas:

"The first nigger to vote will never vote again," read a sign on a black church during the 1946 Georgia primaries.

In Taylor County, Georgia, a black veteran was the only African-American who had dared to vote. For that, he was dragged from his house and shot to death.

In Monroe, Georgia, two days after the election, two black veterans and their wives were pulled from an automobile by a group of white men. All four were shot, with about sixty bullets pumped into their bodies.

Black leaders were incensed.

Paul Robeson, for example, who was one of America's most admired artists.

In a controversial statement made months before the

Korean War, the unapologetic left-winger was quoted by the Associated Press:

"[It is] unthinkable that American Negroes would go to war on behalf of those who have oppressed us for generations," Robeson reportedly said.

Willie Lewis lived far from the headlines.

"I was born in downstate Illinois, but moved to South Bend, Indiana as a boy," said Lewis, an African-American. "It was a pretty quiet childhood, but you had to be smart, too. In the black section, there were plenty of safe areas. On the other hand, I knew that there were streets I couldn't cross. You got educated—found out that trouble could start with only one step. You didn't walk into a white neighborhood uninvited. It just wasn't done."

Lewis, who lives in Elgin, served in the Korean War, working his way up to supply sergeant. He was in Korea for nearly three years.

"I enlisted in 1948, before the war," Lewis said. "There weren't many good jobs out there at the time, not for a black man. I figured that the Army would give me a fair chance at making a living."

Equal opportunity, however, was slow in coming.

Even after their accomplishments in World War II, blacks were often thought of as too scared to fight or too stupid to handle jobs involving complicated machinery.

While more blacks served in the Army than any other branch of the service, racism remained a powerful force—there and elsewhere. Nonetheless, even with the prevailing postwar prejudice, segregation was on the retreat.

According to most historical accounts, President Truman wanted to establish an atmosphere of racial equality in the United States.

Postwar racial atrocities had turned Truman into an eleventh-hour civil rights activist.

"I believe in the brotherhood of man," Truman said. "Not merely the brotherhood of white men, but the brotherhood of all men before the law."

Three military officers under General Alvan Gillem Jr. were ordered to study Army racial policy and prepare a report on how the restructured service could use blacks more efficiently.

The Gillem Board's report, *Utilization of Negro Manpower in the Postwar Army Policy*, was filed in April 1946. It recommended that the military "eliminate at the earliest possible moment, any special considerations based on race."

While progress was being made, it was a stutter-step document, actually amounting to much ado about nothing.

The Gillem Report essentially called for maintaining an awkward status quo. It reaffirmed the goal of limiting black enlistment to ten percent, although acknowledging the success of integrated companies at the Battle of the Bulge. In the future, there would be no more all-black divisions and regiments, but black platoons which would serve within white units. This brand of "integration," however, was not extended to off-duty life. The policy stated that blacks would continue eating and living in separate facilities.

The Gillem Report drew intense reaction from the black community. The reaction, however, was not uniform. Some said President Truman was trying to keep the integration ball rolling; others wanted more movement immediately.

Lewis landed somewhere in the middle.

"When I joined the Army, I signed up for integrated training," Lewis said. "To me, it made no difference what your skin color was. You had a job to do. You had a responsibility to your country."

239

But responsibility is a two-way street.

And to an extent, it appeared that the country was finally trying to level the playing field.

President Truman commissioned another board, also authorized to study racial policy. His Committee on Civil Rights was led by General Electric President Charles Wilson and composed of prominent black and white citizens. It looked at everything from housing to military service.

Its May 1947 report, entitled *To Secure These Rights*, was a groundbreaking document. On the military issue, the report called for an unequivocal end to segregation and any kind of policymaking based on race. Its language provided what may be history's most compelling condemnation of the American military's previous 170 years of bigotry:

> Underlying the theory of compulsory wartime military service in a democratic state is the principle that every citizen, regardless of his station in life, must assist in the defense of the nation when its security is threatened. Despite the discrimination which they encounter in so many fields, minority group members have time and again met this responsibility. Moreover, since equality in military service assumes great importance as a symbol of democratic goals, minorities have regarded it as not only a duty but as a right.
>
> Yet the record shows that the members of several minorities, fighting and dying for the survival of the nation in which they met bitter prejudice, found that there was discrimination against them even as they fell in battle. Prejudice in any area is an ugly, undemocratic phenomenon; in the armed services, where all men run the risk of death, it is particularly repugnant.

Lewis said that the discrimination issue was not especially applicable to his own experiences in the Army.

"Don't forget, I spent a lot of time as a sergeant," he

said. "I was attached to the Eighth Army. For the most part, I didn't see much prejudice there. The men under me—both black and white—listened when I said something. They treated me right. In the military, you're taught to respect someone's uniform."

While Lewis was not directly involved in combat during his time in Korea, he was close enough to the action to hear the shooting and see countless wounded men being brought back for help.

"Supply was part of the rear echelon," Lewis said. "But don't think that we weren't important. We made sure that the men up front had everything they needed, including guns and ammunition. You don't have an army without supplies. The lives of guys in combat can depend on you getting them those supplies on time. I took a lot of pride in not making mistakes. And to this day, I take a lot of pride in having served my country. America isn't a perfect place, but it's the best thing going."

Whenever the Eighth Army moved, Lewis and the supplies he handed out moved, too.

"I didn't have much of a formal education, but I made sure we kept accurate records of everything," Lewis said. "Before Korea, we were living a kind of charmed life. The Eighth Army was part of the peacetime occupation of Japan. Being in supply, we had Japanese civilians assigned to do a lot of our clerical work. They were very good at that. And very polite, too."

Lewis stayed in the Army from 1948 to 1960. He first visited Elgin while on military leave, eventually deciding to make his home here in the Fox Valley.

"My mother was a nurse," Lewis said. "She came up this way from Indiana. They had a job for her at the Elgin State Hospital."

Lewis met his future wife at Second Baptist Church in Elgin.

Willie and Mildred Lewis have been married for more than forty years. They have three children, as well as grandchildren and great-grandchildren.

"Right after the Army, I helped my buddy, who had bought himself a taxicab company," Lewis said. "I was his dispatcher."

And after that, Lewis ended up driving a truck for an area company.

"Day in, day out, I drove a truck for twenty-two years," Lewis said. "It was good honest work. Nothing flashy, but it paid our bills."

In the 1960s, Lewis ran for elected office, seeking to become an Elgin city councilman.

"I lost," he says. "And while I wouldn't want to run for anything again, it was pretty interesting."

Supplying an Army company was also interesting.

"You made your deals," Lewis said. "For instance, you might be out of toilet paper. You called one of the other company supply sergeants and asked about trading them something or another. But everything I did, I did for my men—the guys in our company. I never did try to keep anything for myself. And I never made any extra money selling supplies. I certainly could have, but I didn't."

When he joined the Army, Lewis was making $96 monthly.

"I never intended to get into supply," Lewis said. "If there was going to be fighting, I was willing to fight. My main thing was, I needed a job. Even though there was some discrimination in the Army, it was better than the outside world—better than in the states."

A different type of war was being fought at home. In Montgomery, Alabama, the bus boycott grabbed international attention in 1955, two years after the Korean Conflict ended. In Nashville, Tennessee, a thunderous blast of dynamite shattered a wing of the Hattie Cotton Elementary School, which had enrolled a single black five-year-old girl.

"Yeah, that stuff was really, really terrible, but I was treated pretty well in the Army," Lewis said. "Nothing to it, really."

Others weren't treated as well, however.

Take the case of Major Daniel "Chappie" James, Jr., one of the most illustrious of the new "fighter jocks" who switched from World War II-vintage P-51 Mustangs to jets in the middle of the Korean War. He earned his military pilot's commission in 1943. He went on to become the first black commander of an integrated Air Force squadron, and the first black four-star general.

One of seventeen children, James grew up near the Naval Air Base in Pensacola, Florida. Always wanting to fly, he became a civilian pilot and flight instructor while waiting to make the Air Force Tuskegee quota. At six feet, four inches and more than two hundred pounds, James was a bit big for assignment as a fighter pilot in World War II, but he was a natural for the all-black 477th Bombardment Group. The 477th was activated in January 1944, but thanks to the usual foot-dragging on black bomber crew training, remained stateside throughout the war.

As a young lieutenant, James took part in a series of sit-ins at an officers' club.

"We would start by going into the club ... and ordering a drink and the bartender would say, 'I can't serve you here. We just can't serve you here, this is the Supervisory Officers' Club,'" James remembered in *Chappie*, written by J. Alfred Phelps. "We would reply, 'Well then, we'll sit here until you serve us.' Then they would close the bar. We would leave and later one of our white friends would call us and say, 'Hey, they just opened the bar, come on back.' We would dash back up, and as soon as we walked in, again they said the bar was closed."

By the end of World War II, with Air Force integration under way, James had made it his goal to "get with an integrated outfit and prove that I was one of the best fighter pilots around." He got his chance in 1949 with a fighter-bomber squadron at Clark Field, in the Philippines.

But there were problems.

There was intense hostility toward James and his family from white pilots and their wives. Still, James ranked first in rocketry, second in bombing accuracy and was one of the top gunners in the group, as well as a military baseball and basketball star.

In the spring of 1950, James won the Distinguished Service Medal, when, suffering from severe burns and fractured vertebrae, he pulled a fellow pilot from a runway jet crash. After an extended hospital stay, he rejoined his squadron in Korea.

The Korean War saw fierce air-to-ground combat. Planes flew low, providing the infantry with support: bullets, bombs, napalm and rockets.

Before fighter jets began appearing, most missions featured the P-51 Mustang. James flew eight missions a day.

In October 1950, he was flying in close support of ground forces in Namchonjom, North Korea, attacking only a few yards in front of friendly troops. Calling strike after strike until all ammunition was spent, James was responsible for more than one hundred North Korean dead. After the battle, he was awarded the Distinguished Flying Cross, and promoted to captain.

In late December 1950, having completed one hundred Korean combat missions, James was sent back to the Philippines. He trained pilots on their way to war. Two years later, in 1952, he was a major.

A year after that, James became the first black to

command an integrated fighter squadron in the United States.

In 1960, he became director of operations for the 81st Tactical Fighter Wing.

He flew seventy-eight combat missions in Vietnam and held several leadership positions throughout the Air Force and around the world.

In 1975, James reached the top. He became the nation's first four-star black general.

He died a month after retiring in 1978.

James is buried at Arlington National Cemetery.

When his time comes, Lewis said he wants to stay closer to home.

"Not that I'm in any hurry," he says, smiling. "My health is pretty good. I stop at the VFW in Elgin, maybe have a drink or two—just to be sociable, if you know what I mean."

His voice is vaguely rural. It's warm, too, like the sound of corn quivering in a light summer wind.

Decades ago, after he was honorably discharged from the Army, Lewis learned that not all organizations operate equally. Even those that serviced veterans sometimes discriminated against minorities.

"Years back, I tried to join the American Legion here in Elgin," Lewis said. "In a roundabout way, they told me to start my own post—a post for colored people. The VFW wasn't any better at the time. They didn't want me, either. I got mad—threatened to call the national office. They finally let me in."

More than just let him in, actually. Lewis is a three-time past post commander.

"Things are much, much better than they used to be," Lewis said. "Blacks are accepted today—not by everybody, but by more people than in the past. It's a more democratic country today, especially out of the military."

Lewis said that the Korean War taught him several things, the most important of which involved combat.

"I was never in any actual action, but I saw them boys coming back all shot up," Lewis said. "Their blood was always red. It didn't depend on skin color. Them boys were fighting for the same country."

While not forgetting anyone, Lewis likes to remember the heart and heroism of black soldiers in Korea—especially the ones who didn't make it home. They believed in the ultimate promise of American life. They fought and died for an America that systematically denied them that promise.

"In any war, you have your unsung heroes," Lewis said.

Lewis was one himself. While he was within earshot of the fighting, he never had a shot fired his way. Be that as it may, he served his country admirably.

"Being a supply sergeant, it was like working at a giant warehouse, although this one was under a tent," Lewis said. "When we were busy, we were really busy. And you had an obligation to do your best. No Army can function without supplies. We made sure that the company had weapons, uniforms and everything else the guys needed. You gained experience and you figured out how to work within the system. Try telling some company commander that the supplies he wanted weren't in the right place at the right time."

Tales of glory are balanced by the realities of what it means to be in the Army. As an African-American, Lewis saw the Korean War from a different perspective than the white veterans in this book. And as a supply sergeant, his perspective was turned that much more.

In many ways, even with the problems America faces

today, it is far ahead of any other nation on Earth. Certainly there have been serious missteps in embracing racial diversity. That said, thousands upon thousands of African-Americans have used military service as a launching pad to successful civilian careers and lives of civic engagement.

In part because of Lewis' contributions, as well as the contributions of all veterans, a once shameful racial legacy can be turned into a future filled with promise.

People of every color want something simple. They want an America as good as that promise.

Bud Stout

BUD STOUT

"They kept calling it a police action."

But to the swamped servicemen who were fighting in Korea, it was war.

And a cold, cold war at that.

Burlington's Bud Stout spent more than two years in Korea.

His first tour took place before the war started in 1950. Stout was part of the 1940s peacetime provisional force, intended to facilitate freedom and independence in the newly formed South Korea, with hopes of unifying the entire country—North and South—as an autonomous state.

Later, Stout had an infantryman's view of the war.

He remembers Korea as a land of craggy hills, endless ridges and few natural amenities.

For an area that prides itself on being known as "the land of the morning calm," Korea is ill placed on the surface of the Earth. An ocean peninsula, its neighbors are China, Russia and Japan.

"You never forget the climate," said Stout, who was born in 1930. "The summer was hot and humid. The winter was colder than you could ever imagine. We were outside twenty-four hours a day. That's the way you lived in the Army."

In a typical Korean summer, temperatures can reach

110 degrees and higher, with humidity in the 90 percent range.

Given that type of weather, climbing steep hills with a rifle, pack and ammunition could consume a young soldier, Stout said.

Winters were worse.

United Nations troops never got much farther north than the 40th parallel of latitude, which runs in the United States, for example, from Philadelphia to Denver to Reno.

Weather-wise, not too bad, right?

Think again, at least in terms of Korea, where winter winds seem to come straight from the heart of Siberia, funneled down the Yellow Sea and whipped through the mountains as if by some ferocious frost monster. To try curling up in a sleeping bag or foxhole was to risk being killed by the ubiquitous enemy. To stay out in the cold was to risk freezing to death.

Barren as it is, Korea still has aspects of unsurpassed beauty. But odds are, no non-Korean said a good thing about its climate in the early 1950s.

To Stout, a lifelong area resident, memories of Korea remain a constant companion.

"I think about what we went through," he said. "We fought in rice paddies and on hills. It was a hostile environment. You were tense almost all the time."

That tension was increased because, for the first time in history, the United States was not fighting to win, but to hold its ground—something Stout objected to.

"You can't completely prevail in a limited campaign," he said. "And, bottom line, that's what winning a war is all about."

The Korean War became a test of wills between the free world and the Communist world, between the United States and the Soviet Union, which used surrogates—Red China and North Korea—to do its fighting, although the Soviets were involved in secret air attacks, something that was not admitted until after the Cold War ended, more than thirty-five years later.

Along with the U.S. not fighting to win, Stout also objected to the firing of General MacArthur.

"I never did understand that," he said, referring to the firing, which was initiated by President Truman. "We should have rolled into Communist China—done what was necessary to win. I remember being only about a mile from the Manchurian border, close enough to see it. I still wonder why we stopped. You heard different things, but most of it was just scuttlebutt."

No matter the war, one of the interesting things about combat life is the almost complete and perpetual blindness of individual soldiers to the matters that most immediately affect them.

Stout says he rarely knew what was going on, what would happen next or what the outcome would be.

"You just followed orders," he said. "Sometimes we didn't even know where we were." They thought they knew, however, because there was never a shortage of rumors—all apparently coming from an "authoritative source."

Next to mail and food, rumors are the lifeblood of military existence. And as incredible as it may seem, soldiers never lose faith in them, even the ones generally proven to be greatly exaggerated.

Scuttlebutt often is the only show in town.

But there was much more than a rumor of war at what would become known as the Pusan Perimeter, an early turning point in the Korean War.

The North Koreans had enjoyed the initiative since the war began in June 1950.

The American Army was on the run. And by August 2, all of South Korea, except the rectangular Pusan Perimeter, had fallen to the Communists.

General Walton "Bulldog" Walker, the no-nonsense commander of the U.S. Eighth Army, was told to restore morale among American troops, who were trying to buy time by backing up—giving ground, if you will. In delivering an oratory meant to resurrect Churchill's finest hour, Walker would tell them that they would finally hold the line at Pusan. He said they would stand or die:

> There will be no more retreating, withdrawal or readjustment of the lines or any other term you choose. There is no line behind us to which we can retreat. Every unit must counterattack to keep the enemy in a state of confusion and off balance. There will be no Dunkirk, there will be no Bataan; a retreat to Pusan would be one of the greatest butcheries in history. We must fight until the end. Capture by these people is worse than death itself. We will fight as a team. If some of us must die, we will die fighting together. Any man who gives ground may be personally responsible for the death of thousands of his comrades ... I want everybody to understand that we are going to hold this line. We are going to win.

But to hold the long perimeter around Pusan would require additional troops.

Stout was attached to the 5th Regimental Combat Team, which was sent to back up the 24th Division, among others.

"We were a bastard outfit," Stout said of the 5th Regimental Combat Team. "We went where we were needed. We fought alongside several different divisions— Army and Marines."

Located in southeastern Korea, the Pusan Perimeter was about 50 miles wide and 100 miles deep, backing to the sea on the east and south, with the Naktong River along its western edge and a rugged mountain chain along its northern flank.

The Americans held the perimeter, then turned and went on the offensive. In mid-September, MacArthur launched the bold Inchon invasion. Within weeks, Seoul was liberated and the North Korean Army had been swept out of South Korea. Had the fighting ended at the end of September 1950, the Korean War would be remembered today as one of the greatest triumphs of American arms.

"We had a good chance to win," Stout said of the war. "But politics got in the way of our offensive."

America's apparent allies, the South Korean Army, got in the way, too. Most historians say that it was an inexperienced and incompetent fighting force, especially early on. The long-held military perception is that the South Korean Army was unprepared, uncommitted and didn't do its fair share.

Stout did more than his fair share.

"I'm not looking for congratulations, but I did my part," Stout said.

He became a locksmith after the war, retiring from that occupation years ago.

Bud and LaVonne Stout were married in 1952. She died more than a decade ago.

The couple had six children.

Bud Stout has grandchildren and great-grandchildren.

"What I really enjoy is when the grandkids come over for supper," said Stout, who has epilepsy and needs a walker to get around. "I don't get out much anymore. My daughter, Peg, takes me to church every Sunday. Other than that, I mostly watch television and pick open old handset locks. My record is unlocking one of them seven separate times in a minute. It's an unusual hobby, but don't forget, that's the way I made my living—opening locks."

A virtual shut-in, Stout is a portrait in fragility. His body curls comma-like as he sits through the interview for this book.

Yet in some sense, the frailty of his physical condition is rarely evidenced by what comes out of his mouth.

"I'm a talker," Stout says, the words tripping over one another like a litter of precocious puppies at a kennel.

The canine simile seems appropriate. Stout's most faithful friend is a collie called Precious Lady.

"She's good company," Stout says of his dog. "I've had her for about seven years."

He lives in the house he and his father built four years after Stout returned from the war—returned to the little town he has always called home.

"My dad was a construction contractor," Stout says. "He was a carpenter by trade. This house here, everything is plaster. Real high quality, like my father."

Bud and LaVonne raised their family inside the walls of that house. Through the years, Stout has become something of a village elder. While he is subject to the very real aches and pains, the fears and endless losses that age brings, he also is a man of insight and inspiration.

And a wry sense of humor.

"I'm a self-taught locksmith," he says. "After the war, I worked at Northern Illinois University. You could say that the job just 'opened up' for me. I started there as a carpenter. It used to bother the daylights out of me that security took care of the locks. If they got locked out of something, they'd call me. Being a carpenter, I'd drill the lock out. That bothered me, too. It seemed such a waste. I knew there was a better way to do things, which was why I became a locksmith in the first place. Anyway, I used to tell the professors at the college that I graduated in the 'Top

Ten' of my high school class. Of course, there were only ten of us in the senior class at Burlington High School.'"

Stout enjoys the joke, but there was little to laugh about in Korea.

He won battle stars for five of the ten official campaigns in the Korean War. Not only did he fight at the Pusan Perimeter, but also at Inchon and along the Chinese border.

"In one of those battles, I got myself shot in the neck," Stout says. "I was lucky. The bullet passed right through the side. If it would have hit me straight on, I never would have made it ... After getting hit, I felt inside the wound. I could touch the tendons and cords and things wiggling around. I said to myself, 'This is it, Bud, You're going home.' "

He didn't—at least not right away and not because he had been shot.

"I walked back a few hundred yards to this mobile hospital, a MASH unit," Stout says. "They looked into the hole in my neck, put a couple of stitches in it and sent me back to the line."

Stout speaks openly about what combat was like for him in Korea.

"Guys will tell you that they shot dozens of Communist soldiers," he says. "Usually, that's nothing but baloney. Here's what happened. You're in the dark. You raise your M-1 rifle and you shoot once to the left. You swing it to the front and fire once. You swing it to the right and fire once. There's no way you could tell who you hit or who the guy to the left of you hit or who the guy to the right of you hit."

Stout had a number of unpleasant surprises during the time he spent in Korea, including a rather eye-opening experience, which almost turned deadly:

"One day, I'm out in the open, looking overhead," Stout says. "I could see some of our P-51 Mustang fighters flying in against several North Korean airplanes. I'm sitting there watching them turn and climb and shoot at each other in an area about as big as Burlington and Hampshire, which would be several miles. This was quite a show. But did you ever stop to wonder what happens to all those machine gun bullets the airplanes shoot, the bullets that don't hit their target—that don't hit the other airplane? All of a sudden, zip zip zip, those falling bullets carve a line in the grass right in front of me. I was out of there and hiding underneath a truck before the next line of bullets fell down on me."

Stout says that he came to understand the tenuous nature of existence in a war zone, where life is often tragic and death a release.

"But being young, you don't really believe in your own mortality," Stout said.

What young man does?

Others die. That's one of the laws of death in a war zone.

"Everybody dies" means everybody else dies. Who can conceive of his own nonexistence—if that indeed is what death is all about.

Stout said he didn't think about the "hereafter" in Korea. He thought about the here-and-now.

"When I first tried to join the VFW in Hampshire, they turned me down," said Stout, who was accepted later and twice served as post commander. "You have to admire what the World War II guys did—how they fought for freedom and democracy. After Vietnam, it became popular to call World War II 'the good war.' That's nonsense. There are no good wars; there never have been. But there are wars that have to be fought. Take Korea, for example. The men who went there, we were asked to make sacrifices for a cause. We did it, too."

Stout remembers a great deal about the war.

"I have a lot of pictures," he says, opening a photo album, its pages packed with black and white images of Americans who were in Korea.

Their youth is a moment in time, taken in a war worth remembering.

William Toth

WILLIAM TOTH

"It's war when they start shooting at you."

He once watched John Wayne, wishing to be a hero himself.

But this was no movie. And when the shooting stopped, the dead did not get up and dust themselves off.

They did not walk away.

There were 58,000 Americans killed in Vietnam. Today, most would be middle-aged.

For those who went to war and came back alive, reality sometimes sets in with a vengeance.

Stop and talk to a Vietnam veteran. Most say they think about the war every day.

When William Toth left Vietnam, he was not the same young man who had arrived there in 1968.

For one thing, the country that sent him off to war was not prepared to welcome him home.

Not that he expected it.

Through the mid-1960s and into the early '70s, it was fashionable to be outraged about the war. College campuses were polarization points. Intelligent discussion about American involvement in Vietnam had become virtually impossible.

Adding insult to injury, Academy Award-winning actress Jane Fonda visited the enemy. Even today, she's vilified on bumper stickers at most American Legion posts.

"Jane Fonda was a traitor," said Toth, a longtime local resident.

Some say she should have been indicted and convicted of treason, adding that Fonda's actions constituted nothing less than aiding and abetting the enemy.

She became known as "Hanoi Jane."

Toth says that the antiwar activists didn't bother him personally, but he questions their hostility.

Why was their opposition so abusive?

Why was it turned toward those who served their country?

And why was he called a murderer?

"I thought the war was a noble cause," Toth says, adding that the U.S. was trying to improve the life of people in a conflicted corner of the world.

Food and freedom were among many items America brought to the table.

There was hope for a democratic Vietnam, Toth said.

"How can you win every battle and lose the war?" he asks.

Like other Vietnam veterans, Toth fought two wars—one on the other side of the world and one when he returned home.

"Not that I care, but why were we blamed for the war in Vietnam?" Toth asks, referring to the American men and women who were there. "We weren't the enemy. We were called by our country. We answered that call. A lot of young Americans died fighting for the United States. And the survivors, we became targets of public hatred. That didn't do much for our morale."

No matter how harmful he thought they were, Toth first figured that the protesters were against the war out of principle. How then, he asks, did the same young people who had such apparent principles let the poor and powerless be drafted in their place?

How did they let minority members go as sacrificial substitutes?

Vietnam never strays far from the collective consciousness. The war, which ended three decades ago, remains a litmus test for the generation that grew up in its shadow.

Before joining the military, Toth had graduated from Larkin High School, located on Elgin's West Side. With or without a diploma, he didn't have an ideal upbringing.

"My biological parents had problems—serious problems," he says. "I became a ward of the state."

Toth, a Chicago native, bounced from foster home to foster home. He ended up in Elgin at age sixteen. His new family was really the first family he had. They remained close through the years.

"Right after high school, I enlisted in the U.S. Marine Corps," Toth said. "Thinking back, I didn't have a clue as to what was involved in becoming a Marine. Or what it meant to be part of something sacred."

He found out after arriving in Vietnam. Toth would receive the prestigious Silver Star, awarded for "conspicuous gallantry in action."

Today, Toth looks like a study in maturity—what it is to be an aging Marine. He is on the short side; a strong, stocky man with closely cropped hair.

Sitting sideways at the end of a comfortable chair in the family room of his Hampshire home, he lights a cigarette, taps it against an ashtray and asks about the microcassette recorder, which was used for each interview in this book.

"Are we ready?" Toth asks.

His tone is evenhanded, but guarded, almost as if it

were a clenched fist.

But Toth turns out to be an excellent interview. He comes across as honest and straightforward—refreshingly forthcoming in a no-nonsense sort of way.

"Soft answers aren't any good, not if you want the truth," Toth says.

His truth includes saving several Marines in February 1969, for which he was duly decorated. Their lives were hanging in the balance when Toth retrieved and returned a satchel charge. It had been thrown into an American perimeter, which was swarming with North Vietnamese soldiers.

Having infiltrated the Marine enclosure after midnight, they were firing from behind the U.S. line.

Toth also returned an enemy grenade. It exploded just as it left his hand. He lost his hearing and had a line of shrapnel stapled up his arm and into his neck.

The hearing came back, but buddies didn't.

Toth ended up charging across hostile terrain, killing an enemy soldier in the process.

"We were occupying a defensive position," said Toth, who was with the 3rd Marine Division. "It was called Landing Zone Russell, which was only a couple of miles from the DMZ [Demilitarized Zone]. The enemy came in at night. It was really foggy. By the time the fighting finished, there was hand-to-hand combat going on."

There were 32 Marines killed and 97 wounded at the Battle of LZ Russell, said Toth, who received not only the Silver Star, but also the Purple Heart.

He is an active veteran—a member of VietNow, as well as a number of other organizations.

Eleven million Americans served in uniform during the Vietnam era, yet only one in four made it to Southeast Asia. Of the 2.8 million who did, fewer than ten percent served in the "bush," which was where line infantry soldiers engaged in seeking out the enemy. That's what Toth did before he was wounded and sent stateside.

It was on the shoulders of these veterans that most of the burden of fighting fell in a war that left the vast majority of their peers, even those in uniform, untouched.

Toth and others like him were the tip of an American sword. Some said, however, that the edge was taken off—that the once-sharp sword was dulled by political mismanagement.

"The ideals we fought for were the right ones," Toth says. "And as a Marine, you never turn tail and run."

For most Americans, Vietnam was not even a familiar name until 1964, when the U.S. dramatically escalated its military intervention.

In August, President Lyndon Johnson ordered "retaliatory action" against North Vietnam after apparent attacks on American destroyers in the Gulf of Tonkin.

Few people realized that the United States had been involved in Vietnam since the 1940s, or that it had presided over the creation of South Vietnam in 1954.

The idea was not to create two separate Vietnams, North and South, but to establish the peaceful conditions that would allow for a nationwide reunification election in 1956. Those elections were never held. The United States stepped in to build and bolster what it hoped would be a permanent, non-Communist country—South Vietnam.

Yet, according to some historical accounts, Communism received significant support throughout the country, particularly in the North.

For most Vietnamese, the "Vietnam War" was not a single event, but a long chain of wars of independence against foreign enemies, including the French, who wanted to maintain an imperial presence in Southeast Asia.

For all practical purposes, France made its last stand in Vietnam at Dien Bien Phu. French forces were defeated there in 1954.

The coastline of Vietnam looks like an "S," which runs from the southern border of China to the tip of the Indochina peninsula. Stretching for more than 1,200 miles, it nearly equals the length of the entire Pacific coast of the continental United States.

The Vietnamese sometimes liken the shape of their country to a long pole with baskets of rice attached at each end.

When the country was divided in 1954, some said that the pole had been snapped in two. North Vietnam and its southern allies—the Viet Cong—waged a twenty-one-year campaign to repair the break and reunify their concept of what was a nation.

The United States argued that if it failed to prevent a Communist takeover of South Vietnam, one country after another would fall under the control of America's Cold War enemies.

At home—among those who paid attention to such things—there was widespread support of this argument through the 1950s and early 1960s.

Over time, however, an increasing number of Americans came to believe that their leaders had misled them—that they had lied about the realities of war in Southeast Asia.

Many concluded that South Vietnam was neither a democratic nation nor an independent one, but a corrupt regime entirely dependent on U.S. support, which was delivered in both military and monetary forms.

By the time of the Tet Offensive in 1968, popular sentiment was that preserving South Vietnam was not vital to national security.

What's more, some said that the United States was

itself acting as an aggressor.

Toth says such analysis meant nothing in the killing fields of Vietnam.

"We were always on patrol, looking to engage the enemy," Toth said. "You'd get tired and frustrated, but you had to keep moving."

As a war zone, Vietnam is a land of incredible complexity. On the smallest scale, America's involvement can be understood by imagining a few heavily armed men trudging through the rice paddies and tall elephant grass.

They patrolled the countryside for weeks at a time—waiting and watching.

"When I first got to Vietnam, the nights were pretty tough," Toth said. "There were things that you weren't familiar with, but you had to stay strong. You just didn't let your guard down."

Toth slept on the ground, using his poncho as a sheet. Minutes lay like a terminal illness. Aches became pains, itches became rashes and stiffness set into every joint. The sounds and shadows of the jungle intensified.

It was always ominous, as if impending evil eclipsed the moon.

Bats and birds would fly frantically, moving from one tree to another at the chatter of small arms fire in the distance.

Marines on patrol were understandably apprehensive, ready to strike out at anything.

"The only reason you slept at all was because you were completely exhausted," said Toth, who works as a plumber and pipe fitter today.

He remains extremely patriotic. War was a complicated reality, Toth says. Quite often it proved emotionally wrenching, but like all other life-threatening experiences, combat magnifies the full range of human emotion. It is not unusual to meet veterans who hate having been involved in war but also miss what it brought out in them—the feeling of being fully alive, of having others depend on you, of making history.

Toth was in Vietnam only a short time, starting in December 1968, then leaving in February 1969 after having been wounded during the Battle of LZ Russell.

He was put on a medical evacuation helicopter, brought to a field hospital before being sent home.

During the interview for this book, his voice never cracks. Tears are not part of his equation, although he flashes from delight to disgust, relief to regret.

And nostalgia.

There are, in addition, seemingly special moments through the three-hour interview. On more than one occasion, he stumbled across a long-forgotten memory or a previously unconsidered insight.

"I don't usually talk to anyone about Vietnam, other than a few fellow veterans," Toth says. "You find out that people who have had the same experiences speak the same language."

It is a language of solidarity.

Most Vietnam veterans believe that America didn't lose the war, but quit the war.

"We could have won, but our hands were tied," Toth said. "Either way, this country can be proud of the people who were there. For the most part, Vietnam veterans performed their jobs with pride and valor."

Years after Vietnam, Toth still sensed that there was an urgency to do something—to do anything, he says.

There was unfinished business.

"I heard talk about a group going in to find the remaining prisoners of war, if any at all," Toth said. "I would have reenlisted in a minute for that."

He did, in fact, join the Marine Corps Reserve in the late 1980s.

"If they were going to bring somebody back, I wanted to be part of that," Toth said. "I owed it to the guys who couldn't come home—you know, the guys who were killed in Vietnam. If there were any Americans alive there, I wanted to help get them out."

Toth might not always have agreed with American military methods in Vietnam, but he says that the U.S. was right to resist the terror inflicted on a poor people; right to recognize that the turmoil was caused by the activities of a hostile government—then under the command of Ho Chi Minh—which had clear designs on a territory and people not its own.

The Communists were willing to take that territory by force.

Early in the war, Americans were willing to "stand the test," Toth says, adding that the Marines were willing to risk their lives in a cause completely remote from their own well-being.

In a combat zone, it's what warriors do.

"We never wavered in what we were doing," Toth said, speaking for fellow Marines.

He has visited the Vietnam Veterans Memorial in Washington, D.C. It is commonly called "the Wall."

Toth said he was deeply touched by his visit.

With the addition of six names in 2003, there are now 58,235 names listed on the Memorial. They are arranged in chronological, then alphabetical order.

When the design competition for the Memorial opened, there were four criteria required:

1. Be reflective and contemplative in character.
2. Harmonize with the surroundings.

3. List the names of those who died in the conflict and those who were still missing.

4. Make no political statement about the war.

At last look, there were about 1,200 names on the wall listed as missing—MIA, POW and others.

The first casualties inscribed were Dale R. Buis and Chester R. Ovnard, although the latter's name was misspelled—it should have been Ovnand. The two were military advisers, killed in July 1959 in Bienhoa, while watching a movie in the mess tent. The light had been turned on to change the movie reel and that's when snipers opened fire. The movie was *The Tattered Dress*, starring Jeanne Crain and Jeff Chandler, who was also featured in *Merrill's Marauders*, his last film. The 1962 action picture tells the story of the elite World War II Army unit.

Although 1959 is marked as the beginning of the war on Panel 1 of the Wall Memorial, an Army Captain, Harry C. Cramer, was killed in October 1957 during a training action. His name was added to the wall about a year after the Memorial was dedicated in 1982.

The Memorial is an epilogue of sorts, an article of faith, fitting for disengagement in the face of an aggressive enemy. While not quite defeat, that disengagement left a bad taste in many mouths.

Toth thinks that America should have supported its troops.

"We didn't make public policy, we followed orders," Toth said, referring to Vietnam veterans.

He did more than that, going above and beyond the call of duty, receiving a Silver Star in the process.

Willie and Kim Toth were married in 1998.

Just as her husband had, Kim Toth's father—Weldon "Satch" Ewert—also received the Silver Star. He saw action in Korea.

Willie Toth has two children from a previous marriage. He also has something some Vietnam veterans may never have.

"I'm at peace with what we did in Vietnam," he says. "It was not an 'immoral' war. Our guys didn't die in vain—something I hate hearing. Remember, there's no overall rule of law in the world. Like it or not, we're everyone's policeman. When there's a problem, America is expected to step in and make things right."

As territory, America is little more than the body of land that's bordered by two oceans. The people who inhabit its peaks and valleys provide its soul and spirit.

Toth's spirit, although a bit on the stubborn side, is inspiring.

More than a century ago, Abraham Lincoln highlighted his own love of sincere patriotism:

"I like to see a man proud of the place in which he lives," Lincoln said. "I like to see a man who lives in it so that his place will be proud of him."

Residents of the Fox Valley should be proud of Toth.

After a tough and troubled childhood, he became a U.S. Marine.

He became a hero, too—the genuine article, not some celluloid caricature.

And he has stood shoulder-to-shoulder with other heroes, not only on the line, but also along local parade routes.

What was learned from his service and sacrifice?

Well, to a writer's way of thinking, perhaps Karl von Clausewitz had it down pat more than 170 years ago:

"No one starts a war—or rather, no one in his senses ought to do so—without first being clear in his mind what he intends to achieve by that war and how he intends to conduct it."

On April 30, 1975, when the last American helicopter scurried off the roof of the U.S. Embassy in Saigon as the city fell to the invading North Vietnamese army, the Washington Post said that it was a day of "deliverance" for the United States. In some sense, it probably was.

Deliverance for most Vietnam veterans came years later, however.

"For me, it was during the 1980s," Toth said. "We finally got our parades."

In Chicago, there was cheering and a common call.

"Welcome home! Welcome home!"

Coming home had special significance to those who were in Vietnam.

Fast forward to the current millennium.

Schoolchildren no longer memorize the names and dates of America's major battles. Perhaps that's a good thing. But they should remember that America will remain the land of the free for only as long as it is the home of the brave.

On a foggy night in a faraway land, Toth held his ground. To be brave was no easy matter.

It was a feeling from within, a precious possession.

Courage and character are among America's most cherished virtues.

Schoolchildren should remember that, too.

Tricia Dieringer

TRICIA DIERINGER

"Intelligence is the frontline of national security."

She entered the United States Army in 1972, having enlisted during the Vietnam War.

In some sense, the specifics of that time have been relegated to museums and memorials. Decades have passed. Today, given that two of every five Americans were born after the fighting stopped, Vietnam has become something of a media cliché—a shorthand expression evoking domestic disturbances and a controversial war.

At this writing in 2004, it has become a recurring reference point for America's involvement in Iraq.

But looking back, Vietnam was a complex cataclysm in itself. The war produced a remarkable range of experiences. On one side, dissenters said America was facing a darkening dusk.

Among many on the other side, Tricia Dieringer disagreed.

"I've always been an extremely patriotic person," said Dieringer, a lifelong Elgin resident. "From the time I was a little girl, I knew I'd end up in the military."

Liberty isn't a gift, Dieringer says. It is an achievement—an achievement gained through the steady dedication of a lifetime, during which principles precede privileges.

And achievement is something Dieringer knows all about.

She was, for example, attached to an elite intelligence team that was stationed in Europe.

But before that, she went through basic training at Fort McClellan, Alabama, then to the Defense Language Institute—West Coast. The school, located in Monterey, California, traces its roots to the eve of America's entry into World War II.

As part of her earliest intelligence training, Dieringer went through a 47-week Russian language course—six hours daily. It was not an easy class.

Other languages were just as difficult.

Nonetheless, during the peak of America's involvement in Vietnam—from 1965 to 1973—the institute stepped up the pace of language education. More than 20,000 service personnel studied Vietnamese at the California facility. Many military advisers took a special "survivor" course, which taught them basic communication skills in an eight-week class.

Dieringer would be stationed at the Pentagon and abroad.

"I met some very 'interesting' people," Dieringer said, referring to the years she spent in intelligence. "There are many things that I can't talk about, even after all these years."

On one occasion, she was part of a team that provided translation and escort for Vice President Walter Mondale while he was in Germany.

Dieringer was born in January 1952. Her maiden name was Sherman.

"And I was born at Sherman Hospital, not far from where we lived in Elgin," she says, laughing loudly. "Funny, isn't it? I made my debut as a Sherman at Sherman."

Her father's full name—Merritt Grant Sherman—pays tribute to three Civil War generals: George Wesley Merritt,

Ulysses S. Grant and William Tecumseh Sherman, who is best known for his capture of Atlanta, Georgia and his March to the Sea, which went from Atlanta to Savannah, Georgia.

Sherman was born in Lancaster, Ohio. He was the older brother of John Sherman, the U.S. senator who sponsored the Sherman Antitrust Act.

Their father died when both boys were very young.

Orphaned at age nine, William Tecumseh Sherman would later attend the United States Military Academy at West Point, graduating sixth in the class of 1840.

He entered the Army as a second lieutenant and served through the end of the Mexican War.

He resigned his military commission and became president of a San Francisco bank, which failed during the financial panic of 1857. He accepted a post offered to him by two Army friends from the South. Sherman became the first president of Louisiana Military Seminary. He served in that post until the start of the Civil War, when he resigned and went back north. It's ironic that Louisiana Military Seminary later became Louisiana State University—so the first president of what is now one of the most prestigious and beloved Southern universities was a Yankee general, and a much maligned one at that.

Sherman was hated for cutting a wide path of destruction through Georgia, as well as through North and South Carolina.

"War is cruelty and you cannot refine it," he said, solidifying his reputation as the first modern general.

Sherman's reputation as a contemporary commander stems from his belief in total war, which is the concept that armed conflict involves a struggle not only between competing military forces but also between the societies of the competing states. Within that context, he recognized that a nation could succeed militarily by destroying the opposing side's ability to wage war, and that an army could conduct better campaigns for this purpose by maneuvering its forces against an enemy's economic infrastructure.

Sherman Hospital, where Dieringer was born, has no name ties to the Union general.

The hospital, which was founded by the Elgin Woman's Club, opened its doors in 1888, occupying space in a two-story house donated by local drugstore owner and prominent businessman Henry Sherman.

Dieringer's father was a businessman, too. He owned and operated a dry cleaning store in Elgin.

"I graduated from Elgin High School, my father graduated from Elgin High School and my son graduated from Elgin High School," Dieringer said. "Three generations at the same school. That's almost unheard of today."

Dieringer was one of five children. She was a pompom member at Elgin High School. Later, at Elgin Community College, she was a cheerleader. In addition, she served on the ECC student council.

"I was always involved on a certain level, but I didn't really come to life until enrolling at ECC," Dieringer said. "I was working three jobs, just trying to get my associate's degree. While I loved every minute of it, school got to be a financial hardship. In terms of a career, I thought the military might help, which it did."

Her father was in the Merchant Marine during World War II, having been turned away by other branches of the service.

"Dad was born without an ear," Dieringer said. "When he was sixteen years old, they took some skin off his side and grafted an ear. They also drilled a hole into his head, right where the ear would be. Still, there was no eardrum.

He had wanted to enlist immediately after Pearl Harbor, but was classified 4F—a result of not having hearing in both ears ... He volunteered for the Merchant Marine, running supplies through heavily contested waters."

Merritt Sherman was wounded off the coast of Africa. At the time, those who were serving in the Merchant Marine were not formally recognized as veterans, which would change in the 1990s. Among other things, Congress decreed that time spent on oceangoing vessels from December 7, 1941 to August 15, 1945 constituted "active" military service.

"Dad was my hero," Dieringer said. "We went to all the Elgin parades together. At one of them, I remember pointing to the American Legion, saying, 'Someday, I'm going to be part of that.' Well, my membership remains a proud, proud accomplishment."

Other accomplishments have taken Dieringer around the world.

After graduating from the Defense Language Institute, she had the linguistic aptitude of someone educated at a Russian high school.

That particular course involved another type of education. Dieringer met and married a fellow student, a soldier returning from Vietnam.

Love is one thing; military orders are another matter.

And Dieringer had her Army obligations.

The newlywed went to the Pentagon, getting an overview of what would be her assignment in Germany.

"I served during the Vietnam War, but I'm not a Vietnam veteran," Dieringer says. "People need to understand the difference."

Although not Vietnam by any stretch of the imagination, Germany was a "hot spot" at the time.

Certain criminal elements had a growing support

system there. The Baader-Meinhof Gang gained international attention, becoming Germany's most active terrorist organization.

While Dieringer doesn't discuss specifics, she did hold an important intelligence position during the terrorist group's more than 20-year existence, which began in the early 1970s.

That said, the origins of the gang can be traced back to the student protests of the 1960s. In Germany, those protests often turned into riots. In 1967, for instance, Mohammed Reza Pahlavi, the Shah of Iran, visited the western side of Berlin, at the time a divided city. Exiled Iranians protested, which led to the shooting of a German student who was supporting their cause.

That student was shot by the police.

This event, along with an overall perception of state brutality and increasing opposition to the Vietnam War, brought a group of terrorists together. That group included Andreas Baader.

The terrorists set fire to several German department stores. In addition, through the years, the group was implicated in the killing of high-profile German citizens.

After Baader was arrested, female journalist Ulrike Meinhof published several sympathetic articles in *Konkret* magazine.

Sometime after April 1970, Baader—then recently released from custody—went underground. Meinhof went underground, too. They received terrorist training in Jordan.

All the while, Meinhof continued commenting on their leftist operations.

"If one sets a car on fire, that is a criminal offense," she said. "If one sets hundreds of cars on fire, that is political action."

A manifesto authored by Meinhof used the name "RAF," the Red Army Faction, inspired by the Japanese Red Army, an Asian terrorist group.

The Baader-Meinhof Gang used a red-star logo, which had a machine gun emblazoned across it.

After an intense manhunt, Baader, Meinhof and other members of the gang were apprehended in 1972, but by then a so-called second generation of the RAF had emerged. American installations in Germany were bombed. All U.S. Army personnel were targeted.

"We were very careful," said Dieringer, who was stationed about a half-mile from the East German border, part of a small detachment there.

According to official German documents, both Baader and Meinhof committed suicide while in prison. In each case, however, the cause of death was hotly contested. Conspiracy theorists said that the two were executed by their government.

Dieringer—who was subsequently sent to Augsburg, Germany—has served her government for more than two decades, with a 10-year break between separate commitments, the second of which continues today.

In the 1970s, the Elgin woman became the first female warrant officer in military intelligence.

She continued studying the Russian language, completing a 37-week advanced course, which gave her the linguistic aptitude of a Russian graduate student.

Dieringer also speaks Spanish, German and French.

It was also in the 1970s that she had a relatively close call with terrorists in London. Just two days after she left the city, the Irish Republican Army was named in the bombing of a popular nightspot. Dieringer had been there while off duty.

"To contest terrorism, we need effective intelligence,"

Dieringer said. "That means much more than the latest technology. We need the human touch."

In laymen's terms, among other things, that means more intelligence operatives—men and women who can infiltrate terrorist groups, identify key problems and help guide necessary operations.

In the immediate aftermath of the events of September 11, 2001, demands for intelligence reform were taken more seriously.

Some say that those events cast a dark shadow over the entire American intelligence community.

"As a people, we have a tendency to get complacent," Dieringer said. "But you can't have that characteristic spill over into intelligence."

The key question is why was there no intelligence available to warn of the terrorist attacks on the World Trade Center and the Pentagon.

Security specialists say that no intelligence failure since December 1941 has been as significant. That being the case, going back to the events leading up to the attack against Pearl Harbor is instructive today.

While some say that neither naval nor Army intelligence adequately warned of an imminent Japanese threat in the fall of 1941, Dieringer disagrees, adding an interesting caveat to the decades-old debate about the surprise attack.

"Complacency and inadequate intelligence training leave us as vulnerable today as we were in the days leading up to the Pearl Harbor attack," she said.

According to an Internet source, American military leaders, who expected a Japanese assault on Malaya, gave only general warning to U.S. forces in Pearl Harbor.

One of the major reasons given for the creation of the Central Intelligence Agency (CIA) in 1947 was to prevent "another Pearl Harbor."

Less than five years later, however, the CIA was not able to recognize signs pointing to North Korea's attack on South Korea. Again, the United States found itself at war.

Is there a lesson here?

Dieringer says yes. First and foremost, America needs to understand that there are no easy fixes.

"We need a firm foundation," she said. "We are immediately upset about terrorist attacks, then that feeling fades away. As we're seeing right now in Iraq and Afghanistan, the war on terrorism will not be a short-lived situation. At home and around the world, we need to stay committed to our troops. They're protecting our freedom on a daily basis. Democracy is more than a form of government. It's a way of life. Patriotism is not a one-day, flag-waving event."

After more than twelve years in the U.S. Army, Dieringer left the service for about a decade.

"I had a son to raise," she said, thinking back to 1983.

Brian Schlapkohl, 24, joined the U.S. Navy after high school. He currently serves aboard a nuclear submarine.

"I'm in constant communication with him, but I never know exactly where he's at," Dieringer said, adding that such information is classified—a stipulation she knows inside out.

Dieringer also left the service because her father was ill.

"We were very close," she said. Her father died in 1983, not long after she had returned home from the service.

She returned to ECC, earning a degree, which led to her becoming a registered nurse.

Earlier, while on active duty, Dieringer graduated from an extension program offered by the U.S. Army through Fort Sam Houston Hospital.

In 1995, Dieringer enlisted in the Illinois National Guard as a registered nurse. She was activated in December 2001, helping process troops who would be part of America's war on terrorism.

Dieringer also works as an administrative assistant to the police chief in Gilberts.

"It's a great job," she said.

Her passion remains embedded in the U.S. military and veteran services.

She joined American Legion Post 57 in Elgin more than a decade ago.

"What a truly terrific organization," said Dieringer, who has held a number of important post positions, both locally and on the district level.

She is a past post commander of the American Legion in Elgin. Dieringer also served as an American Legion district commander, which involves overseeing several counties.

In addition, Dieringer has been a featured speaker at numerous events honoring area veterans.

She was guest speaker, for example, at the city of Elgin's September 11, 2002 ceremony, marking the first anniversary of the surprise terrorist attack against America.

Her son joined the American Legion in 1998.

"He's a fine young man, courageous and compassionate," Dieringer said. "Brian has commendable core values—duty, honor, honesty and integrity. Those things are what carry you through the tough times. And they lead you from success to significance."

Dieringer began on that path decades ago. In an even earlier era, her father followed the same road.

"People get ahead by doing the right thing," Dieringer said. "There are no shortcuts in life, not if you're pursuing something special."

Dieringer believes that all men and women should serve in the military.

"First, to challenge themselves to see if they really can 'be all that they can be,' " she said. "And second, to get a better understanding of freedom and the cost of remaining free."

Those who expect to reap the blessings of freedom must also answer the call to support it, Dieringer said.

For more than two centuries, devotion to God and country has nourished the cause of freedom in America.

God and country...

Dieringer has taken those words to heart. In so doing, she has tried to live life according to a consistent code—a code dedicated to honoring both.

Still, it took time to become an overnight success. Along the way, she learned that the difference between good and great is extra effort.

In or out of the military, patriotism bears a familiar face in Elgin. Look closely at Dieringer's photograph.

It tells the story of America—a country of great dreams, a country of opportunity, with wide skies and winds that blow from Canada to Mexico.

Thanks to Dieringer and veterans like her, those winds have always blown on a free people.

William Weir

WILLIAM WEIR

"Effective leadership isn't a flavor-of-the-month."

Flashes from a Wednesday afternoon interview.

He sits at attention, his hands folded on an oversized desk that's in front of him.

But in a moment, Judge William Weir will lean back in his chair. It's time to relax, never mind that he's still at the office—well, in a judicial chamber, to be precise.

He crosses his legs, leaning back even more—as if we were settling in front of a television to watch an arts program.

There is a quiet confidence all around Weir, a longtime St. Charles resident and brigadier general in the Illinois Army National Guard.

"Do you mind telling me about your book?" Weir asks. "How many veterans have you profiled?"

The words are precise. Weir doesn't toss them like confetti, but carefully plunks each one down as if it were a chess piece.

He leans forward, waiting for an answer.

He gets it in short order. Then, seemingly satisfied by the response, we move on to the laundry list of questions that was prepared in advance.

Military rank and judicial standing aside, Weir comes

across as a really good guy. The conversation turns to baseball. His father, William F. Weir, was a professional pitcher for the Boston Braves in the 1930s.

One of the DiMaggio brothers played in the outfield for that team.

And Al Lopez, who later managed the Chicago White Sox to more than 800 victories, was Weir's catcher.

Talking baseball with the general is a reminder of backyard discussions during an earlier time.

William H. Weir is a fan. Our opinions run the gamut. And like others who enjoy the game, loyalties of the heart mean more to us than the economics of the wallet.

With diehard baseball fans, the bottom line is never the top priority.

One minute, the talk is of Barry Bonds and Sammy Sosa. The next breath brings Sandy Koufax into the mix. We decide that the lefty's legacy is secure. He remains the most poetic pitcher in baseball history, delivering strike after strike in a smooth, seamless style. There were no hitches or glitches in his high leg kick.

Weir's father was a lefthander, too. His yearly numbers never approached Cooperstown quality, but he played four seasons among the very best, including Babe Ruth, who ended his career with the Boston Braves in 1935.

The elder Weir played until 1939. He had six career victories, four losses and a respectable 3.55 earned run average.

"After baseball, my dad enlisted in the military," Weir says. "He was a World War II veteran. He saw action at Omaha Beach."

Weir's family has a rich history, which can be traced to Ethan Allen, an officer in the Revolutionary War and leader of the Green Mountain Boys, so named in defiance of the British threat to drive Vermont settlers off the fields and "into the Green Mountains."

It was Allen, along with Colonel Benedict Arnold, who helped the Americans capture Fort Ticonderoga in 1775.

"My grandmother was an Allen," said Weir, who went to Vietnam as a second lieutenant in the Marine Corps.

He had enlisted at a particularly precarious time. Others his age avoided serving America. Many became expatriates, finding haven elsewhere, notably in Canada and Sweden.

"I had an aversion to the whole hippie movement," Weir said. "While they certainly had every right to protest our involvement in Vietnam, I had a problem with watching them burn our American flag."

Weir's mother, having served in the military during World War II, most assuredly agreed with her son.

"Mom was a WAC," Weir says, referring to the acronym for Women's Army Corps. "Our family has a strong military connection."

Family is important to Weir, who was married in December 1969, just four months before he went to Vietnam.

Marilyn Weir recently retired as a schoolteacher.

"She's a marvelous woman," Weir said of his wife, whose parents are lifelong Aurora residents. "Looking back, we really didn't settle in as a married couple until after Vietnam."

Weir was a platoon commander, First Marine Division.

"As a group, we were pretty much seven and eight days out in the bush," Weir said. "From a strategic point of view, we had the defensive perimeter around Da Nang Airbase, which was being used to pound Hanoi and Haiphong. It was critical that we maintain our runway. We did it by establishing a series of fire support bases."

Weir also led a Marine offensive in Vietnam, part of a

larger overall campaign.

"Those young Marines—they were simply magnificent," Weir said. "It was a great honor to serve with them."

His decorations include the Legion of Merit, the Vietnam Service Medal, Republic of Vietnam Service Medal, Vietnam Civil Action Ribbon and Vietnamese Cross of Gallantry.

When Weir went to Vietnam, he believed in what the U.S. was trying to do.

"But bottom line, we were never going to win the hearts and minds of the people there," he says, thinking back more than thirty years. "We never lost a major engagement in Vietnam, but at the end, enemy forces were there, we weren't."

How did that happen? And could it happen again?

"It's something we need to be mindful of today in Iraq," Weir said. "Here in the United States, the military, the government and the people form a holy trinity. When you lose support of the citizenry, then any administration that tries to prosecute a war will be doomed to failure. I don't think we're there yet in Iraq, but it is problematic."

Weir went to law school after serving in Vietnam, graduating from John Marshall in 1977.

"My mother and father always valued education," Weir said. "Back in college at Eastern Illinois University, I might not have been the smartest student, but I was very determined."

Weir was born on the East Coast. His father's company regularly transferred executive employees.

When Weir was in high school, the family moved to Arlington Heights.

He graduated from Prospect High School in 1965.

He met Marilyn Fowler in college.

Weir loved her not only for what she was, but for what

he was when the two were together.

"She was drop-dead gorgeous—real smart, too," Weir said, smiling. "Being with Marilyn made me a better person."

They have been married for more than thirty years.

William and Marilyn Weir have one child, a son.

William Bradley Weir, 28, is a doctor. He also is a captain in the Medical Corps. Although he's doing his residency in Indianapolis, his unit has been called to Afghanistan.

Residency or not, Weir's son might end up getting called, too.

If so, he'll go without reservation, his father said.

"I like to tell Brad—and this is absolutely true—that it takes more schooling to become a general than it does to become a doctor," Weir said, laughing.

He enlisted in the Illinois Army National Guard after his time in the Marines.

Weir moved up through the ranks, graduating from the U.S. Army War College in 1996. Four years later, he was promoted to brigadier general, receiving his nomination from President Bill Clinton.

He was assigned as the deputy commander, 35th Infantry Division (Mechanized).

Weir commands 12,000 men and women.

"My job is to assist the division commander in the formulation, development and implementation of all programs and policies in the 35th Infantry Division," Weir said.

During the week, he sits as an associate judge in the Sycamore Courthouse, where Weir serves Kane, Kendall and DeKalb counties.

Weir was elected to *Who's Who in American Law*. Until his appointment to the bench, he had been a partner with the law firm of Brittain and Ketcham in Elgin. His community commitment extends to a number of area agencies. He served on the board of directors of the Elgin YMCA and the Elgin Leadership Academy, as well as the Summit School for Special Children.

"I've always tried to stay involved, doing whatever I could for as many worthwhile organizations as possible," Weir said. "Service to community and country is a privilege, something I hold very dear."

Leadership is a privilege, too.

Weir was knighted in 2001 by Princess Elizabeth for his military and civic contributions.

He is part of the Knights Templar, formed in 1112 A.D. to protect pilgrims traveling from Europe to the Holy Lands (Jerusalem). Early monastic members took a vow of poverty, which was rare for knights. They also had to supply their own horse, armor and weapons.

The knighthood is indicative of Weir's leadership, as are his other accomplishments.

And great leaders move people. They ignite passion and inspire the best in others.

When media types speak of leadership, they often use words such as vision, strategy and authority. But the reality of being a good leader is sometimes much more primal than that, Weir says.

People are moved by emotion. In Weir's case, he places compassion at the top of his own leadership list.

"I care a great deal about my people," he says. "That concern is fundamental to good generalship."

While the image of an Army general conjures up an elegant uniform and an array of medals, effective leadership involves an ability to help people realize their full potential, which holds true in and out of the military, Weir says.

By all accounts, he looks for results, not salutes.

"Before you can be comfortable with others, you need to be comfortable with yourself," says Weir, a black belt martial arts instructor and a certified dive master with the Professional Association of Diving Instructors.

Perhaps in the military more than anywhere else, people need the cooperation of others to survive.

Good generalship doesn't exist in a vacuum, Weir said. It is not a solitary act. It demands the positive participation of all who serve.

There is a consensus of opinion among military authors that good generalship also incorporates character.

And almost to a man, American military leaders have historically emphasized the importance of character.

Based on the three-hour interview for this book, Weir is quite knowledgeable about the past.

History, he says, is often seen through the prism of biography.

Character comes up again and again.

To General Omar Bradley, who commanded the U.S. First Army in the Normandy landings and later served as head of the Veterans Administration, character meant "dependability, integrity, the characteristic of never knowingly doing anything wrong, that you would never cheat anyone, that you would give everybody a fair deal. Character is sort of an all-inclusive thing. If a man has character, everyone has confidence in him. Soldiers must have confidence in their leader."

General Mark Clark, commander in Italy in World War II, remarked about the qualities necessary for successful leadership: "I would put character at the top of the list. If you want to select an officer for your command, you want one who is confident of his abilities, who is loyal and who has got good character. It is the man of good character that I am going to seek out. There are a lot of people who know the 'smart' way of getting things done, but they also ride roughshod over people that they are supposed to be working with. I don't want that."

Who would?

"Character," said Lucian Truscott, a Corps and Army commander during World War II, "as we used to say when I was in elementary school, is what you are. Reputation is what others think you are ... The two do not always coincide ... I think character is the foundation of successful leadership."

To General Carl Spaatz, first chief of staff of the Air Force and air commander in Europe during World War II, character is having a strong will. "You can't be wishy-washy as a military leader. You must be able to size up the situation and make a decision. Indecisiveness is weakness of character. You must be able to have confidence in what a leader tells you."

General J. Lawton Collins, chief of staff of the Army during the Korean War, stated, "I would place character as the absolutely number one requirement in leadership. By character, I mean primarily integrity. A man whose superiors and, even more important, whose subordinates can depend upon that leader taking action based on honesty and judgment. If he does not base his actions on honor, he is worthless as a leader."

The personal meaning of character to General Albert Wedemeyer, the Army's senior general in China during World War II, was "an officer who stands up under fire, who has the courage to defend his convictions, not arrogantly, not stubbornly, but intelligently. Someone who does not believe he knows all the answers, who will listen to others with different experiences and different knowledge. It means a deep sense of loyalty. Unless an officer has character, nothing he can do can cause his men to love and respect him."

Character can be a combination of many things—personality, presence and clean living, to name only a few. Yet it's very difficult to describe character completely. Leaders come in all shapes and sizes. In the military, temperaments vary from general to general.

It's hard to imagine two men who differed as much as General Eisenhower and General Patton, but both were tremendous leaders of mass armies. Both were men of great character.

Although less celebrated, so is Weir, who won't say so himself. Modesty, after all, is the clothing of talent. And it wears well on the general.

"I've always been honest and hardworking, but don't make me out to be an Einstein—I'm not," Weir says. "Even so, I'd like to think that I've made a difference for my country, which is the greatest on Earth. America means something special. It's another name for opportunity."

With the situation in Iraq at a critical point, America appears to be going through a difficult time in 2004.

Weir, who spent a year in Vietnam, has been down a similar road before.

Although talent develops in quiet places, character cannot. It needs the full current of human life; it needs the stormy billows of the world.

Weir didn't dream himself into character. He hammered and forged it out of experience.

More often than not, it's that way with leaders.

In his judicial chamber, Weir has a collection of military mementos, as well as items of personal inspiration. He likes a good quote, the best of which do not change in climate or currency.

Rudyard Kipling, who won the 1907 Nobel Prize in

literature, immortalized the importance of character in his writing of *If*, a poem of integrity, intelligence and inheritance, printed here in an abbreviated version:

If you can keep your head when all about you
Are losing theirs and blaming it on you;
If you can trust yourself when all men doubt you,
But make allowance for their doubting too;
If you can wait and not be tired by waiting,
Or being lied about, don't deal in lies,
Or being hated, don't give away to hating

And yet don't look too good nor talk too wise;
If you can dream—and not make dreams your master;
If you can think—and not make thoughts your aim,
If you can meet with triumph and disaster,
And treat those imposters just the same,

If you can make one heap of all your winnings
And risk it on one turn of pitch-and-toss,
And lose, and start again at your beginnings
And never breathe a word about your loss...
If you can talk with crowds and keep your virtue,
Or walk with kings nor lose the common touch,
If neither foes nor loving friends can hurt you,
If all men count with you, but none too much;
If you can fill the unforgiving minute
With sixty seconds worth of distance run,
Yours is the Earth and everything that's in it,
And—which is more—you'll be a man my son!

"American military personnel, when properly motivated and competently led, are the finest warriors on the face of the Earth," Weir said. "From Concord to

Baghdad, they never once let America down. They've always made us proud. They represent all that is best in this great nation of ours."

Richard Jung

RICHARD JUNG

"The war wasn't fought only on the battlefield."

When the 21-year-old rural resident went to enlist in the Army, he knew quite a bit about life on the farm, but practically nothing about Vietnam.

Richard Jung grew up in a quiet McHenry County community, not far from the Wisconsin border.

He moved to Lake in the Hills nearly forty years ago.

"Growing up, I was a pretty typical teenager—nothing too dramatic," Jung said. "I played high school sports, stuff like that. As for important issues, I saw things as either black or white. Almost everyone else did, too. You weren't really concerned with much beyond your friends, your car and what was happening Saturday night."

Jung found a job at an Antioch manufacturing plant.

"Work wasn't the greatest," he said. "And with all the talk about Vietnam, I figured it was the right time to enlist. If I didn't do it, I'd get drafted anyway. It seemed smart to get my military time over with, then try to find better employment when I got back."

Good guy-bad guy imagery inspired America.

Like soldiers before and after Vietnam, Jung was what his home, his school and his immediate world had hammered out.

He viewed military service as something honorable, if

not heroic. But as others of his generation discovered, fighting in Vietnam was a totally foreign experience. Men who found themselves humping through the bush never envisioned ending up there.

"I was really just a kid," Jung said. "I didn't know anything about Vietnam until I arrived there in 1965. Before that, you saw things on the news, but when you're that age, who pays attention to world affairs?"

Jung was in Vietnam for ten months. All but two weeks of his time there was spent in the jungle.

"Nightmarish," he whispers, thinking back to that era, which would become the central experience of his life. "It wasn't pretty. I saw the war up close. Civilians were killed, I'll tell you that right at the start. We did things I could never have imagined doing before the war. The Viet Cong did things, too. And after awhile, you started really, really hating them. You killed out of anger, especially after seeing one of your buddies blown apart. The enemy used booby traps, all types of dirty tricks—like land mines made from our own artillery."

Of all the types of mines encountered, Jung said that the "Bouncing Betty" was probably the most feared. The nature and locality of the wounds were what raised apprehension among American troops.

To make a Bouncing Betty, the Viet Cong scavenged American explosive material or fabricated their own, often using U.S. flare canisters. When detonated, a small charge or spring would toss the tube upward to waist height. It would blow up instantaneously.

"I saw some guys cut in half," Jung said. "Others lost their genitals."

While there's virtually no way to determine how many American casualties resulted from unexploded U.S. shells, statistics show that about eight hundred tons of reusable ordnance was available to the North Vietnamese and Viet

Cong each month.

For the most part, other than the remote areas of the Central Highlands, booby traps were almost everywhere in Vietnam. Some sections of the Demilitarized Zone also were free of the deadly devices.

Jung remembers that extreme caution was needed near village entrances and gates, which could be booby-trapped to explode on opening.

At the same time, soldiers were told to be wary of openings to tunnels and around enemy supply stashes— places where booby traps seemed particularly prevalent.

Other likely danger areas included clearings for helicopter landing zones.

Among the Viet Cong, the most common means of employing a hand grenade was to insert one inside an empty can—garbage left behind by American soldiers. The enemy would use the discarded can to hold the grenade's arming spool securely in place, pulling the pin and attaching a trip wire, which, when engaged, would trigger the fuse.

Hand grenades also were encased in mud balls with their pins removed. If a soldier stepped on or kicked the mud ball, what was inside would explode.

Souvenir items such as enemy flags were good indicators of a potential booby trap.

"Anything that looked out of the ordinary was suspicious," Jung said. "A cigarette package in the middle of nowhere, for instance. You wondered, 'How did that cigarette package get there?' Well, odds are, it was put there for a reason."

American soldiers were warned not to follow the same patterns or to frequent the same locations when establishing an evening perimeter.

One soldier went swimming in a little pond after a day of working road security. Just before sunset the next night, he dove into the same section of water. A punji pit—a thicket of sharp sticks—had been planted there. One of the sticks went right through his chest.

"You were always on guard," Jung said. "Sleep was a big, big problem the entire time I was in the jungle. When you did nod off, it was only because you were exhausted. On average, I slept about three hours a day. You were tired all the time, half-conscious some days."

Nights were spent on the ground. Soldiers doubled their knees into the fetal position, wrapping themselves in a poncho or a poncho liner.

In addition, evenings were damp or flooded, depending on the season. And no matter the time of year, mosquitoes rose in clouds to feed from the Americans.

Life in the infantry was neither glamorous nor gallant, not with mines, mosquitoes and many, many other things causing constant mental anguish, Jung said.

An estimated ninety-five percent of the mines and booby traps detected in Vietnam were antipersonnel devices, but vehicles also were at risk.

"The enemy came up with some really unusual booby traps," Jung said. "They'd use anything we left behind. Empty ration cans, batteries—you name it."

Jung sometimes wished he were Tarzan, swinging from vine to vine, above the ground and away from land mines.

"For obvious reasons and whenever possible, you walked in the footsteps of the guy in front of you," Jung said. "But you didn't get real close to him. If someone stepped on a mine, better one dead soldier than two."

Tension increased among American soldiers.

"It was a daily death thing," Jung said. "We were a million miles from home. And we were all young. You start seeing your buddies picked off one by one, you get angry. Anything that moves is a potential target. You wanted to pay people back—you wanted to get even with them for killing your friends."

Jung tried getting even with two small Vietnamese boys.

"We were actually in a truck convoy, which was a treat—you know, not having to walk," Jung said. "These children came to the side of the road. They had hand grenades ... threw them at us. Kids or not, we fired back."

Jung served with the First Infantry Division, the legendary Big Red One, which was constituted in May 1917 and saw significant action in World War I and World War II.

The Big Red One was the first infantry division to arrive in Vietnam, landing at Cam Ranh Bay and Vung Tau in July 1965. By the end of the year, the division had participated in three major operations: Hump, Bushmaster I and Bushmaster II.

In December 1965, the Big Red One defeated the Viet Cong at the Michelin Rubber Plantation, northwest of Lai Khe.

"It was surreal, seeing this massive plantation and magnificent marble home in the middle of the jungle," Jung said. "It was pretty obvious that big business had a stake in Vietnam."

Jung was wounded twice in Vietnam. Among other medals, he received two Purple Hearts and the Combat Infantryman Badge (CIB).

"I was just a survivor," he says, "The real heroes are the guys who didn't make it back."

Jung came home to a hostile America.

"When I arrived at the airport [Chicago's O'Hare International], a group of young people welcomed me back by spitting on my uniform," Jung said. "They kept calling me 'baby killer.' Having left Vietnam only a week earlier, it was a real culture shock."

Jung was married just before going to Vietnam.

Richard and Jan Jung have two children and two grandchildren.

The couple will soon celebrate their fortieth wedding anniversary.

"Jan stuck with me through the tough times," said Jung, who today talks easily about adjustment issues he faced after Vietnam.

That wasn't always the case.

"For years after the war, I'd wake up screaming, standing on the bed at 3 o'clock in the morning," Jung said. "And during the day, I was very short-tempered. I've lost count of all the bar fights ..."

And all the bad nights, too.

Fear started setting in as the sun dropped down. Nightmares came. Long-dead friends died over and over every evening. Memories of blood and burning flesh were a nightly ordeal.

The war within Jung raged for more than two decades.

What was once called Post-Vietnam Syndrome is now known as Post-Traumatic Stress Disorder.

Starting with his wife's intervention fifteen years ago, Jung learned that the only way out was through.

"I went to counseling, started talking to other Vietnam vets about the war," said Jung, who was a truck driver for more than thirty years, recently retiring from the Teamsters Union.

"Although I had a lot of trouble adjusting after Vietnam, I always held a job," Jung said. "Other guys weren't even able to do that."

In terms of readjusting after the war, what was so different about Vietnam?

To begin with, the average age of the men who served in World War II was twenty-six. In Vietnam, a twenty-six-year-old was considered an old man. The average age of those who saw service in Vietnam was nineteen.

Shared burden is another major difference. There was an esprit de corps during World War II. People from all social and economic classes served in the military.

Among many others, Ross S. Carter said so in the preface to *Those Devils in Baggy Pants,* his memoir of the 82nd Airborne in World War II:

> Every level of society had its representation among us. Senators' sons rubbed shoulders with ex-cowboys. Steel workers chummed up with tough guys from city slums. Farm boys ... white-collar men, factory workers, ex-convicts, jailbirds, and hoboes joined.

Furthermore, everyone at home was behind the war effort.

"In Vietnam, half the American people were out protesting in the streets," Jung said. "And the other half, they were out making money, going about their merry way while young guys died every night on TV."

Vietnam vets, Jung said, drew support from one another.

"It was like no one at home cared about us," he said. "But we cared about each other. You felt isolated—cynical, too. You lost faith in a lot of things, including America's leadership at home."

There were no defined goals in Southeast Asia. Conversely, in World War II, the overriding objective was to conquer the Axis countries before they conquered the United States.

In Vietnam, the goals were often political, not militarily obtainable. The perceived purposelessness of the war was felt through the ranks.

Rather than a war with a justifiable ideological basis, Vietnam became a private struggle for survival.

"That's how just about every American individual involved felt about the war," Jung said.

There were no clear-cut combat zones in Vietnam. In classic warfare, campaigns start at one physical point and end when an area of land has been conquered and cleared of enemy troops. Names such as Normandy, Iwo Jima and Guadalcanal resound from World War II. They are among names of places that the U.S. conquered.

Vietnam was fought on an entirely different basis. There were rules about where and when a soldier could shoot, for example. Americans might be dying, but company members sometimes had to check with divisional command to get clearance to fire at an enemy force—often made up of people who had been "friendly" earlier in the day.

"You could be sweeping a village where people were waving at you in the morning, then lose part of your squad to a booby trap there in the afternoon," Jung said. "That kind of stress is incredible. It comes back to haunt you. It makes you bitter, especially when you hear non-Vietnam vets telling you it wasn't a 'real war.' "

War changes the essence of a man. History shows that the atrocities of war are seldom committed by abnormal men. Perhaps the real tragedy of war is that these horrors are committed by mainstream men in situations in which the ebb and flow of everyday life have departed and been replaced by a constant tide of fear, anger and death.

Because blood is everywhere, should soldiers still be judged by civilian rules? Distasteful or not, it's a question grounded in reality.

"We were in a lose-lose situation," Jung said. "Vietnam

burned some of the good things out of you. There's no nice way of saying it."

Despite that, Jung remains a patriot. He loves America. He knows that it is not merely a nation, but a nation of nations.

"We live in a diverse country," said Jung, a longtime member of the American Legion on Algonquin Road in Lake in the Hills. "It's important to keep the memory of Vietnam alive."

America is not a blanket—mass manufactured from one piece of unbroken cloth. It is a quilt, with many shapes, sizes, colors and cuts. And they are woven with a common thread.

As an area veteran, Jung has helped keep that thread tight.

Decades ago, a complex culture withstood the test of an unpopular war. And America remained secure.

For that, thank Jung and others like him.

Do it—do it now. Feeling appreciation and not expressing it is like wrapping a gift and not giving it.

Let an area veteran untie the ribbons.

It's an honor Jung deserves. It's an honor other veterans deserve, too.

Tom Greaves

TOM GREAVES

"We flew all of our low-level missions at night."

Memories can come as a dream—cause and effect nearly nonexistent.

Arranged two weeks in advance, our interview is held on a stormy afternoon.

We will get together at an advertising office, located alongside the Fox River in St. Charles.

It is a working day. And because of the weather, traffic along Illinois 31 is at a standstill. Automobile taillights look like cigarette embers.

After exchanging pleasantries, talk turns to 1972.

Three decades ago, he was a modern warrior, waiting to be hurled off an aircraft carrier.

The starboard bow catapult fired.

And in an instant, his jet bomber became a dark outline on its way to Vietnam.

A state-of-the-art airplane can climb quickly, its engines roaring into the blackness.

Adrenaline rushed through the naval aviator.

Tom Greaves grew up in Geneva. From June to November 1972, he flew ninety-two combat missions over Vietnam, piloting an A-6 Intruder off the USS Kitty Hawk, which was still operational in May 2004. Longer than three football fields, it is America's oldest active aircraft carrier.

Greaves was aboard the Kitty Hawk for half a year, often flying two missions daily.

"I had an entirely different view of the war than the guys who were fighting on the ground," said Greaves, now an Aurora resident. "I did my killing from thousands of feet in the air. There were no adjustment issues after Vietnam. As Navy pilots, we were treated extremely well. We were doing a job, flying our missions. And when we came home, we came home as a unit, with wives and town folk there to greet us … Infantrymen saw things at eye-level. To my thinking, those experiences would be impossible to forget."

After graduating from Geneva High School, Greaves went on to earn a bachelor's degree at Colorado State University.

He was a business major, never interested in aviation until his junior year in college.

"My dad was a B-17 bombardier during World War II," Greaves said. "He was with the 8th Air Force, but he never talked about it much."

As a boy, Greaves, who was born in 1947, regularly vacationed out west with his mother, father and older sister.

"It was a nice upbringing," Greaves said. "We were pretty comfortable."

Greaves' father was a buyer for a nationally known supermarket chain.

"After finishing high school, I wanted to get away from home—going to a Colorado college seemed like a good idea," Greaves said. "But flying for a living never even entered my mind. Three years later, a friend saw something about a private lesson aboard a Cessna. The advertisement said $5. We usually spent that much on beer in an afternoon."

Flying became a passion.

With the draft looming and college graduation at hand,

Greaves decided to enlist.

"With all the fighting in Vietnam, you knew something was going to happen," Greaves said, remembering how he felt about becoming eligible for the draft. "I enlisted in June 1969. By that time, I was intrigued with the flying thing. At any rate, walking through the student union hallway one day, there they were—the Navy, the Air Force, whomever else. I stopped at the first booth, which was the one offering Navy information. I took their test—didn't have to go any farther than that."

Today, Greaves flies for United Airlines.

Personally and professionally, he has logged an estimated 15,000 hours in the air.

"Guess that means I've been flying for a long, long time," Greaves said. "Retirement is getting close."

He is proud of his military background; proud of completing his naval training, which Greaves calls "demanding."

The forward-deployed focus of the Navy requires a great deal of emphasis on combat training—more so than that usually provided for flying units in the Army and Air Force. On average, naval aviators will spend half their time getting ready to fight and staying proficient. While naval aviators fly about the same number of hours every month as their Air Force counterparts, how and when they fly is vastly different. More of their flying highlights actual combat and tactical training. And there is an almost manic devotion to flight safety, requiring an extraordinary amount of study, practice and patience.

Generally speaking, among military experts in the United States, naval aviators remain a national treasure. They are, first of all, among America's frontline combatants.

Like their Marine brethren, when trouble starts

somewhere, naval aviators expect to be the first called.

"The Navy trains its crews hard," Greaves said. "The mental challenges involved in training are really rough."

In addition, flying on and off aircraft carriers lends itself to the establishment of a well-justified mystique. Naval aviators are an elite fighting force.

Sea service requires unique dedication and skill. Greaves, for instance, is blessed with exceptional eyesight and hand-eye coordination, which were pushed to the limit during stressful combat events.

By all accounts, the Fox Valley veteran also has that renowned "right stuff." There is an old saying among pilots that flying is not inherently dangerous, just very unforgiving.

Every time a naval aviator takes off from an aircraft carrier, there's the possibility that the way back home will change dramatically. A ship in hostile waters will often have to alter operations. Clearly, there is much more at stake than an airplane worth tens of millions of dollars. Mastering the stress and strain of such flying requires a special type of pilot.

Greaves said that naval aviators tend to isolate themselves from other branches of the service.

It's a lot like being part of a college fraternity, he said, referring to naval aviation.

And to succeed at it requires a cast-iron ego, lightning intellect and complete concentration.

Living in such a world can create larger-than-life personalities. Independence is valued, although not at the expense of anyone else.

To a certain extent, Vietnam changed naval aviation, especially early in the war. New jets were unreliable—their engines being both underpowered and prone to fires and explosions.

Aviation, always a dangerous profession, became truly deadly. Some Navy pilots began to take on a fatalistic attitude about the odds of surviving, which resulted in a "live for today" sensibility.

This fatalism grew as the war with North Vietnam heated up. Losses of naval aviators flying missions over Southeast Asia were staggering. American pilots faced enemy ground fire, surface-to-air missiles (SAMs) and opposing fighter aircraft.

Best-selling American author Tom Clancy called Vietnam an unwinnable war for naval aviators.

They were saddled by apparently absurd ROE (rules of engagement), as well as equally absurd regulations regarding targets, tactics and weapons use.

Secretary of State Robert S. McNamara and his crew of "whiz kids" devised what was a nonsensical situation, Clancy contends.

In one of the greatest blunders in an acknowledged era of military misfortune, they failed to listen to on-site commanders about how the air war should be fought. Instead, they tried to micromanage the war from a safe distance away.

According to Clancy, this strategy turned into one of the worst military fiascos in American history.

Although denied the means to victory, pilots on aircraft carriers flew daily from Yankee Station—U.S. code name for the operating area in the northern Tonkin Gulf—getting shot down, captured and killed in morale-numbing numbers.

And what was the mission of American aviators? Not to take effective military action that could lead to victory, but to deliver to the enemy "political messages" from American leaders in Washington who did not understand that the enemy had absolutely no interest in those very same messages.

"Our involvement in Vietnam became ridiculous," Greaves said. "We were there for one another, not for the government at home. Still, I wasn't about to run. I did my thing more for the love of flying than for any political agenda."

Greaves flew the A-6 Intruder on missions that targeted bridges, railroad yards, ammunition depots and suspected missile sites.

"It was a very good airplane," Greaves said of the Intruder, a two-seat, subsonic jet with a maximum speed of about 650 miles per hour.

The A signifies an attack airplane. Other letters are used for different designations on military aircraft. The F in F-18, for example, stands for fighter.

The Intruder's ceiling was set at 44,600 feet. Along with the pilot, a bombardier manned the A-6, which worked around the clock in Vietnam, conducting attacks with pinpoint accuracy unavailable through any other aircraft at the time.

With an almost snub-nosed appearance and the two crewmen sitting side by side in the cockpit, the Intruder lacked significant eye appeal. But its all-weather strike superiority and overall versatility made it a naval workhorse.

The Intruder could carry a lot of ordnance, both tonnage and variety, to the target. The aircraft was able to deliver twenty-eight 500-pound bombs, as well as air-to-air missiles, flares and an array of support bombs for almost any ground attack.

"The Intruder's capabilities really stuck out at night," Greaves said. "We had designated targets, and sometimes we flew as low as two hundred feet. If we couldn't find our designated target, we went to a 'target of opportunity,' which was any potential military objective. Our missions generally lasted about an hour and forty-five minutes."

Greaves dropped bombs in the Hanoi area, as well as at other targeted areas in North Vietnam.

"More often than not, I flew at night," Greaves said. "During the day, we'd sleep in a clean bunk aboard ship. Later on, we might get together and watch a movie. In the world of naval aviation, a lot of what we did was almost routine."

And a lot of it wasn't.

Taking off from an aircraft carrier, for example.

"It puts your eyeballs into the back of your head," Greaves said.

His Intruder was fired at on most missions. Greaves had to elude missiles. He had to maneuver around antiaircraft artillery.

Additional dangers also existed.

"There was an incident when we had one of our own bombs detonate early," Greaves said. "Shortly after release, there was a huge explosion behind the airplane. I surmised that it was a malfunction of the fusing."

It's also possible that the bomb might have been hit by ground fire immediately after release, which could cause an early explosion.

Either way, it could have been deadly.

All ordnance was hung externally on the Intruder, Greaves said.

A lot of American aviators went down due to bomb malfunctions in Vietnam.

Greaves made it through the war without a scratch.

Others in his squadron weren't as lucky.

One pilot evidently flew his aircraft into the ground, perhaps trying to avoid enemy fire.

313

The same thing almost happened to Greaves, who had looked over his shoulder at approaching antiaircraft artillery.

"Then, when I turned to face forward, the altimeter was going through two hundred feet on the way down," Greaves said. "A couple more seconds, it probably would have been too late for us to pull up."

Greaves has been a strong supporter of the Air Classics Museum headquartered at the Aurora Airport in Sugar Grove.

"The museum teaches kids an appreciation of the military and of aviation," Greaves said.

He has an adult daughter who lives in Colorado.

Greaves has worked at United Airlines for more than a decade, flying out of O'Hare International Airport. Before that, he flew for two other commercial carriers.

He captains a Boeing 737 for United.

Greaves says that he has no regrets about killing other human beings in Vietnam—no matter that they died up close or at a distance, death cancels everything.

"When someone's shooting at you, it gets kind of personal," Greaves said, echoing a sentiment shared by other veterans profiled in this book. "We carried out our assignments. And when war is involved, people are going to die. Like it or not, that's just a fact of life."

War stories tend to emphasize peaks and valleys at the expense of the great level plain between them. Combat engenders extreme emotion, good and bad.

But battle is only one side of what went on in Vietnam.

Greaves' story reveals yet another facet of the American experience. No country can remain free if it acquiesces in what it knows to be wrong.

To be an ongoing success, government of the people must depend on the interest, intelligence and morality of the people themselves.

As Greaves gets up to leave the interview, we shake hands.

Given the tone of our meeting, it is an American gesture, locking together a unity of purpose.

Unity, however, does not necessarily mean uniformity.

In the United States, the endless echo of voices is the price people pay for the right to hear the music of their own opinions.

Decades ago, Greaves served to preserve and protect those opinions, which, when heard together, strike up a joyful noise—the sound of America.

Souphanh Rattana

SOUPHANH RATTANA

"Here in America, dreams can come true."

It is his family's flag—ownership of which is seen by both the dawn's early light and twilight's last gleaming.

Those broad stripes and bright stars belong to them, just as they belong to those who have been in the United States for generations.

America means more than good geography. It is based on unity of freedom, not uniformity of opinion.

One heart, one hope, one flag flying from sea to shining sea—such sentiment requires eternal vigilance.

Souphanh "Pon" Rattana joined the U.S. Marines right out of high school, serving as a reservist until being activated for the Persian Gulf War in November 1990.

He was in the Middle East a month later, remaining there through April 1991. During that time, Rattana was promoted from private first class to lance corporal.

When he left the Marine Reserve in 1996, he was a sergeant.

He received an honorable discharge.

"I wanted to do something significant—something to pay back America," said Rattana, an Elgin resident who was born in Laos. The landlocked country is in the center of Southeast Asia.

Situated between Thailand and Vietnam, Laos is

predominantly agricultural, with farming accounting for more than 50 percent of the country's gross domestic product and 80 percent of its employment.

Laos became increasingly involved in the developments defining Vietnam in the 1960s and 1970s.

In addition, civil strife turned the Laotian landscape into a broad-based battle zone. The old order, under the reign of King Savang Vatthana, engaged incoming Communists, a guerilla-led movement that became known as the Pathet Lao, which translates to "Lao Nation."

The Pathet Lao received support from North Vietnam.

Rattana's father was a police captain, a married man with two young sons.

He was part of the established government, making him a potential target for the Communists.

"Everything seemed set, then everything crumbled," said Rattana, who was five years old when the Communist regime gained control of Laos in 1975.

By that time, the Laotian people were on intimate terms with warfare.

North Vietnam had succeeded in turning the entire terrain of Southeast Asia into a battleground.

As early as 1963, North Vietnam had expanded the Ho Chi Minh Trail through eastern Laos and garrisoned it with support troops.

The U.S. began bombing Communist-controlled areas in Laos.

Some said it was a "secret war," violating the terms of a 1962 Geneva agreement. Questions arose about so-called clandestine involvement inside Laotian airspace. American airmen killed or captured in Laos, for example, were often officially listed as lost in "Southeast Asia."

Clandestine or not, by the early 1970s, U.S. aircraft had dropped nearly 2.1 million tons of bombs on

Laos—which is slightly smaller than the state of Oregon—nearly equaling the total tonnage dropped by American air forces during all of World War II in both the European and Pacific theaters. Most of the bombs were dropped on the Ho Chi Minh Trail, which had grown into a major transportation route for the North Vietnamese.

Meanwhile, political revolution was tearing Laos apart. Rattana's father fled to Thailand.

"My father knew that they would be looking for him," said Rattana, referring to the incoming Communists. "He had to leave us behind temporarily. If we would have all gone together, others in the government might have known what we were planning. We wouldn't have made it out of Laos."

To a certain extent, the ruling right-wing party was trying to keep control of a deteriorating situation.

Rattana's father made it to Thailand, leaving his hometown, Vientiane—an administrative city with an estimated population of 550,000 people today. It was considerably less than that thirty years ago.

Vientiane is about forty miles from the Thai border.

"One evening, after we were asleep, my mother woke us up," Rattana said. "My brother and I were very quiet. She said we were going to meet my father. We could only take a few things, mostly the clothes on our backs. We walked to Thailand. I don't remember a lot about that event, but I do know that we stopped several times."

Laotian police were out looking for them, apparently wanting to force Rattana's father back to Vientiane.

Rattana's mother moved her children along an underground railroad of sorts. Sympathizers hid them during the day. They walked at night, finally finding the head of their family.

"I guess it took two or three days for us to reach him in

Thailand," Rattana said.

The family lived there for nearly a year, staying together in a refugee camp.

"I don't remember much about it," Rattana said. "When you're just a little kid, almost anyplace you can run around is fine. But I know that leaving Laos was very hard on my mother and father."

Before coming to Elgin in 1985, the Rattana family first found a home in Virginia.

"In getting to the United States, we were sponsored by a Christian family," said Rattana, who is a Buddhist, as are most Laotians. The Communist country relaxed religious controls more than a decade ago—a gesture of recognition to the majority of its remaining citizens.

The Rattana family stayed in Virginia for less than a year. An aunt and uncle had settled there earlier, making the transition to the U.S. somewhat easier.

Still, there were difficulties.

Rattana's father found work in a factory—far from the prestige he enjoyed as a government official in Laos.

"My mother worked at the same place," Rattana said. "In trying to make ends meet, she and my dad didn't have much time together."

At home in Laos, his mother had taught classical dance.

"My parents sacrificed everything for their family," Rattana said. "They truly embody the American dream."

By 1979, they had moved to Hanover Park in search of better employment opportunities, as well as to be included in the growing Laotian population in Chicago's northwest suburbs.

Rattana's parents had a third son, their first and only child born in the United States.

Family faces are magic mirrors. When caring parents look at their children, they have an opportunity to see the past, present and future.

Rattana's father found a job as a forklift operator at U.S. Can, where he has been for more than two decades. At this writing, retirement is just around the corner.

Rattana's mother stayed home with the children.

The three boys attended area schools. Their English is impeccable.

"I was a little bit of a geek growing up," Rattana said. "I played violin in middle school. I also played in the high school orchestra."

Excuse the colloquialism, but there is nothing geeky about being a Marine.

He enlisted in the Marine Reserve after graduating from Elgin High School in 1989, just four years after the Rattana family members became American citizens, something bestowed upon all of them at the same time.

"Coming out of high school, I wasn't sure about things—what I wanted to do with my life, for example," Rattana said. "But no matter my choice, I was sure about honoring the personal commitment I made to this great country of ours. America took us in. That meant everything to my mother and father. They didn't want their children growing up in a Communist country."

Freedom provides oxygen to the soul. It is the breath of life worldwide.

Even so, it's easy to take freedom for granted when you've never had it taken away from you, Rattana said.

American freedom is backed by the Bill of Rights, an acclaimed document as clear as anything this side of the Ten Commandments.

In the United States, people have the right to be wrong.

"One of the reasons I enlisted in the reserves was that I wanted money for college," Rattana said. "Later on, I found out that college really wasn't for me."

He had enrolled in general studies courses at the University of Illinois Chicago.

The reserves required Rattana go through basic training, then give the Marines one weekend a month and two weeks every summer.

On the night that he was called to active duty, Rattana was home eating dinner with his parents. He was surprised by the telephone call.

Kuwait had been invaded by Iraq.

To say that his mother and father were nervous would be an understatement, Rattana said.

He would soon be on an airplane heading for the desert of Saudi Arabia, which had little love for Iraq's leader, Saddam Hussein.

Saudi leaders feared that their country could be Iraq's next target.

Desert Shield preceded Desert Storm.

Rattana's reserve unit was sent to the Middle East to provide support for the Marine Corps. Among other things, they worked as carpenters, construction laborers and electricians, setting up camp not far from a strategic Saudi city.

The work was exhausting.

Rattana was with the 8th Engineers, attached to the 2nd Marine Division.

U.S. President George H. Bush had drawn a line in the sand, sending the 82nd Airborne Division into Saudi Arabia. Further aggression would not be tolerated. What's more, Saddam Hussein did not belong in Kuwait and would not be allowed to stay there.

Rattana was part of the third invasion wave, which pushed enemy troops back toward the center of their country. He operated what was called a "Ninja" bulldozer. It was used in tearing down sand berms built by Saddam

Hussein's forces as a defense perimeter in the event of a ground attack against Iraq.

Rattana's job put him atop the specially designed dozer, which was reinforced to withstand mine explosions.

"Along with knocking down the berms, which were much smaller than we expected, we were assigned to remove mines hidden in the sand," Rattana said. "The closest call I had was when one exploded about fifty feet from me. No one was hurt."

About twenty miles away, oil fires blazed on the horizon. They had been set by fleeing Iraqi troops.

North of Kuwait City at a place called Mutla Ridge, a caravan of death twisted into the desert. What was a chunk of the Iraqi army was now a cemetery of burned-out tanks and trucks. In some of the trapped vehicles, motors still idled. Others contained corpses of Iraqi soldiers, burned beyond recognition at their steering wheels as they tried to escape from American bombers and attack helicopters. The scene reminded one journalist of a latter-day Pompeii.

Saddam Hussein's army was in tatters as it fled Kuwait.

Almost all international fingers pointed at the Iraqi dictator, blaming him for the slaughter of his own army.

Some said that the Persian Gulf War was a descent into madness. Saddam Hussein had his Iraqi troops invade Kuwait, a much smaller neighboring country.

Beginning on August 2, 1990, more than 100,000 Iraqi troops took control of Kuwait's capital, Kuwait City, seized the country's rich oil fields and forced the Kuwaiti royal family into exile.

The Kuwaitis, taken by surprise, never had a chance. The Iraqis seized control of government buildings, the international airport, the central bank and the royal palace.

Saddam Hussein's explanation for what he had done changed from day to day. First he said that the Kuwaiti people had risen up against their rulers. Then he said his army would withdraw once a new Kuwaiti government had been installed. Finally, he annexed their land. Kuwait, he argued, had been carved out of what should have been Iraq by British colonists and should never have existed in the first place. From now on, he said, the country that used to be Kuwait would be the nineteenth province of Iraq. It would stay that way forever. If not, it would be turned into a "graveyard."

Saddam Hussein also claimed that the pretext to the attack on Kuwait was its "aggression" against Iraq. Baghdad charged, for example, that Kuwait wanted to destroy the Iraqi economy by flooding the oil market and driving prices down. This, according to the Iraqi dictator, was part of a conspiracy with the United States and Zionism intended to undermine Iraq's military program.

For several months, heads of state and diplomats from a host of countries tried to persuade Saddam Hussein to remove his troops from Kuwait. His continued refusals eventually convinced the United States and the United Nations to use military force against the invading Iraqi army.

The war that ensued was short and decisive. In January 1991, Saddam Hussein heard the thunder of Desert Storm. His army felt the lightning.

The U.S. military and additional U.N.-sponsored forces destroyed Iraq's industrial and war-making facilities, crushed the Iraqi army and liberated Kuwait in just forty-three days.

The Gulf War was significant for many reasons. In the U.S., the military success sparked feelings of pride and confidence among Americans.

Some said that the ghosts of Vietnam had finally faded away. They would appear again the next decade, however, with America's involvement in another war against Iraq.

In addition, Desert Storm was the first instance in which Arab countries joined foreigners fighting other Arabs. A sense of optimism existed. Perhaps the Arab world's united hatred of Israel might ultimately give way to peaceful pockets of coexistence. In hindsight, that decade-old optimism vanished quickly, disappearing like the coin in a magic trick.

Saddam Hussein's army would rise again, although it would disappear again, too. Operation Iraqi Freedom would wind up bringing the dictator down in 2003. Nonetheless, in 2004, serious problems still exist in Iraq.

For Rattana, most memories of the Gulf War era are positive.

"I remember when we came home," he begins. "We landed at an airport on the East Coast. Walking through the terminal, people just started shaking our hands. Everyone was cheering."

Beyond that, he has saved all the letters sent from his then nine-year-old brother and the boy's classmates, who were Elgin elementary school students at the time.

Rattana received the letters while in the Middle East.

"It made you feel good, knowing people back home were behind the troops," Rattana said.

Other things weren't good at all.

While Rattana saw no combat action in the Gulf War, he did see the ravages of battle—an Iraqi soldier still seated in a Jeep with his head torn off; bloated corpses strewn along the roadside.

"They are what they are," Rattana said, referring to those images of war. "Still, you don't like to see such suffering, enemy or not. Even in victory, there wasn't a lot of hootin' and hollerin' going on."

Rattana remains appreciative of his home in the United States.

"My parents, my brothers ... we all love Elgin," he said. "The Laotian community here is strong. We're all extremely supportive of America."

Rattana said he still mists up when he hears the national anthem.

He walked to freedom as a boy. Today, he walks a daily mail route.

"I'm a letter carrier for the Post Office right here in Elgin," Rattana said. "I really enjoy my job, the people I work with and the people I meet out on the street."

Rattana is an active member of American Legion Post 57, located on Elgin's East Side.

Among other positions he has held there, Rattana is a past post commander.

When the older of Rattana's two younger brothers was married, he held his wedding reception in the legion's banquet hall. It was a traditional Laotian Buddhist ceremony with more than two hundred guests.

"I guess my day will come—you know, the whole marriage thing," said Rattana, who was still single at this writing in 2004.

The Laotian Buddhist ceremony certainly celebrated America, a country that allows diversity.

America's fate is to remain one, yet many.

In light of their coming to America, the Rattana family honors the plurality of the United States, which gains strength through diversity.

And if this country can stay strong in the future, that diversity must retain the clarity of a pioneer axe.

Throughout America's history, there never have been two opinions exactly alike—no more than two hairs, two fingerprints or two grains of sand.

Diversity is a universal American quality.

It's what Rattana defended during Desert Storm.

It's what many have died for, both before and after the Gulf War.

Trudy Hall

TRUDY HALL

"We were part of a total team effort."

Frailty thy name is woman?

Sorry Shakespeare, you're a bit behind the times.

That said, it remains a startling photograph—at least to a male writer who was born in the 1950s.

The U.S. soldier stands in full battle gear, an M-16 slung across a strong shoulder. And what's so startling? Well, the enlistee is an attractive blonde, her hair tucked into an Army helmet.

Of the 540,000 Americans who served in Operation Desert Storm, nearly 41,000 were women—more than 7 percent of the U.S. forces in the theater.

It was the largest deployment of American military women in history. They did just about everything, serving on land, at sea, and in the air—everything except engage the enemy in face-to-face fighting. Yet even that dividing line was subject to the capriciousness of war.

Women piloted and crewed jet planes and helicopters across battle areas, refueled fighters in mid-air, serviced high-tech equipment on the ground and loaded laser-guided bombs onto the F-117 Nighthawk—a stealth attack airplane, also known as the Frisbee and the Wobblin' Goblin.

They directed Patriot missiles, drove trucks, and served

on naval repair and replenishment ships.

Fox Valley veteran Trudy Hall had an interesting assignment.

The Elburn resident repaired radios and telephones, mostly mobile units used to maintain command communications during Desert Storm.

She was rated an expert with her M-16.

Hall, who was born in 1968, enlisted in the U.S. Army at age twenty.

"I was looking for a career," said Hall, a Wisconsin native. "We had an Army recruiting station in our town, but that was it in terms of having a place to sign up for military service. Anyway, when I joined, no one expected we would be going to war—not that I would have changed my mind about enlisting. Personally, patriotism means a lot."

It's not just holding the flag, but making it the most moral in the world.

Women have helped accomplish that.

Even today, while women cannot take part in actual ground combat, commanders stopped trying to remove them from fighting areas during Desert Storm.

The changes did not come easily or without considerable controversy.

For females in the military during Desert Storm, the dangers associated with war were clear early on.

In February 1991, U.S. patrols found an abandoned American truck near the Saudi-Kuwaiti border. Two GIs were missing, one of them twenty-year-old Melissa Rathbun-Nealy of Michigan. She was later released along with other American POWs.

American women were helping defend a Saudi Arabia that treated its own women with what Westerners would call contempt, not allowing them to drive cars or even show their faces.

According to an Internet news site, thirteen American women died during the Gulf War, including Major Marie T. Rossi, an Army helicopter pilot. She was buried with full honors in Arlington National Cemetery.

Women were truly equal in death.

And they brought historic change to the American military.

"We don't need special treatment because of gender differences," Hall said. "Women are capable of doing quality work and are willing to accept the same risks as men."

Right or wrong, many Americans have held onto conventional notions about protecting women.

Before Desert Storm, for example, debate over women in combat raged through much of the 1980s. The Supreme Court upheld the military's right to exclude women from the draft largely because they were presumed unfit to serve in combat. But with little notice or fanfare in the early 1990s, female soldiers began performing roles that took them ever closer to danger areas once the fighting broke out.

During the administration of President Bill Clinton, Congress repealed laws that barred women from serving as members of combat aircraft and warship crews. The following year, Secretary of Defense Les Aspin repealed so-called "risk rules" restricting women from certain jobs if they were subject to hostile fire or capture.

Although the military still bars women from fighting per se, it no longer tries to keep them out of harm's way.

"Individual courage isn't an issue," Hall said. "In positions where women are as able as men, they should be given the exact same opportunities."

Hall was married in November 1998, three years after

leaving the military.

Craig and Trudy Hall have no children.

"Craig and I are from the same small town in Wisconsin," Hall said. "We knew each other, but didn't date until I got out of the service."

Today, Trudy Hall maintains medical equipment, handling the electronic upkeep on X-ray machines, for example.

She has a degree from the DeVry Institute of Technology, which has locations in Chicago and the surrounding suburban area.

Degree or not, work has been a constant struggle, Hall said. She was wounded during Desert Storm, although not in a strictly traditional sense.

In the years since coming home, her health has been brutalized by Gulf War Syndrome, a medical condition of uncertain origin that affects many veterans of Desert Storm.

"No matter what has happened to me, I'm proud that I served my country in the Middle East," said Hall, who was there for five months. "In a very real sense, we were defending America against tyranny."

While the seeds of Saddam Hussein's dictatorial regime were never really harvested here in the United States, no one knew where the tyrannical taskmaster's aggression would stop.

One of the commonest expressions around is that America cannot be the world's policeman. But guess who gets called when someone suddenly needs a cop?

Hall was in Kuwait, Saudi Arabia and Iraq during Desert Storm.

"I wasn't shot at, but we were always aware of missile attacks," Hall said.

Early in the conflict, Saddam Hussein began firing his Soviet-made SS-1 missiles, nicknamed "Scuds," into Saudi

Arabia and Israel. Originally the Scuds, which carried a two-thousand-pound warhead, had a traveling distance of only 186 miles. The Iraqis managed to make improvements, which extended that range to nearly 500 miles. And those improvements made the missiles a threat to much more of the Middle East, including interior targets in Israel.

However, the Scuds were very inaccurate and often missed their intended targets by as much as several miles. While limiting their effectiveness as a military weapon, the inaccuracy gave the missiles more power as a terrorist tool. They created an overall atmosphere of tension and anxiety.

The United States and United Nations combined couldn't completely eliminate the Scud menace simply by bombing the missiles' launch pads. Many of the Scud launchers were mobile, carried from place to place on the backs of large trucks. Generally, the Iraqis were able to hide their launchers long enough to fire missiles, although American airpower caught up with a number of the traveling launch units.

In addition, the U.S. countered Scud attacks with an advanced Patriot air defense system. During Desert Storm, a Patriot station consisted of a mobile launcher equipped with four missiles and a radar trailer.

After a Scud was launched, the Patriot's radar system tracked the flight of the enemy missile.

A Patriot antimissile was fired. An advanced guidance system in the missile exchanged information with computers in the radar trailer, allowing the Patriot to zero in on the incoming Scud. As the two weapons neared each other, the Patriot exploded into a shower of metal fragments that destroyed the Scud.

Hall had been subject to Scud attacks while in the Middle East.

She also was exposed to various chemical pollutants, many of them probably undetected.

"Remember the oil fires?" she asks, not needing to wait for an answer. "We never knew what we were exposed to. It was always so sooty. Day was night. God only knows what that stuff did to us."

Starting in February 1991, Iraqi forces unleashed environmental terror by setting ablaze more than half of Kuwait's oil wells. The action provided an insight into Saddam Hussein's "terrorist deterrence."

Knowing defeat was imminent, the Iraqi initiative was called a "scorched earth" policy—the systematic destruction of those things that the enemy would find most valuable. Teams of Iraqi soldiers set fire to more than 600 of Kuwait's 950 oil wells. Thick columns of smoke and dust blotted out the sun, creating twilight at noon across much of Kuwait.

Hall had the requisite special suit and gas mask, but American military personnel were exposed to a variety of nasty substances, not all of them completely understood— then or now, more than a decade after the fact.

Furthermore, American military men and women eventually had to take their safety equipment off. No one knows what was lingering in the air.

In the 1980s, Western intelligence reports indicated that the Iraqis had amassed between two thousand and four thousand tons of chemical weapons. In an attempt to both cripple and terrorize the enemy, Saddam Hussein used poison gas against the Iranians in the Iran-Iraq War. He also used chemical weapons on the Kurds, Iraq's largest ethnic group, in northern Iraq to suppress Kurdish protests and rebellions.

In the fall of 1990, some Iraqi diplomats warned that Saddam Hussein would not hesitate to use the same weapons on Americans or other "foreign invaders."

U.S. commanders prepared for the worst, having issued

special protective gear to their troops.

Hall has serious health issues today. She says that they are a direct result of her time in the Middle East.

"I'm always tired, regardless of how much I sleep at night," she said. "My joints ache, I have nocturnal seizures and very bizarre lapses in memory."

Hall has been through several sleep studies. Some say she should be on permanent disability.

Medication hasn't helped much, if at all.

"My doctor has told me again and again that he doesn't want me working, but I certainly can't afford to go without a paycheck," Hall said. "If I were receiving war-related compensation, things would be better."

Hall's condition is frustrating. So is the lack of help she's getting from the government.

It took years for the military to stop brushing aside claims of illness from Desert Storm veterans. Not surprising, some say, adding that the medical condition is inexplicable.

Today, even though the U.S. Department of Veterans Affairs recognizes that the condition is serious, Hall's claim for injury compensation still hasn't been processed.

It's a claim she filed in 1996, as Hall's ever-worsening illness interfered with her job performance.

Although an eight-year wait for benefits would probably be inconceivable if she were dealing with a private insurer, Hall has plenty of company. Thousands of veterans like her have waited years, even decades, for VA benefits.

Some say they're fighting an apathetic bureaucracy.

"I never had any of these symptoms before the war," Hall said. "Why won't they believe me?"

Although there were limited combat casualties during Desert Storm, within months of returning from the war, military members began complaining of illnesses and symptoms, including those that Hall has.

Along with headaches, chronic fatigue and memory loss, symptoms include digestive disorders, rash, arm numbness and respiratory problems.

According to published reports, these symptoms are most common in Desert Storm veterans, but have been seen in every war in which the United States has participated.

Hall is on a waiting list for benefits, which needs to be approved by the Veterans Administration.

The VA spends $60 billion a year taking care of veterans and their families. Six million Americans receive monthly pension and disability or death compensation checks from the VA.

Just two years ago, in 2002, more than 4.5 million people were treated by VA health care centers, out of a total of 7.5 million people enrolled in the VA medical system.

There are various benefits and classifications of entitlement. The information could fill a book, but veterans are often unaware of what's available to them.

"When I got out of the Army, they didn't give you anything at all about applying for certain benefits," Hall said. "It wasn't really explained."

After serving their country honorably, some veterans feel a bit betrayed by the VA.

In terms of Desert Storm, some say that doctors treat the condition with only cursory consideration.

"Gulf War Syndrome is very real," Hall said.

Her condition is one of the newest members in a family of hard-to-figure illnesses. Quietly epidemic, long-running though not life-threatening, these ailments include chronic fatigue syndrome, fibromyalgia and multiple chemical sensitivity.

Veterans are diagnosed without conventional measures of a disease in their bodies. Objective findings are either lacking or inconclusive. Doctors determine that their patients are sick all right, but they more or less have to take the patients' word on the nature and degree of pain.

There's nothing more exasperating than being ill and having someone say you're not that sick, Hall said.

Whose fault is it when people lose their health for reasons that doctors don't understand?

The longer such group illnesses fester unresolved, the more they become politicized, lending to the patients both a growing sense of strength and a growing sense of being wronged.

It's a double-edged sword.

Hall just wants to feel better.

"What I'm going through today is much more difficult than basic military training," she said. "You just hope that there's some justice in the way we're treated."

In *Falcon's Cry: A Desert Storm Memoir*, Major Michael Donnelly, United States Air Force (Retired), describes the feeling of betrayal veterans experienced after the Gulf War:

> For despite the fact that over 110,000 Desert Storm veterans are sick—and despite all evidence pointing to U.S. troops having been dosed by low levels of Iraqi nerve agents and exposed to chemical weapons' fallout—the Pentagon adamantly denies any connection between their illnesses and their service in the Gulf War.

Hall's condition is an invading enemy. It has made its home in her body, turning it into an occupied zone. Gulf War Syndrome is a parasite on her health.

That said, she keeps going and going, rolling up her sleeves with all the vigor of a world-class cook confronting a brand new kitchen.

She is an active member at Batavia's Veterans of

Foreign Wars post, where she is chaplain.

Desert Storm forever changed the nature of warfare. By establishing early air superiority, then relying on a sophisticated system of weaponry, the United States was able to bring the war to the enemy before the enemy could launch anything other than a limited offensive.

But it wasn't just the nature of warfare that changed with Desert Storm. The very nature of fatalities and casualties changed, too. The enduring effects of the Gulf War, which was so lightning quick, are yet to be tallied.

Ultimately, only time will tell the truth. History has a way of weeding through the trivial, uprooting loose ends and irrelevancies.

For years and years, the Pentagon denied that Agent Orange caused cancer, birth defects and early deaths for thousands of Vietnam veterans.

Gulf War veterans converse on the Internet, telling one another their stories, talking about the health issues many of them face on a daily basis.

Their accounts can be found with the click of a mouse.

The American public, owing so much to Gulf War veterans, should pray that the mouse roars.

In keeping with what they did for America during Desert Storm, veterans deserve support from the very same citizens they fought for.

Salute those courageous men and women, heroes all, so that their suffering may not go unattended, so that their sacrifice will not have been in vain.

Hall has proven that she was ready, willing and able to accept the risks and responsibilities involved in defending a nation.

She has earned the right to be treated with respect.

In America, giving opens the way to receiving.

And as a veteran, Hall has given a great deal.

Now it's her turn to get something back.

Hall's story concludes with a passage from The Holy Bible, abbreviated from the King James Version:

A Prophecy About Babylon

An oracle concerning the Desert by the Sea:
Like whirlwinds sweeping through the southland,
An invader comes from the desert,
from a land of terror.

A dire vision has been shown to me:
the traitor betrays, the looter loots.

At this my body is racked with pain,
pangs seize me;
I am staggered by what I hear,
I am bewildered by what I see.
My heart falters,
fear makes me tremble;
the twilight I longed for has become a horror.

Isaiah 21:1-4

Richard Dunne

RICHARD DUNNE

"When that telephone call comes, you have to get going."

Welcome to the Ready Reserves.

Heroes reveal the promise of human nature. They are able to honor an entire generation and the glory of their times.

Heroes help make America a better place.

Military service can cast a spell. It is, in part, one of experience—of strange places, of unfamiliar responsibility, of excitement.

Of danger, too.

To understand the modern American reservist, readers must understand the tradition of citizen soldier, sailor, airmen and marine.

The use of a part-time military force to supplement a regular or full-time force is as least as old as the Middle Ages.

Yet, America's concept of what it is to be a reservist remains fairly unique.

"For me, the key is patriotism," said Richard Dunne, a longtime Elgin firefighter. "I think it's important to place yourself in the service of America."

At age eighteen, after graduating from a Chicago Catholic high school, Dunne joined the Illinois Air National Guard.

"I couldn't afford to go college on my own," Dunne said. "The reserves paid every penny of my college tuition."

Later this year, Dunne, a Chicago native who was born in 1961, will receive his bachelor's degree in fire science management.

"I picked up a couple of associate's degrees along the way," Dunne said. "It's been a long run."

His entire military career has been spent as a reservist.

Dunne married his childhood sweetheart.

"We were both involved in scouting," Dunne said. "Other than that, I was a pretty typical teenager—going to the high school football games, hanging out afterwards with the guys."

While he went to St. Patrick's High School in Chicago, Dunne was raised in Elmwood Park, immediately west of the city. He has been an Elgin firefighter for more than sixteen years.

Richard and Judy Dunne were married in 1984. They have three daughters.

"Judy has seen me through the ups and downs involved in each of my two careers," Dunne said, referring to being both a firefighter and a reservist. "It's my wife who took care of everything at home—our girls, all the household particulars. She is absolutely indispensable to our family."

When he first enlisted in the Illinois Air National Guard, Dunne was an electronic installation specialist—"a telephone lineman would probably be an easier way of putting it," he said. "I spent nine years with that unit. I loved it. I loved the guys."

Dunne always liked electronics. He scored well on the military aptitude test in that field, but his first career choice was firefighter.

But funding for college dictated his military choice.

"The Air Guard didn't have a fire department," Dunne

said. "The Air Force Reserve did, but the Guard paid better college benefits. I went with them."

Dunne went on to become the first firefighter in his family. He also is a licensed paramedic.

While not slighting the military, he has a passion for his primary profession.

"From the time I was a kid, I wanted to be a firefighter," Dunne said. "There are physical dangers and psychological pressures associated with the job, of course. But I truly believe it's what was intended for me. There's a camaraderie and deep loyalty in a good department, which we have here in Elgin."

Firefighters form a fraternity, Dunne said. He likens it to the military, where everybody, black, brown or white, wears the same uniform, all assembled for a common purpose—an armed forces fellowship, if you will.

"We've got great people in the Elgin Fire Department," Dunne said. "I've been around for quite awhile now. You spend so much time with other firefighters, everybody becomes like family."

Threaded through the life of a firefighter are inevitable tragedies. Dunne has been there. He has felt the blistering heat of a burning building. He has heard the crunch of broken glass at an automobile crash scene.

On New Year's Day about a decade ago, he was there when a mother and four young children died during a fire.

It's a hard, hard reality, yet there is some satisfaction in a job well done.

By its very nature, firefighting involves risks and rescues.

So does military service.

During Desert Storm, America went to rescue an entire nation.

On July 17, 1990, Saddam Hussein angrily accused

Kuwait and the United Arab Emirates of conspiring with the United States to cheat on oil production previously set by the Organization of Petroleum Exporting Countries (OPEC).

At the same time, evidence began accumulating about a large military buildup by Iraq on its disputed border with Kuwait. On July 24, and in response to its request, two U.S. aerial-refueling tankers were made available to the United Arab Emirates as a way to keep patrol aircraft aloft. It was a precautionary measure.

A short-notice U.S. naval exercise in the Persian Gulf was also announced.

In the early morning hours of August 2—the very day that President George H. Bush was to deliver an address in which he would discuss the broad outline of his proposal to restructure the armed forces—two Iraqi Republican Guard armored divisions attacked across the Kuwaiti frontier. Separate assaults were made against the palace of the Kuwaiti royal family and key government facilities by commando teams and a special operations force.

Dunne, like other reservists, had little reason to take particular note of those events, which were far away in desolate Arab countries.

How could that affect reservists personally?

Even when the president declared on August 5 that the invasion of Kuwait "will not stand," there was little apparent reason reservists needed to be anxious. After all, the U.S. was at peace and the large reductions in the number of career military professionals being called for by several members of Congress had not even been decided upon, much less taken place.

Furthermore, there was substantial precedent for the widespread belief that political leaders were more than a bit reluctant to turn to reservists in a time of crisis.

In the mid-1970s, however, military planners began to assign increasing responsibilities to National Guardsmen and reservists pursuant to the new "Total Force Policy" of the Department of Defense.

Dunne has more than twenty-four years as a reservist, including time in the Air National Guard and the Air Force Reserve.

When he switched from the first to the second in 1989, he was recruited into an air evacuation squadron, which specialized in treating and transporting wounded troops.

"Because I was already a paramedic, I was able to bypass tech school," Dunne said, referring to his assignment with the medical evacuation team. "But that didn't diminish my skill level."

Dunne has lived in Elgin since joining the fire department in October 1987.

"Before that, I spent two years as a volunteer firefighter," said Dunne, who was paid $8 an hour while working with a Chicago-area department. "You were regarded as an 'on-call' employee."

At the same time, Dunne was working at a paper plant.

"After getting married, I worked as a warehouseman," Dunne said. "The money was good, but it was just a job, nothing really more than that."

Dunne wanted a career.

He found one in Elgin.

"I think you should support the community that supports you," Dunne said. "I believe you should live in the city that you protect, even though firefighters aren't required to live in Elgin."

He has helped protect America, too.

How did Dunne get called to active duty?

He smiles, taking time to puff on a cigar. Words roll easily, like string from a big ball of twine.

"Well, that's an interesting story," he begins. "January of '91. We fought a fire on Fremont Street. It was in the basement. I made the basement with another firefighter. I came out of the fire and was sitting on the bumper of Engine 1. So, here comes one of the older guys. He tells me to start rolling up hoses, which I did. I only had about four years on the job, still the new guy, really. All of a sudden, I'm not feeling well."

Dunne and another firefighter went to the ambulance to get oxygen, fearing that they'd been exposed to a chemical agent in the basement fire.

"Our fire captain sent us to the hospital," Dunne said. "We started to argue, but he insisted."

Tests were taken at the hospital. While waiting for the results, Dunne received a telephone call.

"It was the Air Force Reserve," Dunne remembered. "My sergeant said, 'I've got to read something to you.' That's when I got called to active duty."

Dunne recalls the words, reciting them without hesitation:

"By order of the president of the United States, you are hereby ordered to a period of active duty for one year," Dunne says. "Anyway, I'm at Sherman Hospital sucking some oxygen when I got called to the Persian Gulf War. Not too many people can say that."

Dunne's wife was pregnant with their second child.

"When you're told to go, you go," said Dunne, who was in Saudi Arabia within days of being informed that he had been called to active duty.

"I was in the Middle East for only a short time—just a couple months," Dunne said. "I was lucky. There were guys from my unit who stayed significantly longer—until about September — nine months in all."

Dunne flew on only one assignment, which was a

strategic air evacuation mission to Germany.

There were nearly ninety wounded Americans on the flight—amputees and severe burn victims, among others.

It was not a typical day.

"The rest of the time I was on call, waiting in no-man's-land—waiting and waiting and waiting," said Dunne, who was stationed at King Khalid Military City (KKMC).

The military city is in the northeast corner of Saudi Arabia, just two hours from the Kuwait and Iraq borders.

The theater of operations for Desert Shield, which preceded Desert Storm, was Saudi Arabia, a country of 840,000 square miles, most of which is uninhabited desert. The environmental extremes are inhospitable to people and equipment, compounding the demands and difficulties of maintaining military operations.

Most of the area surrounding KKMC is not the stark but beautiful desert seen in *Lawrence of Arabia*, which featured windswept sand dunes and soft footing.

Instead, the hard, flat Saudi surface appeared to touch the horizon. Dunne remembers miles and miles of packed, pebble-strewn sand and dirt.

KKMC is in a religiously conservative area.

And that's saying something. Islam itself is a conservative religion.

"We were originally supposed to follow the 82nd Airborne and the 7th Corps," Dunne said. "They were to advance and stop. We'd deploy in after them."

The American fighting force moved faster than anyone expected, finding less resistance than anticipated.

"Our evacuation unit actually arrived before the ground war started," Dunne said. "But for all practical purposes, it was over before they needed us."

In planning for Desert Storm, military experts expected up to 240,000 American casualties—dead and wounded.

347

The Gulf War, however, was the first in which air power inflicted such a decisive defeat on a field army. By the time the land war began, which means by the time Allied soldiers were put in harm's way, the war was virtually over.

Although estimates vary, it seems sure that somewhere around 100,000 Iraqi soldiers in and around Kuwait were killed by Allied air attacks.

Coalition military deaths were estimated at 378 for the entire engagement.

U.S. forces suffered 148 battle-related and 145 non-battle-related deaths.

It is scarcely surprising that, once the land war started, large chunks of the Iraqi Army—perhaps most of it—simply decided not to shoot back.

Iraqi troops were tired and lacking in morale.

In spite of the overwhelming victory, many people in the United States said that the win was incomplete. The Allies had failed to remove Saddam Hussein from power, which would wait another decade.

Nonetheless, the Allies were so successful that they were in a position to dictate whatever cease-fire terms they wanted from the Iraqi strongman.

General Norman Schwarzkopf set up a meeting between Allied and Iraqi commanders. On March 3, 1991, a little less than six days after the fighting stopped, they met at a captured Iraqi airfield near the Iraqi-Kuwaiti border. The tent in which the meeting took place was surrounded by more than fifty tanks draped in U.S. and British flags.

General Schwarzkopf made an impressive entrance, arriving in a squadron of six Apache attack helicopters.

Two Iraqi generals appeared in open jeeps and entered the tent with Schwarzkopf and the commanders of the Saudi, British and French forces.

After the two-hour private meeting, Schwarzkopf said that there was agreement on all matters.

The most important term was the safe release of Allied prisoners. Within three days, the Iraqis released them to the Red Cross.

Terms also demanded that the Iraqis provide information about the location of their explosive land mines in Kuwait.

Dunne downplays his role in the Middle East, saying that he was ready but not really used.

"There was just that one mission to Germany," he says, referring to the air evacuation of wounded Americans.

Still, lives hung in the balance. Reservists played an important role in Desert Storm, providing support in any number of situational operations, including combat.

Dunne served as a medical technician on that one flight, augmenting the primary evacuation crew.

"I helped treat and care for ambulatory patients," Dunne said. "There are sixteen different things that can happen to a body on an airplane."

As an airplane goes up and down, air expands and contracts, for example.

"You treat patients differently in the air," Dunne said. "With air expanding and contracting, a person's esophagus can get torn out. There are also dehydration issues on an airplane."

Dunne goes on to list a half-dozen different changes the body experiences in flight, each one of them a potential problem for a wounded soldier.

Dunne received a Kuwaiti Liberation Medal for the time he spent in the Middle East.

"Entering military service is one of the most important decisions a person will ever make," Dunne said. "Personally and professionally, it has helped me a great deal. Being a reservist has been both challenging and rewarding. I've always tried to do my best for this great country of ours."

And in so doing, the Fox Valley veteran has become another area success story. He has risen to the rank of senior master sergeant in the Air Force Reserve.

In addition, Dunne is an active VFW member.

He is past post commander of VFW 1307 in Elgin.

Currently, Dunne is working with the Department of Homeland Security, having taken an approved leave of absence from the Elgin Fire Department.

He is doing administrative field work for FEMA, the Federal Emergency Management Agency, which is under the aegis of Homeland Security.

"That's one of the reasons why I can't comment much on the situation in Iraq today," Dunne said, referring to the ongoing Iraqi Freedom operation. "Everything would have to be approved."

His assignment with FEMA takes Dunne to fire departments around the Midwest.

He follows up on allocations made to local departments since September 11, 2001—a day that changed the world.

After a fire department in some small Midwestern town receives federal funding for emergency equipment, for example, it's Dunne's job to make sure that the money was used accordingly.

"The work has been very interesting," Dunne said. "As a firefighter, it's an opportunity to see what different departments are doing in terms of serving and protecting their individual communities."

And some of those things might benefit Elgin in the future.

"When appropriate, I'll certainly pass on what I've learned," Dunne said. "We already have an excellent fire department in Elgin, but you're always looking to get even better."

Reservists are looking to get even better, too.

Today's reserve force is a large modern organization that's critical to America's defense.

The National Guard can trace its history to 1636. That year, the General Court at Boston issued an order stating that all military men within the jurisdiction of the court were to be ranked in three regiments. Those Massachusetts units are among the oldest military groups in the world.

During the Revolutionary War, which began at Lexington and Concord on April 19, 1775, more than 164,000 militiamen from the thirteen colonies served under the command of the former Virginia colonel, George Washington. Without the militia, American independence could not have been won.

In America, the most important public office is that of private citizen.

While the Continental Army, with militia support, fought the main battles of the war, other militia regiments kept British forces in check by harassing and raiding—thus limiting the royal troops to the cities. Many of today's Army National Guard units carry battle streamers embroidered with the names of the battles of the Revolutionary War.

More than one million men and women make up today's reserve forces.

The image of today's National Guard began to emerge in 1903, when congressional legislation required that the government play a more active role in organizing, training and equipping the National Guard in line with standards established for the regular Army. The Guard's involvement in aviation began in 1911, when New York's First Company, Signal Corps, became the first National Guard unit to get a plane off the ground. Soon thereafter, Guardsmen in Missouri and California established flying units. But it was not until 1915 that the National Guard's first federally recognized aviation unit, the 1st Aero Company of New York, came into being. About a year later the new aviation unit was called to active duty.

The Guard was called into federal service in 1917 for World War I. At that time, more than 379,000 Guardsmen were ordered to active duty.

Illinois Guardsmen formed the 33rd Infantry Division in France.

Dunne understands that call to service.

He has answered it in the past. He is ready to go if called again in the future.

"America is an ideal," Dunne said. "And as a citizen of this country, it is my responsibility to defend that ideal."

It is his right, too.

Part of what makes America great is its belief in tomorrow.

America exists as a frontier, which is never just a place, but a way of life—found somewhere just over the horizon, somewhere around the next bend.

Dunne believes in the youth of today. He believes in the enduring character of this country, created out of inspiration, perpetuated by strength and sacrifice.

Here on Earth, God's work must truly be the work of the United States.

And American ideals will survive only if they are regularly replenished by the very faith that gave them birth.

Travis Cotner

TRAVIS COTNER

"We witnessed history."

It was a bombing campaign called "shock and awe."

Star Wars was waged on Planet Earth.

Operation Iraqi Freedom, which helped open the 21st century, was a push button event.

It ended Saddam Hussein's horrifying regime.

More than a decade earlier, Desert Storm had been a military masterpiece—electrifying ferocity in a one-sided scenario.

But Saddam Hussein had avoided international prosecution after that earlier event. What's more, by all accounts, he paid little if any attention to the coalition that certainly could have dethroned him. The Iraqi dictator didn't miss a beat, however, marching to his own diabolical drummer for another twelve years.

And through it all, he tried to satisfy his personal and territorial appetites. Saddam Hussein savored the feeding frenzy that powered his regime. He enjoyed eating with defiant impunity and a tyrannical taste for absolute power.

All that came crashing down during Iraqi Freedom, launched in March 2003.

Saddam Hussein heard an entirely different drumbeat.

Technological advances altered the rhyme and rhythm of war. Gone were most traditional combat concepts, replaced, for one, by supersmart bombs programmed weeks in advance. There was added explosive power packed in every one of them. These new and improved weapons were guided by special computer commands, which, in the future, might be directed from the White House basement.

But back to 2003.

Iraqi forces were overwhelmed again. No surprise, really. There was never anything especially efficient or effective about Saddam Hussein's military, except, that is, for an ability to kill its own people.

A coordinated ground invasion would follow the sophisticated Allied air attack on Iraq.

Travis Cotner, twenty-two years old at the time, arrived in Baghdad with the U.S. Marines in April 2003. He was attached to the First Regimental Combat Team.

"When we first entered Iraq, everyone thought that we'd finish things there in a few days," said Cotner, a lifelong Elgin resident who grew up on the city's far west side, which meant attending Burlington Central High School, from which he graduated in 1999.

Marine bravura aside, finishing up operations in Iraq would take longer than the few days Cotner originally anticipated.

He wasn't alone in his thinking.

Many thought that the war would be a mere cakewalk.

In the diary he kept while in Iraq, Cotner, who was trained as a radioman, tells the story of aggressive action against all who resisted. Others were treated with decency and respect.

"We were there to help liberate a country, not kick it around," Cotner said. "I conducted myself appropriately at all times—the way you're supposed to as a U.S. Marine. We have a proud tradition. When you fight, you fight to win. But there's room for compassion, too."

Cotner was in the southeast section of Baghdad.

"It wasn't too bad," he said. "We had snipers, of course, but the war wasn't as intense there as in other parts of the city."

History shows that every fighting force prefers a particular battle style. The North Koreans and Chinese employed massive infantry assaults, then settled into trench warfare. The Viet Cong were skillful with mines, booby traps and sappers—guerrillas who wriggled through the barbed wire of a perimeter at night, leaving behind a timed charge.

In Somalia, native tribes swarmed to battle with AK-47 assault rifles and rocket-propelled grenade launchers, commonly called RPGs. In the first Gulf War, the Iraqis had tried to employ armor equipment. They were not successful.

In Iraqi Freedom, Saddam Hussein had again equipped his military with artillery and tanks, which they abandoned at almost every road junction. Even the machine gun, a staple since World War I, was not used much.

The weapons the Iraqis consistently employed were the AK-47 and the RPG, armed with antipersonnel and antivehicle warheads.

First the military, then the insurgents, figured that an entire nation equipped with urban weapons could coerce an American withdrawal, as occurred in Mogadishu two years after Saddam Hussein's forces were chased out of Kuwait.

Cotner said that assault weapons were as common as flies in Baghdad. Dependable and easy to use, AK-47s and RPGs were ideal to dispense to the ill-trained Fedayeen, an Iraqi paramilitary force loyal to Saddam Hussein.

Formed in 1995 by Saddam Hussein's son, Uday, the Fedayeen had an operational strength estimated at about 40,000.

U.S. forces remain troubled by the Fedayeen, which

translates to "men of sacrifice." Some have been trained to carry out suicide attacks. During Iraqi Freedom, the paramilitary members proved far more successful than any unit of the Iraqi army.

"You didn't know who was who," Cotner said. "Someone wearing a black robe might wave at you. Another person dressed the same way starts shooting. On some street corners, people would be cheering and whistling, like we were part of a passing parade. You see a lot of billboards with Arabic advertising. In the working-class neighborhoods, things look old and shabby, but in the richer areas, there were nice two-story stucco houses. Trees and green shrubbery lined the streets."

Luxury automobiles might be hidden behind high walls. Judging by their material trappings, Saddam Hussein loyalists lived pretty well, Cotner said.

The Elgin native, who is unmarried, joined the Marine Corps three years prior to Iraqi Freedom, enlisting in March 2000.

"I wasn't much of a high school student," Cotner said. "I should have done better academically, but I goofed around a lot. Nothing that was against the law, just stupid stuff teenagers do. In joining the Marines, I was looking for a real challenge."

According to family and friends, the Marines made Cotner a responsible young adult.

He agrees.

"You learn that the team is more important than any one individual," Cotner said. "And any member of the team who won't cooperate becomes a liability. You can't have that, not if you want to be part of something special."

Allied forces were something special in Iraqi Freedom.

The U.S. Marines marched into Baghdad just three weeks after leaving Kuwait. They entered the Iraqi capital, then took possession of the palaces built by Saddam Hussein.

Hand in hand with that, they deployed into attack groups, forming firing lines and advancing against Iraqi strong points.

Although Cotner wasn't with the first invasion wave, he did get a close look at the gun and run approach of Iraqi forces.

Living through that experience is the making of a Fox Valley veteran.

And as is the case with other veterans of the Middle East operation, Cotner helped turn the page in Iraq's next chapter.

On April 9, 2003, Iraqis in Baghdad attacked the statue of Saddam Hussein in Firdos Square. They started with a sledgehammer and a rope.

Cotner was not there, but other U.S. Marines were. They decided to help out. A short time later, despite orders not to show the American flag, a Marine draped the deposed dictator's face with the Stars and Stripes. It's an image the Arab media focused on. The flag was replaced with a pre-Gulf War Iraqi flag, then the statue was toppled.

So was Saddam Hussein's evil reign. He went into hiding, only to be captured eight months later.

After toppling Saddam's statue, frenzied Iraqis stomped on it, then rode the detached head through the streets.

"I'll never forget the sights and sounds of Baghdad," Cotner said. "It was good getting home, but what we did in Iraq—going in and helping remove Saddam Hussein—that was worth more than I could ever put into words."

Cotner completed his active duty with the Marines in March 2004.

"Right now, I'm trying to find a job as an electrician or as a pipe fitter—something in the trades," he said in June

2004. "I need training, but hard work won't slow me down. I'm not afraid to get my hands dirty."

Blue collar, white collar—there are no menial jobs, only menial attitudes.

And there's nothing negative about Cotner, who was born in April 1981.

"Yeah, I try to stay upbeat," he said, smiling.

In Iraq, he managed to stay alive.

"My mom and dad were worried, just like all military parents," Cotner said. "There weren't any casualties in our unit. I'm really grateful for that."

Early on in Iraqi Freedom, there was a separate sort of danger at home in America. The war was brought into the nation's living rooms in real time. Never before had U.S. citizens seen and heard frontline correspondents providing play-by-play reports on an almost nonstop basis. While they detailed events on-air, artillery blasted and small arms fire rattled in the background.

War has been broadcast before, of course, with Vietnam and the first Gulf War being obvious examples. But with the increase of cable coverage by 2003, Americans were provided round-the-clock chronicles on Iraqi Freedom. Reporting was unprecedented, with unedited material reaching the small screen. Those images went worldwide.

That said, danger lay in the depersonalization of a war which, when delivered at a distance, looks less real than a video game.

Cotner, who has one older brother, came to know the faces of war.

"You really, really hated it when innocent civilians got hurt, especially children," he said. "I remember these two boys—brothers, about grade school age—who were caught between Iraqi forces and our Marine unit. They, the two kids, were wounded, but both survived. You never forget seeing such pain. And their crying ... it could break your heart."

People need to pay attention to the faces of war; otherwise the horrors get lost.

They are remembered whenever humanity shines through.

"Not that it's up to me, but I fully approve of what we're doing in Iraq," Cotner said. "Even with all the trouble today, you always support the troops. They're there for us. They're there to do what's right. Rebuilding a country takes time. It costs so much."

It costs much more than money, Cotner said.

It cost lives, which is the ultimate price people pay for liberty.

In the truest sense of the word, liberty cannot be bestowed, it must be achieved.

And wasn't that America's motivation in Iraqi Freedom?

America wanted to help an oppressed people, giving them an opportunity to share in the promise of liberty, to start earning it in this new millennium.

And what about weapons of mass destruction? The notorious WMDs. The search supposedly continues. If the weapons don't exist, who would say that Iraq isn't better off without Saddam Hussein anyway?

For all practical purposes, even if Iraq's WMD capability had been voluntarily wiped away before the 2003 invasion, history still shows Saddam Hussein developed and used weapons of mass destruction on a scale that was without parallel. He employed chemical weapons at least ten times from 1983 to 1988, for example, killing thousands upon thousands of Iranians and Kurds, his own people.

Although Iraq never possessed nuclear weapons, it

wasn't for lack of effort. By the 1980s, the country's nuclear program had progressed to the point that it threatened the security of Israel.

The Israelis weren't waiting for the sky to drop down on them. They didn't need an eye-opening revelation. On June 7, 1981, they launched an air attack against Iraq's nuclear reactor and research facilities at Osirak.

The mission was a success, sending Iraq's nuclear weapons program so far back that Saddam started turning to chemical and biological agents instead. However, during the Iran/Iraq War—which began in 1980 and ended in 1988—the Iraqis returned to their nuclear initiative. They wanted to develop a twenty-kiloton nuclear weapon, which would be comparable in power to the American bombs dropped on Hiroshima and Nagasaki in 1945.

After the first Gulf War in 1991, the Iraqi nuclear program was set back again. Although Allied operations were successful, they were never enough to put "paid in full" on Iraq's nuclear receipt. On several occasions, Saddam Hussein's underlings were caught red-handed trying to buy forbidden items such as aluminum tubing, used in the development of super-modern weapons.

The so-called Butcher of Baghdad earned his reputation early on. According to published reports, on July 18, 1979, just five days into his new presidency, Saddam Hussein ordered a meeting of over three hundred Baath Party senior officials.

The Baath Party was founded in Syria in resistance to centuries of occupation of Arab lands, first by the Ottoman Empire, then by the British and French.

Saddam Hussein became a junior member of the fledgling party in 1957.

A decade later, the Baath Party gained control of Iraq. Saddam Hussein became one of the regime's top enforcers, a strong, strapping bully who eventually emerged as an effective number two to President Ahmed Hassan al-Bakr.

When the president stepped down, he handed power over to Saddam Hussein, whose name means "the one who confronts."

That's just what he did at the Baath Party meeting in July 1979. The new president presided over an Iraqi inquisition, taking those in attendance by surprise.

Wearing his military uniform and puffing on a Cuban cigar, Saddam Hussein, who was a sturdy six feet two inches in height, listened as one of his henchmen announced the discovery of "a painful and atrocious" plot to overthrow the Baath regime and its new leader.

Saddam Hussein stepped to the rostrum, revealing details and inviting the plot's alleged instigator, Muhyi Abd al-Hussein Mashhadi—who had just emerged from a grim and grotesque visit to one of the Baathist torture chambers—to reveal further details. Promised his life, Mashhadi confirmed all.

Some sixty party leaders were taken away to be killed as Saddam Hussein videotaped the arrests. He was now in complete control of Iraq. In a final grand gesture, indicating the new regime's demonic direction, the dictator demanded that unindicted delegates volunteer to serve on the firing squads.

Mashhadi himself would be shot, regardless of his confirming testimony and promises made by Saddam Hussein.

"The world will be a safer place without Saddam," said President George W. Bush years later.

Cotner, the area Marine trying to start out in the work world at age twenty-three, would agree.

So would most Americans, including those opposed to U.S. involvement in Iraq, which continues through June 2004, when this profile was written.

Shannon Sterk

SHANNON STERK

"You were worn out at the end of every day."

Smoke over Baghdad became a familiar sight.

War was on.

"At night, the entire sky looked like some strange painting," said Shannon Sterk, an Elgin resident who was part of Operation Iraqi Freedom. "I never got real close to the fighting, but we were able to see almost everything from our base."

Baghdad burned as coalition forces pounded their targets, the first installment of "shock and awe."

Sterk, who was born in 1981, was a cook in the U.S. Marines. She was assigned to an air wing support squadron, responsible for refueling and repairing attack helicopters.

"We were inside Iraq," she said. "The desert gives you very little protection. You had to be mentally tough to survive."

The Fox Valley veteran is the youngest of six children, and the only one who went into the military.

"I graduated early from Larkin High School," Sterk said. "It's January of 1999—too late for spring registration at Elgin Community College, which was going to be my starting point. I wanted a career. I wanted to make a real difference. And to be completely honest, in looking around, I didn't see that happening here. I needed to get away from home. I needed to do things for myself."

Without funding for four years of college, Sterk, who is single, decided to enlist in the Marine Corps, having first considered the Navy.

"I figured my best bet would be the military," she said. "I liked the structure of the Marine Corps. When I talked to the recruiter, things went well. I decided to enlist."

Sterk served in the U.S. Marines from February 1999 to July 2003, five months longer than the typical four-year enlistment period.

She was weeks away from being discharged when Operation Iraqi Freedom changed everything. Sterk was handed an automatic extension of her military time.

"I was preparing to come home," Sterk said. "Instead, I was sent to the Middle East. But you can't complain, not when you're trained to accept changes, even at the last minute. Being a Marine, that's the way things are at times. You adjust ... What would you do otherwise?"

Sterk's unit, first stationed in Kuwait, then outside Baghdad, grappled with vicious sandstorms and unwanted surprises.

Early on, the Marines were attacked by Iraqi missiles, for instance.

"We went into the bunker thirty-two times that day," Sterk said. "Sure, I was a little scared, but you have a job to do. It's all about being responsible, looking out for fellow Marines."

Leaders live up to their obligations. And the best of them keep their feet on the ground by having responsibility on their shoulders.

Sterk was promoted to corporal before leaving the Marine Corps.

"I went in as a follower," she said. "I'd do just enough to get by. Today, that's not good enough. I've learned leadership skills. I've gained a lot of confidence in myself and in my ability to get things done."

American women were able to get things done during Iraqi Freedom. According to recent Defense Department statistics, 200,000 of the nation's 1.4 million active-duty military personnel are female.

In 2003, American women made up about fifteen percent of the units striking Iraq from land, sea and air.

Sterk said female Marines "have what it takes," adding that ongoing battles for gender equality are put aside when war is at hand.

"Men and women were working side-by-side in Iraqi Freedom," she said. "Americans can move mountains. It's just getting everyone on the same page."

Without question, Iraqi Freedom was an unqualified military success. Yet the operation represented more than a triumph of superior strategy and planning.

The war was won on the sharp end by individual soldiers, sailors, airmen and marines. They risked their lives for friends, family and country. They will bear burdens beyond what other Americans might experience.

It is the veteran who will have nightmares. It is the veteran who upheld the virtues of faith, freedom and courage.

They are American virtues. It is an America, by and large, that lives in peace and freedom, far from the terror and tyranny with which so much of the world struggles.

And it is an America that needs to see the bigger picture, as do people worldwide.

War is an abomination, a terrible tragedy—just talk to the veterans who have fought them. Burning oil wells, nerve gas and nuclear winter threaten everyone.

Twentieth-century cinema played with the idea that the only way to abolish war forever was an outside threat—often an attack from a distant galaxy. Think of

Independence Day, the 1996 sci-fi saga. Alien aircraft hover over the Earth, apparently planning an invasion, which unites the world.

Movies employ themes that work when they speak directly to precise problems—the world will not do away with war unless an unfriendly force threatens its very existence, for example.

In June 2004, war itself is that threat. From Boston to Baghdad, Detroit to Damascus, citizens of the world breathe the same air, drink the same water, eat fish from the same sea.

When threats to those resources come from war, how can reasonable human beings ignore the shared danger?

"Reasonable," of course, is the operative word.

How many readers think that Saddam Hussein is a reasonable human being? He's in custody, which undoubtedly is a good thing.

But what about Osama bin Laden, said to have masterminded the terrorist attacks of September 11, 2001?

Sterk, who was not yet twenty-one years old when the Twin Towers collapsed and the Pentagon hit, thinks that terrorism jeopardizes her future, as well as the future of the world.

"Everything changed that day," she said. "I was watching the news. We didn't believe it. Our base was immediately locked down. Security measures got really tight."

Sterk was in North Carolina on the day of the attacks.

With an emergency existing, she was assigned to a security squadron, told to put everything else aside.

A short time later, Sterk boarded an airplane for Kuwait, taking on additional duties, as well as the task she was trained to do

In the Middle East, she was among about forty-five cooks assigned to feed 1,500 Marines.

"It was an important experience, but I wouldn't want to go through it all over again," she said, referring to her time in Iraq. "We were ordered over there. In the Marines, you follow orders—period, end of story."

America's story in Iraq continues at the time of this writing, June 2004.

An interim Iraqi government is supposed to be in place by the end of the month.

Currently, Lakhdar Brahimi, special envoy of United Nations Secretary-General Kofi Annan, has been holed up in an Iraqi office for four weeks, working to help piece a government together.

The new government's task sounds so simple: hold Iraq together, and lay the groundwork so reasonably fair elections can be held at the beginning of 2005, just seven months away.

Getting there won't be easy.

And, by all accounts, there's no Plan B.

To succeed, the new government will have to sell itself to the Iraqi people. The sale will include convincing citizens that the leaders form an autonomous body with real authority rather than functioning as a puppet organization ordered around by an occupying power.

According to published reports, with the publicity surrounding abuses at the Abu Ghraib prison, many Iraqis no longer trust the United States.

They remain skeptical of an eventual U.S. withdrawal out of Iraq, something Brahimi himself addressed during an interview with *Time*.

I am telling Iraqis, if you expect that on the 30th of June, midnight, 135,000 American soldiers are going to evaporate out of some Aladdin's lamp out of Iraq, then that is not going to happen. And what I'm also saying every day is, you need to sit down now as a sovereign

369

government to see what the American soldiers are going to do, what they are allowed to do, what they are not allowed to do, and how they are going to be phased out of your country.

Sterk said she is troubled by the situation at Abu Ghraib, but thinks that the attention is focused on "a few bad apples."

American Major General Antonio Taguba's report on Abu Ghraib details a prison in disarray, especially at command levels.

Sterk said she was both happy and sad at leaving the Marines.

"I met people from all over, different backgrounds and all that," she said. "I really grew up while in the Marines. Being back home, I've run into a few of the people I was friends with in high school. They're pretty much doing the same stuff as always. I'm not trying to sound mean, but they haven't progressed much—they haven't grown up. I guess I've become a mother hen. In the military, you become close with your peers. They have your back, you have theirs. You have to become brothers and sisters. You learn to respect people. You learn to put your differences aside. If not, you won't make it ... In Iraq, the bonds were just extraordinary."

Today, Sterk works at a home improvement store, attending ECC at the same time. She hopes to transfer to a four-year college, perhaps Northern Illinois University.

"I'm in pre-med," Sterk said. "My goal is to become a physical therapist. And down the road, I'm hoping to open my own practice, specializing in helping veterans. Being a veteran myself, I've got some insight into their emotional makeup, which would make it easier to help them with their physical therapy."

As this book is wrapping up in mid-June 2004, it is not

entirely clear what will happen in Iraq. Attacks on American military personnel continue. The number of Americans killed in Iraq long ago surpassed the number killed in the first Gulf War.

Some say that the current U.S. administration and its military advisers should have been better prepared to handle the intractable problems raised by victory. Perhaps part of that failure has been a relatively recent reluctance to involve the U.S. military in nation building and peacekeeping.

The United States' record of nation building has not been a high point of military or civilian competence over the past forty years. General William Westmoreland, commander in Vietnam from 1964 to 1968, neglected the tasks that lay beyond defeating the Viet Cong and the North Vietnamese in battle. His successor, General Creighton Abrams, did care, but by the time he took over it was too late to win the war, much less the peace.

Like almost every other American, Sterk said she hopes for peace in Iraq, as well as worldwide.

Not only was she in harm's way while outside Baghdad, but she gave up the creature comforts people take for granted in the United States.

"You work sixteen-hour days, from sunrise to sundown," Sterk said. "The weather was always a factor. It would have been nice to take a shower. It would have been nice to have a little privacy when going to the bathroom, but that's not how things were in the desert."

How things were...

The events of September 11 forever altered the view that the United States is immune from the troubles besetting the rest of the world. Continuing American operations in Afghanistan represent an unobstructed realization: both air and ground forces must be enlisted in the fight against terrorism—a definite departure from the "distant punishment" approach of the Clinton administration.

While it was well and good to overthrow the Taliban and try to clean out the nest of bin Laden-led terrorists, the question arises: what are U.S. forces to do in Afghanistan once they accomplish their purely military mission?

In the spring of 2004, Army Ranger Sgt. Pat Tillman was killed in Afghanistan. A former football star, his death whistled across America, raising the hair on the back of its neck.

Tillman was wealthy, but left privilege for pride—pride in an America he had called home.

Tillman put humility before honor. He listened to his inner voice, and now belongs to the ages.

In a much less celebrated case, Sterk listened to her own inner voice.

It brought her to the U.S. Marine Corps. Country and community should thank her. She served honorably.

She came home alive, but others didn't.

"I think about that all the time," Sterk said, her words sounding sad, like the tolling of a funeral bell. "I feel blessed being back home."

Just last year, she lived in a miserably hot, humid climate, knowing that the desert could turn into a free-fire zone at any moment, no matter how far from Baghdad— five minutes or five hours, time ticks away when incoming missiles are approaching.

The same scenario could repeat itself—today, tomorrow or next week. American troops endure exhaustion, danger and fear for a relatively small salary and the promise of returning home to a nation that, they hope, will accept and appreciate the depth of their sacrifice.

Nearly forty-five years ago, presidential candidate John F. Kennedy came to the Fox Valley asking for votes.

In 1960, he addressed a large noontime crowd,

speaking to them from an improvised dais at the intersection of DuPage Street and South Grove Avenue in Elgin. According to local historian E.C. "Mike" Alft, the appearance produced little change in local voting behavior. Richard Nixon carried Elgin Township by a count of 15,487 to Kennedy's 5,924, not far from three-to-one.

Kennedy carried Illinois, however—although by less than one percentage point. And he carried the national election.

He was inaugurated as the thirty-fifth president of the United States on January 20, 1961.

His brief presidency, cut short by an assassination, was still long enough to provide America with a renewed faith in itself. Across the country, people lifted their heads just a little bit higher, thinking that the United States was on the brink of an amazing era.

Minorities and majorities alike would share in the blessings of liberty that the Constitution secures.

Not since Abraham Lincoln, not since the darkest days of the Civil War, had the language of the presidency been instilled with such vision.

When Kennedy spoke, words were like scattered seed. And finding favorable ground, they unfolded in vitality and strength, opening in the light of American aspirations.

He molded language into a banner for patriotism. Ultimately, that's what has propelled this book, which closes with a quote from Kennedy's inaugural address.

The words serve as a reminder. Then, as now, they involve a fresh appreciation for an unending American dream:

Ask not what your country can do for you—ask what you can do for your country.